LIFE
LESSONS
&
TRAVELS

STEPHEN D. EVANS

AN AUTOBIOGRAPHY

Ordering Information:
For details, contact Stephen D. Evans at stephen452@netzero.net
Print ISBN: 978-1-66786-011-4
eBook ISBN: 978-1-66786-012-1
Printed in the United States of America on SFI Certified paper
First Edition

Introduction/
Acknowledgements

Some of us realize what we have while others don't. Priorities for the masses seem skewed toward materialism. Are we individuals following our own path or lemming-like creatures influenced through the likes of social media and characters claiming to have all the answers?

Far be it from me to pretend to have the explanations. However, I do believe that my life experiences, as outlined in this book, provided me with a solid foundation. Life struggles, opportunities, and reality impressed upon me the importance of certain traits. Early on, I developed the habit of checking claims out for myself. Simple enough and mostly accomplished through keeping up with current events verified through reliable media sources.

The traits I've learned to be most beneficial to life are belief in God, honesty, genuineness, loyalty, and responsibility. It took me a while to realize that God was in my corner and is a true Father to us all. Several God-guidance examples are in this life story. The most prevalent was his leading me to my wife Sandie. Both of us had difficult marriages preceding our involvement. If the timing hadn't been what it was and Sandie wasn't given the patience to wait for me, I would have missed out on the love of my life. A truer partner there couldn't be. She's my best friend, lover, and companion. At the writing of this book, we've been together over thirty years, and my love for her continues to grow daily. Only God!

This book is dedicated to my family—my wife Sandie, my daughter Janette, my older son Shawn, my younger son Scott, and my two new-daughters Olivia and Julie. Family is important to me. All have brought significant meaning to my life and for this I'm truly grateful. To date, Sandie and I have been blessed with eight grandchildren. Julie and Kenny, thank you for Amanda, Kenny Jr, Taylor, and Matt. Olivia and Cesar, thank you for CJ & Emily. Scott and Berna, thank you for Deacon. Shawn and Yucco, thank you for Axel. May life be as blessed to all of you as it has been to me!

Everyone mentioned in this book contributed to my life experiences in one way or another and for that I thank them. Special thanks go out to my wife Sandie who supported me during this project and provided her superb proofreading skills. It's my hope that readers find enjoyment in one fortunate individual's life path with experiences, good or bad, that I would not have changed for anything.

Table of Contents

Chapter 1 | Ancestors

MY GRANDMOTHER

My grandmother was born in Franklin, Indiana, on August 16, 1897. Marjory Huffman Young Strobel lived to be eighty-three years old, passing away on the island of Maui, Hawaii, on June 11, 1981. The one word that comes to mind when I think of her is regret. Regret, as my grandmother was a heroine to me and I regret not having spent more time with this wonderful person, getting to know her and our family heritage better. The one word I'd use to describe her character is "principled."

She was a loving, caring person but stood by her principles for the benefit of those around her. It was all the more troublesome for her as she was a single parent during the challenging years of raising my mother and uncle. She married her first husband, John Sandy Young, when she was twenty-four years old. Grandmother lost her first husband a scant seven years into their marriage, leaving her with two young children, ages six and two. Her second husband, Ralph J. Strobel, loved and wanted to marry her but she insisted on waiting until her two children were older and more set in their life choices before remarrying. Grandmother waited until mother was nineteen before remarrying and was married to her second husband for thirty years, before he passed in 1975. In retrospect, I'd say that my behavior mirrored her "principled behavior" while raising my children. On occasion after occasion, the handling of my children's behavior was not the "easy way out" but rather reflected what would hopefully prepare them for adulthood.

Grandmother was ahead of her time in many ways. During the Second World War, she became a draftsman. In our current world, she'd be referred to as a draftswoman to point out that she was filling a role that was traditionally a man's job. She was active throughout her life, working in her profession until retiring at the age of sixty-six. My mother and uncle characterized her as having a wonderful sense of humor, a smile for everyone, and always setting a good example.

Full disclosure—the below account is based on conversations with other family members and friends and not from a direct accounting by grandmother:

My mother met my paternal father when she was approximately eighteen years of age. Paul James Thayer was in the navy at the time and was a handsome man with an engaging personality. Grandmother didn't feel he would adequately provide for mother or that the marriage would last. Besides which, she wanted more for mother (college) as she·entered the prime of her life. Mother fell head over heels for him. In retrospect, I'd say this was one of the happiest periods of life for my mother as I have a photo of her with a genuinely happy smile on her face. Grandmother's position on the relationship was that if mother continued, "She'd have to sleep in the bed she made." In other words, continuation of the relationship wouldn't receive support from grandmother. The rest, as they say, is history as mother married my bio-father, Paul J. Thayer, and had me, creating other challenges mentioned later in this book as the marriage was indeed short-lived.

A special treat for my brother and me was visiting grandmother and Ralph Strobel (her second husband) at their country home outside of Greencastle, Indiana. The entrance to their home was off a one-lane road onto a gravel driveway that dipped down into a gully. Once we turned into grandmother's driveway, we looked for their dogs that welcomed us with wagging tails while acknowledging our entrance. Our minds drifted as we imagined the wonderful treats awaiting us in grandmother's home. Grandmother was a magnificent cook and every meal she cooked seemed special. To this day, we remember the extraordinary cookies Grandmother would bake for special occasions and package in attractive tins.

Another admirable trait of my grandmother was communicating. To my knowledge, she never forgot a birthday, anniversary, or special occasion of a family member. Once in the family and known by her, you were always in her life. I remember my uncle Jack and his second wife Joanne divorcing around my senior year of high school. My aunt Joanne had two young sons from a previous marriage and Grandmother kept in touch with the three of them after the divorce. She wrote numerous letters and cards to family members and would always sign them "God Loves You and so do I." I can't help but believe that she's now with God in his kingdom.

Left: Grandmother Marjory Young with her first Husband, John Sandy Young. Center: Uncle Jack, Grandmother, and Mother. Right: Grandmother.

MY MOTHER

Despite my mother's problems, there was never a doubt in my mind that she loved me. The first of two children, she was born Dorothy Jean Young on October 22, 1925. Mother lived seventy-one years, passing away on November 3, 1996. Having me so young presented Mother with a number of challenges.

She met and fell in love with my bio-dad, Paul James Thayer, marrying him over objections from her mother and soon thereafter had me. Grandmother wanted Mother to prepare for a better life at that point while having reservations about her husband-to-be. The short courtship and the first months of marriage to my dad was probably the happiest period of my Mother's life. I left home for good at age sixteen and while I have a few memories of Mother's happy days, they were by far the exception rather than the rule. I have an old photograph of her with my dad, taken during their courtship and Mother looks happier there than any other time I've witnessed.

My dad left Mother for another woman before my first birthday and Mother divorced him on December 2, 1946, a mere five months after my birth. I feel this absolutely crushed Mother, leading to a deep depression that she never fully recovered from for the rest of her life. I had very little contact with my dad following the separation during my formative years. Some of this was due to my dad's character and some due to my Mother's desire to keep me from him. While Mother held bitterness toward my dad as long as I can remember, she didn't openly discuss him in front of me.

Being a single parent at such a young age in the mid-1940s presented a horrendous handicap for Mother. Society in general frowned on women in this category, classifying them as promiscuous. So much so that during my early toddler years, Mother seriously considered letting a distant relative living on a farm in the country adopt me. This never materialized for reasons unknown to me.

Mother married my stepfather, Forrest Harlan Evans, on October 21, 1949 when I was three years of age. My stepfather brought a one-and-half-year-old son into the marriage, Floyd Leon Evans. We initially lived in the city of Indianapolis, Indiana, but shortly after the marriage, my uncle Francis got my stepfather a job at the naval depot in the small Indiana town of Crane. The population of Crane, Indiana, as recently as 2014 was only 184. This wasn't farm life but it wasn't far from it.

We lived in Crane in the early 1950s for four to five years and one of my Crane memories of Mother pertained to a broken arm. During the fifth grade, I fell out of a tree and broke my right arm. Being right-handed, this handicapped my writing. Mother offered to and, in fact, wrote my homework for me during the entire period I was incapacitated. I certainly felt privileged at the time. Mother and my stepfather worked hard not to play favorites between my mother's son and my stepfather's son. However, being children, my stepbrother and I couldn't help to feel that my stepfather favored him, while my brother thought Mother favored me, realistically or not.

Following Crane, Indiana, we moved back to the city, Indianapolis, Indiana. Mother was a homemaker for most of this period while I graduated from grade school #39 and attended my freshman and junior years of high school at Arsenal Technical there. She worked an odd job here or there to help make ends meet. One of the odd jobs I remember her having was as a laundromat attendant. I visited her there a couple of times and remembered being proud of her for running the laundromat. Mostly, I remember her during this period in a depressed state confined to her favorite chair in the living room reading magazines while smoking cigarettes and drinking Pepsi.

We didn't do much together as a family. My stepfather worked two jobs as long as I can remember to provide for us. Mother and my stepfather were poor money managers and it seemed we were constantly in debt. One example of poor money management was our grocery purchases. While living on the near east side of town in Indianapolis, Indiana, on English Avenue, the majority of our grocery shopping occurred across the street from us at a ma-&-pa owned neighborhood convenience store. This meant we paid more for our daily needs than if we shopped at one of the major supermarkets.

Mother didn't drive so on the rare occasion when we went anywhere as a family it was when my stepfather was off work and then it would be primarily to visit family. One memory of a family excursion sticks in my mind and was a testament to our constant lack of funds. The four of us went to a drive-in movie theater. Kids were free, so for my brother Floyd and me, there was no charge but adults were charged admission. My stepfather and mother worked it out where she would hide in the trunk of the car to get in without paying. Once we were inside the drive-in and settled, my stepfather removed mother from the car's trunk.

My brother and I performed most of the household chores. We didn't receive a weekly allowance so we either earned money on our own outside of home or asked Mother for money. Mother's canned response would be to ask if all of our chores were done. It seemed she would inevitably find just one more task for us on such occasions. As my stepfather was working so much my mother became the disciplinarian. Her method was to warn my brother and me and then provide the ultimate threat of "wait until your father gets home." My stepfather, being exhausted most of the time, didn't take any time to determine whether what Mother said was true or not. If Mother said we were guilty of any offense my stepfather took the belt to us without hesitation. My brother Floyd and I received strict corporal punishment.

For the most part, my brother and I were on our own for meal preparation, which meant cereal for breakfast the majority of the time and sandwiches for lunch if we were home. We weren't home for lunch much. On a typical day to avoid household chores, my brother and I would rise before Mother and leave the house for the day. We'd roust up neighborhood friends for baseball or sporting events at the park. One dinner memory is a pot of beans being made and kept on the stove for a week or so, which we helped ourselves to.

Mother was happiest when she was with my aunt Helen, her closest friend. Aunt Helen was married to one of stepfather's brothers, George. My

6

mother was normally with aunt Helen on the rare occasion that she'd go out. Aunt Helen drove, providing transportation for her and Mother.

Mother and my stepfather subsequently had two daughters in life. Marjie (named after my grandmother) was born in 1958 and Becky in 1964, providing me with two half-sisters from my mother's side of the family. By second-hand accounts, this "second family" worked well initially, with my Mother and stepfather even attending church on a regular basis. However, a few years down the road saw them fall into similar life patterns that Floyd and I experienced minus the corporal punishment and level of household chore responsibility that my brother and I had.

During the period that Mother and my stepfather were raising their "second family," I was deep into a hotel management career, causing me to move with my own family on numerous occasions. The geographical location of my family during the mid-sixties through the early eighties prevented a close relationship with my parents, meaning I didn't get to experience the growth and development of my two half-sisters, and my parents didn't have the opportunity to be close grandparents to my children.

Sometime in the 1970s, Mother and Father moved to Hawaii with the promise of a home to be given to them by my uncle Jack. For unknown reasons, the home exchange didn't take place. Mother and my stepfather stayed in Hawaii until my stepfather passed away in 1980. Mother moved back to Indiana sometime after my grandmother's passing in 1981.

When she returned from Hawaii, Mother lived primarily with my youngest sister Becky and her family on Arsenal Street in Indianapolis. Eventually, she was moved to an assisted living facility in relatively close proximity to Becky. Mother was diabetic and didn't watch her health closely, which eventually led to more health problems for her. I was living in Chicago at the time as a single parent after going through a divorce from my second wife.

I was dating Sandie Sinck then, who would eventually (blessed that she waited for me) become my third wife. Sandie would accompany me on some Indiana trips to visit relatives on my side of the family. I tried to see

Mother when visiting Indiana. Mother liked Chinese food and on one such visit in November of 1996 we brought her some Chinese food for lunch from one of her favorite Chinese restaurants. We stayed with my stepbrother Floyd and his family on that visit and early the following Sunday morning, on November 3, we received a telephone call informing us that mother had passed away from congestive heart failure. To this day, I'm grateful to God that we were in Indianapolis and saw her the day before she passed.

Left: Dorothy Jean Young's High School Photo.
Center: Dorothy Jean Young and Paul James Thayer.
Right: Mother with her one-year-old son Stephen.

MY DAD

Full disclosure—Most of what follows regarding my bio-dad is from secondary sources. My bio-dad left my mother before my first birthday and wasn't really a part of my life during my formative years.

My dad, Paul James Thayer (nick-named PJ) was born in 1926 and died in 1993. His dad's name was Francis Thayer and his mom's name was Mary. My dad had three siblings, a sister named Marian, a brother named Charles, and another brother named Francis after his dad. Probably he and his siblings weren't shown love, affection, or security reassurance during their childhoods. Apparently, alcoholism ran rampant in the family. Several of the Thayer children's uncles were serious alcoholics.

According to Betty Bartlett (Buses), my stepmother, my dad's second wife, his childhood environment probably fueled his actions as an adult. He had only a tenth-grade education, having gone to grade school's Mc Kinley Elementary School 39 and to Arsenal Technical High School in Indianapolis through his sophomore year. While it's believed that his sister Marian is still living, his brother Francis was killed at Luzon in World War II and his brother Charles committed suicide.

Paul Thayer joined the Navy when he was eligible. He met my mother Dorothy Young shortly after joining the Navy, sometime in 1945, and after a very short courtship they were married. I was their first and only child born July 18, 1946. My dad met his second wife sometime during 1946 and they married on February 22, 1947, a mere two months after his official divorce from my mother. My stepmother described him as handsome, likable, very clean, neat, and smart. They were married for ten years and eleven months although as his second wife states "he wasn't home enough for them to talk much." He broke a lot of hearts.

His short education coupled with early-sustained instability habits limited his employment options. After the Navy, he started work in a factory, which was short-lived, and held job after job with numerous unemployment periods in between. He had two daughters from his second marriage, Sheryl Thayer, born on June 3, 1947, and Sharon Thayer, born on July 5, 1949, providing me with two half-sisters from my dad's side of the family.

He was in prison on at least one occasion when he was caught stealing money from one of my half-sister's schools. In today's world, he would probably have been diagnosed as bi-polar. His Veterans Administration documents revealed that he was neurotic and chemically dependent. His best friend, Bud Burleson, described him as being plagued by demons.

During my second marriage, my family and I visited him when we could in Indianapolis. He didn't go out much at that juncture of his life and actually lived like a hermit, going out only for necessities. We did get him out on one of our Indianapolis treks. I secured tickets to an Indiana Pacers basketball game and encouraged him to go. I remember the two of us, along with my brother Floyd and brother-in-law Joe, had a grand time that evening. My bio dad was found dead by one of my half-sisters during the sixty-seventh year of his life, sitting up in a chair in his living room with the blinds drawn.

Paul Thayer and Me.

Sister Sheryl, her daughter Denise, Sister Sharon, Step-Mom Betty.

MY UNCLE

My uncle, John Sandy Young, was born on January 8, 1929, in Indiana and passed away on July 19, 1990, in Hawaii, at the age of sixty-one from metastatic carcinoma (cancer). He was named after his bio-father, Sandy Young, who'd passed away while my uncle was a toddler.

It's not an understatement to say that my uncle turned my life around. He was a lifeline for me as a teenager, not realizing the wrong road I was traveling. He was living and working in Phoenix, Arizona, when I first lived with him. Following runaway incidents, numerous all-night adventures without my parents' knowledge of my whereabouts, a stolen car incident, and other infractions, my mother had just enough of my shenanigans.

For her health, marriage, and her peace of mind, she convinced my uncle to let me live with him and do my sophomore year of high school in Arizona. This worked out well enough that my uncle also offered to take me in during my senior year of high school when he had later moved to Hawaii. He offered a waiting plane ticket for me in Los Angeles from Los Angles to Hawaii with the stipulations that I first make it to Los Angeles and then later work for him once in Hawaii to pay back the cost of the ticket.

My uncle went from high school to the Army before completing college. At twenty-two years of age on leave from the Army, he was driving home in bad weather and skidded on the road, ending up veering off the road into a creek with his vehicle turned upside down. The accident resulted in permanent paralysis to him from the waist down. I lived with him for two years and knew him for forty years and never once heard him complain of his handicap. He never let his handicap prevent him from enjoying life. Whether it was swimming without the use of his legs or playing ping-pong against the unhandicapped, he gave it his all preferring that his friends and the public didn't pity him for his handicap.

The earliest memory I have of my uncle Jack was when I was around twelve years old. He had my stepbrother and I visit him and his wife in Chicago. My aunt was the most beautiful woman I had known to that point. Their accommodations were modest but gave me the impression of riches.

They showed my stepbrother and me a wonderful time during the visit, which was for several days. My aunt took my stepbrother and me to see the Chicago White Sox play the Baltimore Orioles. To this day, I like the Chicago White Sox. They also took us to the Chicago Museum of Science and Industry, where a captured German submarine was and still is an exhibit. Who would know that some twenty-five years later I would be living in Chicago?

My uncle and aunt's Arizona home was a modern three-bedroom, two-bath, and two-car garage house but it had seemed like a castle to me. They had an outdoor built-in swimming pool, which, due to the weather, could be swum in nearly all year-round, day or night. Their automobile was a later model convertible and I was impressed not only with the car but also the fact that they rarely had to put the top up. Their car was modified, so my uncle could drive it hands only using a stick lever by the steering column.

Following in the footsteps of his mother, he became an architect. His Arizona home had an office that he worked out of. Trying to emulate my uncle, I thought of becoming an architect for a brief period and unsuccessfully attempted mechanical drawing classes in high school. My uncle and aunt entertained regularly, always including me in their dinners and get-togethers. Several of their friends they knew from college were handicapped. My uncle went to Purdue University and for its accessibility features transferred to the University of Illinois at Urbana Champaign where he graduated. The University of Illinois at Urbana Champaign is one of the most accessible college campuses in the world.

He was a life model to me and after a few months into my new living arrangement, I realized that there was so much more in life than I had been exposed to. Witnessing his success in spite of his handicap modeled to me a better lifestyle. His drive and passion for life encouraged me to reach higher in life.

My uncle was always improving himself. He was a Bridge Life-Master early on and participated in Bridge tournaments all around the United States for bridge Master Points. He taught me the game and playing with him I won a Master Point. While living with him in Phoenix, I was able to earn some money by going with him and working at local Bridge Tournaments. He also belonged to a national organization called Toastmasters. They met regularly and were required to prepare and give a speech once a month. He loved his mother, my grandmother, and made sure she was taken care of after his stepfather passed away. Years after the passing of his stepfather, he moved his mother from Indiana to Hawaii to be closer to him.

He wasn't particularly close to his sister, my mother, but was obviously close enough to take me in on two separate occasions. To this day, I remember an evening with him, which made a lasting impression. We were in Phoenix and it was later in the evening when we just started conversing about life and my troubles. We talked most of that night and not only did I feel listened to but also extremely valued as an individual as in my mind at that time I was the most important person to him.

On another occasion, we were traveling between Arizona and Indiana and he let me drive for long distances at a time even though I didn't have my driver's license. I never once doubted the trust and confidence he had in me, which made me believe in myself even more.

After his divorce from Sandy, he moved from Arizona to Hawaii. I felt bad for him that he was losing our beautiful aunt and often wondered why. He never divulged the reasoning but I subsequently learned that my aunt was seeing another gentleman and became pregnant by him.

This led me to hypothesize that my aunt wanted a child or children of her own, which my uncle, due to his handicap, was unable to provide. His move to Hawaii was accelerated by the gift he got from one of his friends, which was a TV station on the island of Maui. At the time, his friend, Cecil Heftel, owned the island-wide KGMB TV affiliate. My uncle worked the station for a few years while designing and building his dream home on the Big Island of Hawaii. These were exciting times in Hawaii, as the state had just recently become the fiftieth state of the union.

Shortly after moving to Hawaii, my uncle remarried. His second wife, Joanne, had two sons from a previous marriage. Joanne, Steve, and

David were part of the household when I joined them for my senior year of high school. While retaining the life-experiences learned in Arizona, this visit didn't go as well. My uncle and new wife, for reasons unbeknownst to me, were not getting along. This coupled with the antics of a hormone-raging sixteen-year-old (me) who still had a few exploits up his sleeve, like drag-racing their automobile late at night, led to my uncle suggesting that I quit high school in favor of joining the army. This led to a disagreement between us, and I subsequently lived with others to finish my high school education.

Shortly thereafter, my uncle and new aunt were divorced and my uncle took on a totally different persona. He grew a beard, wore flowery clothes, smoked marijuana, and had lots of late-teens, early twenties' individuals in and out of his home. Through this tumultuous period of his life, he became a strong advocate in the state for handicap rights, leading a Maui chapter, working tirelessly while gaining new, warranted accessibly rights for the handicapped in the state of Hawaii.

While we didn't share the same values for a period then, the life-lessons my uncle provided and modeled during the time we were together in Arizona have stuck with me for a lifetime. My uncle gave me a second chance in life and for that I'll always be grateful.

Left: Uncle Jack with Grandmother Strobel before his accident.
Center: Aunt Sandy.
Right: Aunt Sandy and Uncle Jack with their German Shepard.

MY STEPFATHER

My stepfather, Forest Harlen Evans, was born in Jasonville, Indiana, on July 12, 1923, to Arthur and Beulah Evans. He died at the early age of fifty-seven on Maui, Hawaii, on September 18, 1980. He came from a large family, having four brothers and eight sisters. I believe that coming from such a large family and being one of the older sons inhibited his education. Not sure how far my stepfather went in school but later in our lives my stepbrother and I learned that he couldn't read or write as an adult. On the rare occasion that he would read to us, we learned that he was actually telling us a story while pretending to read.

He was a single parent for a short time as he gained full custody of my stepbrother following an incident where his wife left my stepbrother alone as a baby for a period. He married my mother on October 21, 1949, in Indianapolis, Indiana. Thus, my stepbrother Floyd was one-and-one-half years old and I was three when his father married my Mother. It may have been somewhat a marriage of convenience as both Mother and stepfather were single parents at the time. My stepfather adopted me in April of 1951.

During my middle and high school years, I remember my stepfather being a hard worker. He held down two jobs most of the time. His longest and main employment stint was with Ford Motor Company. He worked on the assembly line at the factory a few miles east of us when we lived on English Avenue in Indianapolis, Indiana. One of the secondary jobs he held was at the local amusement park, running one of their two roller coasters. When my brother Floyd and I could make it out to the amusement park, my stepfather would let us ride his roller coaster for free. That was quite the treat to us.

For the thirteen years I lived under the same roof with my stepfather, I don't remember any signs of affection between him and my Mother. I didn't think of it at the time but later in life I realized that due to his laboring, he never had the time or energy to spend quality time with either my stepbrother or me. Thus, my brother and I didn't learn how to hunt, fish, or camp from our father.

It was as an escape that we became adept at sports, specifically at baseball and basketball. Sports relieved us from our unending daily household chore list. We would gather a group of neighborhood boys and play from the moment we awoke in the morning all day until dark. Floyd became quite the athlete at both the grade school and high school levels.

Father dished out punishment for infractions my mother would accuse us of. He was too tired to determine our guilt or innocence. If mother said we did something worth being punished for we knew the thick army belt with grommets was in our future as soon as he got home.

He had health issues in his late forties and early fifties, probably resulting from the extraordinary amount of work he did to provide for his family. A home offer from his brother-in-law led my stepfather, Mother, and two younger sisters to Hawaii. The home offer never materialized, but I'm convinced the Hawaii move increased his life span. From my perspective, he was happiest during those last years in Hawaii. He was more open and friendlier than at any other time of his life, which I'd experienced. Anyone knowing him during that period spoke highly of him.

Looking back, I believe that my strong work ethic came from his modeling in that regard. For that and his adopting me, I'm most appreciative.

Left: Toddler Stephen and Father.
Center: Young Sister Marjie.
Right: Young Sister Becky.

Sisters Marjie and Becky.

Chapter 2 | 1946–1955

M other gave birth to Stephen Douglas Thayer, who weighed six-and-a-half pounds on July 18, 1946, in St. Vincent Hospital, located at 2535 N. Capitol Avenue in Indianapolis. The hospital outgrew its older facilities and in 1974, moved to 2001 West 86th Street.

Four and a half months after my birth, my mother and bio-dad divorced on December 2, 1946. I never learned specifically what caused the divorce although during the time of my birth my bio-dad was seeing other women. It was nearly three years later that Mother married my step-father. During the divorced period, I can only surmise that Mother had an extremely difficult time. She gave birth to me before her twenty-first birth-day by a man she was in love with, divorced, and faced life as a divorcee with a baby in the mid-1940s when society frowned on that type of behavior.

I learned from an older cousin, Mary Lou, much later in life that her parents nearly adopted me when I was one or two years old. Mary Lou was an only child and we nearly became brother and sister. Mary Lou's parents, Frank and Mary Ellen Guerkie, lived on and ran a farm outside of Roachdale, Indiana. What a different lifestyle this would have presented me growing up in the country on a farm versus living in the city. This had to be a tremen-dously difficult decision for Mother, who decided against the adoption.

It was around this time that my soon-to-be stepbrother had a horri-fying experience. Floyd Leon Evans, born on March 31, 1948, was left alone as a baby in his crib for two days. The neighbors heard insistent, constant crying coming from the apartment that he lived in with his mom and dad. He always remembered the flashing red lights from the police patrol cars coming to his home to investigate. This incident led to his father obtaining full custody of him as he was at work while his mother was supposed to be taking care of him. Instead, he learned later, his mother was out drinking and partying.

Thus, both my Mother and Floyd's father were single parents when they met. They married October 22, 1949 creating an instant blended family. Unfortunately, I don't know how they met or how long the courtship lasted. It obviously worked from the standpoint that Floyd and I had both a mom and a dad. Additionally, Mother had the security of a provider and my stepfather had a partner to watch Floyd and me while he worked.

I was nearly five years old when my stepfather adopted me on April 4, 1951. The adoption papers stated that my bio-father hadn't paid child support for two years and that I was a "dependent and neglected child." In my earlier years, I never gave a thought about being adopted. To my knowledge, my stepfather was my dad and of course Mother was my mom. I was too young to think differently. I'm sure Floyd felt the same way.

It was later in 1951 or early in 1952 that we moved to the small country town of Crane, Indiana. Crane is located approximately ninety miles southwest of Indianapolis. The 2010-census indicated a population of 184. We moved there as my stepfather, through one of his brothers, secured a good-paying job at the Naval Depot located there. Crane was the type of sleepy town in which you didn't lock your doors and parents let their children roam liberally without fear.

My first through fifth grades were attended at the school in Crane. I was an average student and at that time didn't get into much trouble. During this period, Floyd got into more trouble than I did. Floyd grew quickly and in no time was the tallest, biggest kid in his class. This led to incident after incident, as the other older kids seemed to always think they had something to prove and would start fights. Floyd had the path to the principal's office memorized.

Our childhood there was great. On non-school days, we'd be out all day and most of the evening until we heard either my mother or stepfather calling us. We'd enjoy the typical hide and seek, tag, and other children's games. Marbles were big at that time and both Floyd and I had our own collections and would spend hours challenging and playing the neighbors for their best marbles. We also had a fairly large collection of comic books that we'd go door-to-door and trade with other kids. Additionally, we'd spend days at a time playing Monopoly. The town (probably sponsored by the Naval Depot) showed free outdoor movies that we'd rarely miss. The movies were projected onto the side of a building in the central area of town. Heaven was watching one of these movies while consuming a root-beer float.

A peculiar incident occurred when I was approximately eight years old and Floyd was six. We were outside playing when a car pulled up next to us. A man and a woman exited the auto and the woman, after surveying the situation, walked up to Floyd. "I'm your mother," she proclaimed to Floyd. Of course, being six years old, Floyd had no idea how to respond. To Floyd's knowledge, my Mother was his mom. He knew no differently. Needless to say, that when Mother and my stepfather discovered this going on, you'd think an international incident was occurring. We were told to go into the house but could hear loud shouting and serious arguing going on for what seemed like an eternity. Floyd's mom and her then husband left and that was the last we heard of her for many years.

A little later that year, Floyd and I experienced what we called "the ten-penny incident." Family visited us and before leaving accused either Floyd or me of taking ten pennies from them. In those days, if we were accused of anything, the assumption was that we were guilty. My stepfather dispensed the discipline in our family. There was no middle ground here. We knew the penalty would be a good whipping. No child liked to be whipped but it's especially difficult to take when you know you're innocent. Floyd and I confided in one another that neither of us took the money. I convinced Floyd that to avoid this unwarranted punishment we should run away. Thus, an eight-year-old and a six-year-old stuck out our thumbs to hitch hike to Indianapolis.

The plan was to find Floyd's mom and stay with her. Of course, we had no idea of the enormity of Indianapolis or where to even begin looking for her. We got a couple of rides. A gentleman picked us up on our last ride and drove us to Bloomington, which was over thirty-five miles from Crane. He obviously knew that we were runaways and took us to a police station. We told our story to the officers there and pleaded with them to tell our parents not to whip us. While waiting for our parents, they brought us ice cream and life was good. Our parents arrived and after talking with the police officers and agreeing not to spank us, we left. That didn't last long. We were smacked as soon as we got into the car and got the whipping of whippings when we got back home.

Prior to moving back to Indianapolis an incident occurred in Crane that garnered national news. Ronnie Weitkamp, the three-year old brother of a friend of Floyd and me, went missing on October 11, 1955. The total community along with armed forces personnel scavenged the entire Crane community and surrounding areas looking for little Ronnie Weitkamp. It's estimated that over 2,500 Marines, sailors, and civilians participated in the exhaustive search. Nearly two months later on December 4, three local teenagers in a wooded area north of town discovered his badly decomposed body. Foul play was doubted as investigators were under the impression that Ronnie died of starvation and exposure. It's an event I'll never forget. Ironically, over sixty years later while touring the Civil Rights Museum in Montgomery, Alabama, I came across a Montgomery newspaper dated December 5, 1955, exhibited to reflect the country's mood at the time and it had Ronnie's sad story on the front page!

This was a very confusing period of my life. Not understanding or appreciating the family dynamics brought on through the divorce and subsequent remarriage of my Mother was disorienting to say the least. I'm sure my brother Floyd had similar sentiments. Conversely, it was also a time of great innocence, living in an area that for the most part was shielded from the wickedness a big city can bring. It had to be comforting to our parents that living in such a rural setting provided a secure, safe environment for their children as well as themselves.

Where else could an eight-year-old experience a free chocolate Coke at an authentic soda fountain? On one summer day, I wandered into Crane's only soda fountain without any money and sat at the counter. There were a couple of teenagers there that were making fun of me. I don't recall what they were chiding me about but the female attendant behind the counter came to my defense and even provided me with one of my favorite beverages of that time, a chocolate Coke. Life couldn't have been much better for an eight-year-old of that time.

Left: Floyd Early-On. Right: Floyd and Stephen—Brothers around 6 and 8.

My Crane First Grade Class Photo.

Chapter 3 | 1956–1965

This period of my life was one of numerous growth experiences. My parents moved back to the big city, Indianapolis. I experienced puberty along with the challenges it provided for both my parents and me. Mischievous, adventurous, exasperating, creative, imaginative, and responsible are all words that could be used to describe me at one point or another in time during this era. I graduated from grade and high school, hitchhiked south to Louisville, north to Chicago, and cross country from Indiana to the west coast; married at eighteen years of age; and was a teenage parent before my nineteenth birthday.

Shortly after I'd completed my fifth grade in Crane, Indiana, we moved back to Indianapolis. I'm not sure why as the job my stepfather had was a good one at the Naval Depot. We lived with my stepfather's brother George and his wife Helen while searching for our own place. Aunt Helen became Mother's closest friend and when Mother was out of the house, she was nearly always with her. Aunt Helen and uncle George had two children (our cousins) with whom Floyd and I became very close. Mary was the oldest and Johnny the youngest. Of the four of us, I was the oldest, Mary and Floyd were about the same age, and Johnny was the youngest. Due to our mothers' closeness, the four of us also became chummy.

An incident comes to mind when the four of us ranged in age from seven to ten years old. Mother and Helen went shopping and took the four of us kids with them in the car, which was a common occurrence. We were left in the car while they went into the store and to pass the time, we would yell expletives at individuals as they walked past the car and then duck down so they wouldn't know where the foul language was coming from. One lady figured out what was going on and waited for our mothers to return to the car. That night, Floyd and I learned firsthand what soap tasted like.

Somewhere around 1956, we moved to 1555 English Avenue. I believe we rented this house, which I would live in off and on for the next six years. English Avenue was a busy city street with lots of traffic located less than two miles from the center of Indianapolis. Our home was one block from another major street that ran perpendicular to English Avenue, State Street. It was bordered on two sides by busy alleyways. On more than one occasion, we'd wake up in the morning to discover an automobile or two had crashed into our garage. One evening, an auto hit the side of our house, shaking it to its foundation while we were watching TV.

Our English Avenue residence was a modest two-bedroom, one-bath home with a kitchen, living room, and sitting room. We settled into a routine soon enough, if you could call it that. The sitting room was probably initially a third bedroom as even though it didn't have a door, we used it as such at times. An old coal stove that Floyd and I would have to fuel every so often heated the home. Coal deliveries were made via a truck through an opening leading to the basement off the alley. A couple of days after each delivery, you could see black soot from the coal on tables, chairs, and surface tops. We had a bad roach infestation problem. Turning on the lights from a completely dark state sent these detestable creatures scurrying in all directions.

We had one of those old wringer washing machines and clothes were hung out on our clothesline to dry. Floyd and I did most of the household chores and I remember many a day taking clothes off the outdoor line, which were frozen solid due to cold weather. Not unlike other families of that era, Floyd and I took weekly baths, not daily showers, for conservation purposes.

My parents were poor money managers, making some bad financial decisions where we always seemed in need of money. For most of this period, my stepfather worked two jobs. His main employment at this time was at the Ford Motor Company, with him working on the assembly line. This was hard, grueling work but a great paying job for someone who didn't make it past the sixth grade in school. I learned much later in life that my stepfather couldn't read and that to get the job at Ford he had to rely on one of his brothers to complete the required paperwork.

To save money, Floyd and I would get our haircuts at a barber college, where we would walk over a mile to get to. Students there learned the art of cutting hair. We had to get either a burr (all hair cut off) or a Hollywood (just a patch of hair left on the front) so we could wait longer between haircuts. Occasionally, we'd get home haircuts.

Mother, for the most part, didn't work. She was a stay-at-home mom. This was around the time I noticed Mother going in and out of depression, which I later attributed to her not getting over her failed first marriage. She would get up very late each day, which allowed my brother and me to leave the house beforehand. Mother was a heavy smoker and drank a lot of Pepsi Cola. Her daily routine after rising would be to sit in her chair in the sitting room, reading magazines while drinking Pepsi and smoking Kool cigarettes. She would stay up most of the night doing this, go to bed, and begin the same routine the next day. Mother wasn't much of a cook although when she put her mind to it, she did fine. Floyd and I were on our own a lot for meals, eating cereal or whatever we could easily heat up. Every so often, Mother would cook a large pan of navy beans and these would stay on the stove for us to heat up, as needed. We'd heat them up for several days until maggots became visible when you raised the lid.

For our sixth through eighth grades, Floyd and I went to grade school number 39, located six or seven blocks from the house. Unknown to me, my bio-dad went to this same grade school. We walked to and from school each day regardless of the weather as my stepfather was already at work and Mother didn't drive. As a matter of fact, Mother never learned how to drive.

I was an average student two grades above Floyd.

Floyd was somewhat of a celebrity at the school. He was quite the athlete in all school sports which, appropriate or not, afforded him great latitude in school tardiness, participation, etc. Apart from being a gifted athlete, Floyd was always big for his age. By the time he was in his sophomore year of high school, he was nearly 6'5" tall, with a solidly built frame. He set several grade school sport records, some of which may even stand to this day. The one grade school sport I excelled in was track. I wasn't the fastest runner in the school but fast enough to make the track relay team.

Floyd and I would leave the house as early as we could in the morning and not return until we absolutely had to. We were now definitely living in the big city. With each succeeding year there, by necessity, I became more and more street wise. The big city taught me an early 'street wise' lesson the first or second Christmas we were there. My uncle had given me a golden yellow Voit basketball that I immediately fell in love with. We had a basketball rim attached to our garage and despite the cold temperature I went outside to shoot with my newfound treasure. Another boy came along and we started playing one-on-one until one of my parents called me to the house. Knowing it wouldn't take long, I told this kid whom I was unfamiliar with to shoot the ball and I'd be right back. You've probably guessed what happened. Yes, he left with my brand-new basketball, never to be seen again. I roamed the neighborhood for several days after that, trying to find my basketball with no success.

I loved sports and played baseball in several leagues while going out for my high school basketball team at two of the three high schools I went to. I didn't possess the natural skills that Floyd did, but I was never accused of not hustling and giving it my all. During my sophomore high school year, I caught the attention of the basketball coach for having the knack of getting bloody during each practice. Whether it was a school or outside sporting activity that either Floyd or I wanted to participate in we had to find our own way there and back.

Floyd and I, along with our friends, would play baseball at a park located about four blocks from us from the time we left the house in the morning staying until nightfall when we could no longer see the ball. One day, we were playing baseball in our backyard, which at the time seemed huge. One of us hit the ball through a window of the connecting walkway to our basement. Afraid to own up to this abominable deed, we instead stuffed the perfectly round hole with newspaper. It was actually several months before this misdemeanor was discovered. We received quite a whipping for this, making me realize the infraction was closer to a felony.

My brother and I found the ideal retreat for us at a Boys Club located five blocks from our home on English Avenue. It was inexpensive to join and we spent many hours there playing pool, basketball, climbing rope, etc. It was an outlet that allowed us to burn off energy while meeting other boys in our neighborhood. There was a middle-aged lady in a booth just inside the door to check cards upon entry. My friends and I would play pranks on her, and I remember one incident where I pretended I was being choked by an unseen attacker. This put quite the scare into her as the entire building was put on alert!

We played enough pool there where my skill level advanced enough to allow me to represent our Boys Club for my age group in a state tournament played at Indiana University. I didn't fare well in the tourney but the university made a huge impression on me. So much so that, although I never attended college there, I became and still am an ardent IU basketball fan.

Four years before leaving for my sophomore year of high school in Arizona, my third half-sister was born. Thus, I was twelve years old when Marjie (named after our grandmother) came along and had very little interaction with her. A crib was placed in the sitting room for Marjie, and I remember coming home from school one day to find Marjie standing up in her crib with her diaper off and feces everywhere: on the walls, her crib, and on her. Somehow, it became my responsibility to clean that debacle up. Prior to Marjorie's birth, I had two half-sisters from my bio dad, Sheryl and Sharon, but had very little contact with them also. Marjie was the first of two children born to my Mother and step-dad. As they waited so long for Marjie, I'm guessing that this may have been an accident.

While having responsibility for most of the household chores, Floyd and I did not receive an allowance. To have money for events and recreation, we either had to ask our parents for it on a case-by-case basis or work for it outside of the home ourselves. In a lot of these cases, it was simpler and more expedient to earn our own money. I got involved in several schemes to finance my desire to participate in and attend camps, movies, and organized baseball or just to have money to buy things.

While doing what most kids did to earn money by collecting pop bottles, shoveling snow, cutting grass, running errands, etc., I also got involved in some interesting and sometimes dangerous arrangements for my age. When we had particularly heavy snowfalls, I'd cut school to take advantage of the snow-shoveling moneymaking opportunity. Not as common then as later in life was the selling of magazine subscriptions. I'd sell a canned "working my way through school" pitch to potential door-to-door customers, which proved quite successful. Another ingenious exploit at the age of twelve or thirteen was selling eggs door-to-door making five cents for each dozen sold. Floyd and I met a man who sold eggs from his car in various neighborhoods. We actually rode in this man's car trunk (with the trunk open) through neighborhoods far from home without our parents' knowledge. When we got bored or sales weren't going well, we'd throw eggs at houses from the back of the car.

On another occasion, I was able to secure an ice cream wagon pulled by a bike to sell ice cream on a commission using a fake ID. I sold most of the product and then ditched the wagon/bike in a nearby creek. At thirteen or fourteen, I'd work randomly, unloading semi-trucks of fruit at a station about a mile from home.

My closest friend during this period was Steve Verhines (more about him later). Steve and I worked various odd jobs to earn money. One of these adventures has stayed with me for years and I still have the scar to prove it. Steve and I, at ages thirteen and fourteen, were helping to set up carnival rides for one of those small neighborhood outfits going through town over a weekend. A platform we were lifting fell wedging my thumb between it and the track it was mounted on splitting the area between my thumb and finger open. It was a bloody mess and the man who hired us was, of course, terrified that he'd get into trouble as we were under age to be performing that type of work. There was no permanent damage done thank goodness, but while this was going on my thought process was centered on how I was going to hide this from my parents to avoid punishment!

As a pre-teen and teenager with practically no structure, I created my own activities, sometimes good and sometimes bad. Steve Verhines and I were inseparable during this period. It was a given that wherever I was he was and vice versa. We did everything together and for this period of my life I was closer to him than my own brother. Alonzo Baker hung out with us frequently but wasn't with us on all of our adventures. Like most kids our age, we'd spend nights at each other's homes. A favorite pastime of ours at that time was to see who could go the longest without sleep. When Alonzo or Steve would fall asleep, I'd place a substance in one of their hands (shaving cream, ketchup, etc.) and tickle their nose to always-hilarious results. During some of these evenings, we'd walk down to the Twin Drive-In Theater located about a mile from where we lived and sneak in. This Drive-In had a seating area in front of the concession stand with speakers where we would sit in an attempt to meet girls. We'd get their names and phone number so we could continue desired relationships.

We'd cut school every now and then and of course would then fill the day with mischief. One day in particular stands out. We stayed most of this day at Alonzo's home as both of his parents worked. His place was in the next block from Steve Verhines' home. Steve's older sister was home that day for some reason so we decided to prank her. We called every delivery service we could think of from pizza shops to flower deliveries for orders to the Verhines residence. As each delivery was attempted, we'd watch the action from Alonzo's home. Once we hid while a police car drove by. We thought it'd be funny to yell, "What are pennies made of? Dirty copper!" The policeman didn't' think it funny and actually got out of his patrol car and chased me. I was scared out of my mind and ran ever so fast through alleyways and between houses before losing him.

One exploit nearly cost Steve jail time. On another day while cutting school, we were in Steve's neighborhood and noticed an ice-cream truck running down his block. The back of the truck was open at a particular juncture so we decided to jump into the back to see what ice cream may be available to us. Nothing was obvious to us, so we jumped back off the truck. A few days later, Steve was questioned as a suspect of a robbery to that truck on that day. He was identified by one of his neighbors as jumping onto the truck. Neither of us took money from the driver that day. We suspect that the driver took the money himself and used our incident as cover for his story.

Another adventure landed me in jail for a few hours.

A neighborhood friend of mine, Bobby Carmack, who was eleven and I was thirteen "borrowed" Bobby's uncle's car. Neither of us was old enough to drive and, of course, Bobby's uncle wasn't aware that we took the vehicle, and reported it stolen. We were pulled over and taken to the closest police station. Our parents had to come down to get us out. This proved to be the beginning of a series of incidents that eventually led to my parents sending me to Arizona to live with my uncle to complete my sophomore year of high school.

My freshman and junior years of high school were spent at Arsenal Technical High School. At that time, it was distinguished as one of the most populated high schools exceeding over 4,000 registered students. Commonly referred to as Tech, it was located on a seventy-six-acre parcel that originally served as a Civil War Arsenal. Due to the significance of the school's facilities and history, Arsenal Technical was placed on the National Register of Historic Places in 1976.

When I was fourteen years old, Steve Verhines, Alonzo Baker, and I created quite the adventure for ourselves. It was over our school spring break and each of us told our parents that we were staying with the other's family for a few days. Our parents didn't know each other and thus didn't bother to check out our story. The three of us decided to hitchhike from Indianapolis to Louisville. Apart from having a few dollars between us, we had no concrete plan on what we were going to do once we got there. We made it down to Louisville without incident. We came upon a junkyard just within the city limits and decided to sleep there a couple of nights in the back of a box truck. Our first meal there was dinner at a downtown White Castle. Hamburgers at that time went for 10¢ each, helping to stretch what little money we had. Our money ran out quickly as we felt compelled to play the juke box there. Our only nourishment option at that point if we wanted to continue our trip was the pilfering of food.

Two specific scrounging instances come to mind during the trip. The first was at a gas station that doubled as a convenience store. We worked out a chain operation scheme where one of us heisted food items from the store and passed them to a second team member stationed in the men's bathroom where he then passed these items through the window down to the third outlaw in our group waiting outside. The second incident occurred at an outdoor fruit stand. Alonzo, Steve, and I were mulling around this fruit stand. Alonzo and Steve each stuffed an apple or orange into their pocket. I don't know what made me do what I did next but in front of me was this large stalk of bananas. I picked it up and Alonzo and Steve's eyes nearly popped out of their heads. The three of us took off running, escaping to the safety of the box truck we were staying in to enjoy, excuse the pun, the fruits of our labor.

The return trip from Louisville to Indianapolis was much more challenging than the trip down. Unbeknownst to us the Louisville school system was not on its spring break. While hitchhiking, we had to constantly elude the police. We'd spot a patrol car approaching and have to toss our bags over the fence, run into the woods, and wait for the patrol car to pass before returning to the highway. We had to pull this maneuver on several occasions before finding safety in rides distancing us from the city. We returned home without further incident and felt comfortable that we had gotten away with our little secret venture. A few weeks later, the three of us were on my front porch chatting and reminiscing about our trip. Unfortunately, my next-door neighbor overheard our story and informed my parents who eventually made it known to Steve's and Alonzo's parents.

Oh yes, there was hell to pay for that escapade but it also was one of several experiences that will stay with me for my lifetime.

As a teen, I had my share of love (and puppy love) interests. My first Indianapolis neighborhood love (I'll call her Amy) and I went with each other for about a year. She was the sister of a friend of mine. I'd stay overnight with him and when everyone was asleep Amy and I would end up together. His parents were very kind to me. Apart from being with Amy, my favorite time during these visits was the breakfasts Amy's mom would make the following morning. I have never forgotten her banana pancakes.

I met another companion, Lynette, through a high school classmate friend. We weren't exclusive to each other but were serious when we were together. We went with each other for about a year with some of this time overlapping with my involvement with Amy. At any rate, Lynette had moved to Chicago and this seemed an appropriate destination for Steve and me on several fronts. So, about a year removed from our Louisville adventure, Steve Verhines and I ran away from home. I had Lynette's address and without her knowledge or parents' consent felt we'd be welcomed to their home in Chicago. We were typical teenagers from the standpoint that we felt life owed us more than we got. That plus getting in trouble for various outlandish acts led us to the decision to strike out on our own.

This time, unlike Louisville, there was no made-up story so our parents knew something was amiss when we didn't return home. They called the police and an alert was put out on us. Our trip up Interstate I-65 to Chicago was relatively simple. However, once arriving, the enormity of Chicago was overwhelming. That first night, we slept on the beach of Lake Michigan. I was prodded early the following morning by a nightstick wielded by the largest policeman I've ever seen. Lying down and looking up at this giant after just waking up was downright scary. We did locate Lynette but of course couldn't stay with her and her parents for long. We returned home after a few days without being captured by the police.

Story within a story—**Angel over My Shoulder?**

It was 1961 and I had worn on my parents' patience one too many times. Several incidents led me here and I don't remember the one that made my parents realize they needed a break from me for their sanity. I believe it may have been my Chicago adventure where my closest friend, Steve Verhines, and I ran away to from Indianapolis. We were gone for over a week. We being fifteen and fourteen years of age, our parents were worried sick and even had the police looking for us.

The crowd I was running around with at this point was troublesome to say the least. Their main claim to fame was whatever they could get into. I'd been in on part of their planning efforts but never an actual misdemeanor or felony. It was just a matter of time before I was sure to be arrested along with my brood of friends.

Corporal punishment failed to work on me at his stage of my life (believe me when I say my stepfather tried). Grounding was of little use as I would simply sneak out of the house. After consulting with various family members, my Mother made arrangements for me to live with my uncle in Phoenix, Arizona, for my sophomore year of high school. This in itself had to be a stretch for her as she and her brother, while not distant, were not really close. Reading between the lines, I'm surmising that my Grandmother intervened with my uncle on my Mother's behalf.

At any rate, arrangements were made, and I was destined for the first time in my life to not only live out of my home state of Indiana, but nearly 1,700 miles away! It wasn't entirely foreign to me as my brother and I had visited my uncle there before. Of course, visiting versus living there are two different stories. While it came to me as somewhat of a shock, I looked upon it as an adventure. I idolized my uncle, a successful architect with a beautiful wife and lovely suburban home complete with an in-ground swimming pool! During my childhood, while living in the city the closest I came to a swimming pool was a public pool nearly a mile away, to which my brother and I walked. Unable to even afford air-conditioning, living in a lovely home with central-air and a pool in the backyard would be heaven.

My parents took me to the Greyhound Bus Depot downtown for my journey from Indianapolis, Indiana, to Phoenix, Arizona. Mother, being concerned for my well-being over such a long journey, befriended a gentleman who was going most of the way on the same bus. She asked him if he would look over me during the trip. He was a nice enough fellow and sat next to me for the trip.

We talked during the trip while the bus made a few stops. Eventually, I fell asleep. I'm not sure how long I was out but when I woke up the gentleman was gone. After a period, I checked the bus's restroom and he wasn't there. I then checked every seat on the bus and he hadn't changed seat locations. Concerned, I went to the bus driver and asked him if we had made any stops since the last one I could remember. The bus driver indicated that we hadn't made any stops and that nobody had gotten off!

It's a mystery that I've never forgotten. Every piece of eyewitness testimony and evidence that I could gather proved to me that he was real. I can only surmise that during this event as well as some other life experiences, someone was watching over me.

End story within a story

The final hitchhiking adventure that Steve Verhines and I adventured together was coupled with my permanently leaving home. I was seventeen years old and obviously a handful for my parents at the time. While I don't remember specifically whose idea it was for me to leave, my parents were okay with my leaving home. My uncle Jack whom I stayed with in Arizona for my sophomore year of high school told me that I could stay with him for my senior year of high school in Hawaii. He indicated the he'd have a plane ticket waiting for me in Los Angeles and I would have to work for him after my Hawaii arrival to pay him back. It was my responsibility to make it to Los Angeles. Having succeeded on two previous hitchhiking adventures, I was able to convince my parents to allow me to undertake this trip. My Mother even wrote me a permission note. Not wanting to go it alone, I spoke to Steve and he was more than willing to undertake this venture with me.

Steve's plan was to remain on the west coast while I traveled on to Hawaii, which had just become our fiftieth state four years earlier. I knew very little about Hawaii but dreamed it to be a paradise that would forever take any perceived or real troubles I had away. My mythical vision was that beautiful bare-chested Polynesian maidens would greet me as I departed the plane. But first, Steve and I had to make it from Indianapolis to the west coast so I could claim my ticket and get on that plane.

We didn't leave right away. We first performed some odd jobs to earn money for the trip. This plus some money gained from our parents gave us the confidence to attempt this feat during the summer of 1963. It was an expedition that created several memorable experiences. An excursion of over 2,000 miles necessitated complete trust between Steve and me. We made a pact to look out for one another on this journey and one of our covenants was that one of us would always be awake when we were with others.

One of our first rides was with a group of hillbillies that, unbeknownst to us, were intoxicated. We were thrilled when they stopped for us and mentioned that they were going all the way into Missouri. We were elated that one of our first rides was going to take us so far along our route. Shortly into this ride, we learned that our ride benefactors were inebriated due to the chances they were taking while driving. Both Steve and I just sat back and felt that whatever happened would happen. Miraculously, the ride ended event-free, launching us a couple of states into our undertaking.

Being short of cash, we slept outdoors beneath a highway overpass one night a few more states into the trip. A kind gentleman gave us a rather long ride a few states later and even paid for a motel room for us overnight. This man we learned that night was from the LGBT community. While his sexual orientation was with other males, we made it clear to him that it was not ours. We spent another night in the foothills overlooking Albuquerque, New Mexico.

Under the "strange but true" moniker, our most unusual ride occurred between somewhere in New Mexico and Phoenix, Arizona. An elderly lady stopped and picked us up. The usual casual conversation took place as we drove along. I felt like I'd seen this woman somewhere before and the feeling was mutual with her. After some initial background questioning, we discovered that she was my Algebra teacher at Carl Hayden High School in Glendale, Arizona, during my sophomore year!

Phenomenally, we made it to our west coast destinations without incident. It was ironic that we encountered more difficulty on both our Louisville and Chicago adventures than we did on this 2,000-mile potentially treacherous journey. I even had an unneeded permission note in my pocket. That's life; you never know what lies ahead.

Saying goodbye to Steve was bittersweet but excitement pulsed through my veins as I boarded the jumbo jet in Los Angeles. This was my first ever plane ride and it was to, of all places, Hawaii. At this stage of my life, I was a huge James Bond fan (my first son was named after Sean Connery), and when the stewardess asked me what I wanted to drink, without hesitation I requested a martini. It looked to be such a cool drink on the big screen as well as on TV shows. The stewardess, I'm sure, knew I was underage but probably felt it would be a lesson taught if she served me. She did and it was the most horrible concoction I had ever tasted in my life to that point. Looking back on this, I could just picture the stewardess laughing at the disgust on my face after my first sip. The rest of the flight was uneventful although I wasn't feeling at 100% due to the martini incident. As you probably guessed, bare-chested maidens were not waiting to greet me at the conclusion of my flight.

Nevertheless, I was in Hawaii, a Polynesian paradise, and I was flying high on cloud nine. My uncle lived in his dream house that he'd personally designed. It sat at the top of a hill off the main highway approximately halfway between Kona and Kealakekua, Hawaii, on the Big Island. Beautifully landscaped, it had an outdoor courtyard situated between the bedrooms and living space/kitchen. The newly built home also had an in-ground swimming pool. Between my sophomore and senior years of high school, my uncle Jack was divorced from his first wife and remarried to Joanne who had two sons from a previous marriage. Joanne's sons were named

Steve (the oldest) and David. So to avoid confusion in the household, I went by my middle name Doug, short for Douglas. In retrospect, this probably wasn't the best of timing for my uncle to take on his seventeen-year-old nephew while acclimating into a new marriage.

My uncle had relocated to Hawaii following his divorce from Sandy, our first aunt. I'm surmising that he wanted to get far away from Arizona and the sad memories it held for him. He had a friend, Cecil Heftel, who at the time owned the CBS TV affiliate (KGMB) for the state of Hawaii. Cecil Landau Heftel "Cec" was born and raised in Chicago. He graduated from Arizona State University and attended the University of Utah and New York University. His Hawaii Company was called Heftel Broadcasting. He served in four succeeding Congresses representing Hawaii from 1977 until his resignation in 1986. He unsuccessfully ran for governor of the state of Hawaii. I mention his background deducing that my uncle originally met him in either Chicago or Arizona. Cec provided my uncle with the Maui portion of KGMB TV, which probably also contributed to my uncle's desire to relocate to Hawaii.

The rest of the summer of 1963 found me acclimating to my new surroundings and environment. In short order, I decided that a trip around the island should be in the cards. Having previously conquered hitchhiking trips to Louisville, Chicago, and the West Coast from Indianapolis, I set off to hitchhike around the island. The island of Hawaii is one of the eight major islands in the Hawaii chain. It's also known as the Big Island due to its size as its 4,028 square miles makes it larger than all of the other Hawaii islands combined. It's a fascinating location as in the winter you could ski on top of the 13,796-foot Mauna Kea and then drive to the beach and surf enjoying a tropical climate. Even with its size in relation to the other islands, it of course paled to areas within the United States mainland. I navigated the entire island within a day, as it's only about 225 miles to go completely around it. While reveling in amazement at my new environment in short order, I felt land-locked. Unlike living on the mainland of the United States where if desired, you could hop into a car and travel hundreds, even thousands of miles, this was not possible in Hawaii. That's an adjustment I'm not sure I ever made.

During that summer, I developed a friendship with Jeff Faye. Jeff was going into his junior year at Konawaena High School and I was going into my senior year. Unknowing at this time I learned later that there were only three Caucasians at my new high school. Konawaena High School was populated with Japanese, Filipino, Chinese, Koreans, Portuguese, and of course Hawaiian students. Hawaii was indeed properly labeled "The melting pot of the Pacific," with these numerous ethnic groups in residence. It was rather ironic, however, that even at this early-stage full-blooded native Hawaiians were in the minority in their own state. Marrying into other races had dramatically reduced the pure native Hawaiian population.

Adjusting to my new high school was difficult on a few levels. First, the school year for Konawaena High school differed from all other Hawaii and mainland high schools. This was to allow students to help their parents on Kona Coffee farms. I tried picking coffee beans and it was tough work. I think the school year has since realigned to more of a traditional year. By far, my most difficult adjustment was the prejudice I experienced. Locals then, and I believe even now, don't like Caucasians. They felt Caucasians were ruining Hawaiian lands as well as the local lifestyle preferring high-rise hotels, for example, to land conservation. The locals refer to Caucasians as Haoles. The term haole is usually considered to be a neutral descriptive term. However, it's used in Hawaii mainly with disparaging intent, arising from a distrust of foreigners or outsiders. It took me several months to develop the trust of the locals in my new high school. There were cliques there by race, which made the process even more challenging. Needless to say, we three Caucasians at our high school formed a strong bond by necessity. Looking back on this, it was a tremendous growth experience for me.

My activities during my senior year at Konawaena high School were typical for a seventeen-year-old. I went out with my friends, attended local and school functions, and, while not to the degree experienced back on the mainland, got into my share of exploits. I went out for my school's varsity basketball team but didn't make it. I've always felt that I was better than several of the guys that made the team but either due to my race or the fact that I was a senior with just the one-year of eligibility remaining, wasn't selected. It was highly disappointing as it would have been an excellent extracurricular activity for me. My youngest half-sister Becky was born back in Indianapolis around this time, but it would be several years before I ever saw her.

An exhilarating experience occurred for me during this year. My uncle awakened me very early one morning to announce we were going to drive across the island to take in the eruption of the Kilauea Volcano. Having no experience with erupting volcanoes, my reaction was one of indifference. My preference was to get more sleep. My uncle won that disagreement, so we went on a volcano excursion. Witnessing one of the world's wonders was a magnificent sight to behold. Seeing lava and fire spout several hundred feet into the air during darkness was a once-in-a-lifetime experience. From that day forward, I've encouraged anyone who has the opportunity to see the Kilauea Volcano in action even if it means having to catch a flight from a neighbor island to do so. Its eruptions are sporadic, so when they occur, you need to take advantage of the opportunity.

One of my exploits while living with my uncle led to me moving out of his house. One evening while the household members were all away, I snuck out and took my uncle's Plymouth Fury drag racing. While I accounted well at the races, my uncle found out. It may have had some-thing to do with rocks settling into the hubcaps. Having to deal with me while working on his recent marriage eventually proved too much for my uncle. He gave me an ultimatum of either joining the military or moving out. This was during the Viet Nam War and, apart from my desire to finish high school, I had no inclination to become part of that conflict.

So I moved out, living with friends I knew or met through my uncle, until settling in with a family named the Peacocks whom I'd met through my uncle. They had boarding-like rooms detached from their home, which were perfect for me. Their son, Robbie, was a couple of years older than me and was attending Dartmouth College in New Hampshire. He was a nice enough fellow and we went wild boar hunting together one day in the mountains. His dad was quite the athlete. He taught me how to body surf by taking me to the infamous "disappearing" white sands beach and having me go out far enough out into the water that I either had to catch a wave in or suffer the consequences.

One of the girls in my class caught my eye and we began dating. Eileen Kiyoko Morinoue of Japanese ethnicity was my age and lived in Holualoa, Kona. Her parents were old-fashioned, believing in Japanese traditions. Eileen's mother (Ayako) was a homemaker. Her dad (Kukicha— all his friends called him "Sako-san") was a highly talented pool player, and he played around the island for money. He had his own personal pool cue made specifically for him, which he carried around in a case. During our courtship, Eileen became pregnant. There was never a doubt in my mind that the correct path for me to take would be to marry Eileen and support her and my soon-to-come-into-this-world child. I would have a high school diploma when my child was born without known job prospects but I knew that somehow we would make it work. Discussing this with Eileen's parents was one of the hardest tasks I'd had to undertake at that point. Her parents were intimidating to me and wanted her to go to college. Eileen was also disappointed as she was looking forward to attending college. They took it better than I imagined and in a few months Eileen and I would get married.

I don't remember whether Eileen's parents wouldn't allow us to live with them or we just thought it best to strike out on our own. At any rate, we never lived with her parents but rather rented a place in the same town where her parents lived. Job prospects were limited at that time, providing me basically with two broad options: either construction work or the hospitality industry, which was blossoming into a major Hawaii industry. I chose hotel work and was able to obtain a position as a busboy at the Kona Inn Resort in Kailua Kona. It was ideally located just off the ocean in a central part of Kona. The Kona Inn Resort was well known at the time as it hosted the Annual International Billfish Tournament. My Kona Inn employment came close to never materializing as the resort's general manager indicated that he nearly nixed my hire because I misspelled "restaurant" on my employment application.

Thus, my first position as a married expecting dad was a busboy, where I worked for $1.40 an hour plus gratuities paid to me by the waitresses and waiters I bussed for. It was challenging work as I worked split shifts and a six-day workweek. Labor laws were much more relaxed those days. A typical workday had me punching in around 6 am for a breakfast shift, leaving around 9 am, and returning for a lunch shift from about 11 am to 2 pm. After a three-hour or so break I'd return around 6 p.m. for a dinner shift. I worked in the main restaurant, which took advantage of Hawaii's tropical climate. The restaurant had a roof covering the dining area with large openings on three sides of it to allow trade winds through.

On April 14, 1965 at 12:06 pm, my daughter Janette Dorothy (named after my mother) Tamiko Evans was born at Kona Hospital. Experiencing fatherhood for the first time was quite amazing. Your baby is so small you're initially afraid that holding her the wrong way will injure her. All parents probably think the same way but my daughter was perfect in every sense of the word. I was excited and proud but also felt a renewed sense of responsibility for this beautiful little creation. It was important to me to properly provide for this little bundle of joy. In the all-too-common standard household those days, Eileen was a stay-at-home mom, maintaining our residence while I worked to provide for our family. Not happy with my then income level, I decided to make a major employment change involving my family. Three months removed from my nineteenth birthday; we relocated fifty miles away to the Hapuna Beach area so I could take a position at the brand-new Mauna Kea Beach Rockefeller Resort as a waiter.

When it opened in July 1965 with 154 guestrooms, Mauna Kea Beach Hotel owned by Lawrence Rockefeller was the most expensive hotel ever built. Praised by travel writers and critics worldwide, it was named one of the "three greatest hotels in the world" by *Esquire* magazine, one of the "10 best buildings of 1966" by *Fortune*, and presented with an honors award by the American Institute of Architects in 1967. Unheard of in those days the resort and golf course were built at a cost of 27 million dollars. Mass tourism was still new in Hawaii. Statehood and the jet plane had arrived together a little more than five years before. It had standard resort amenities: a golf course, tennis courts, swimming pool, restaurants, and lounges. Situated on a remote section of the island by the town of Kawaihae on one of the world's most beautiful beaches the resort even avoided placing TVs into their guest rooms until a 1995 renovation.

This move was somewhat of a gamble considering that Eileen and I were both just nineteen, with a baby less than one year old. The move also distanced us from the close family support of Eileen's parents. Help from my parents could not happen as they live more 4,000 miles away. My hourly wage as a waiter was comparable to that of my previous busboy position but I expected to earn more in gratuities and hopefully advance into hotel management there. While not feeling close to God at this point in my life, I am now and have been for many years a believer. This is one of the many instances that I believe God interceded in my life and led me to this opportunity.

It was at Mauna Kea Beach Hotel that I like to say I earned my PhD in hotel management. While at Mauna Kea Beach Hotel, I worked in several positions learning the industry from the ground up. Beginning as a waiter I advanced to other positions including: Accounts Receivable Clerk, Revenue Auditor, Food & Beverage Auditor, Night Auditor, Room Service Manager, Restaurant Manager, and Beverage Manager. Fascinated with the industry and the potential it offered, I enrolled in the Educational Institute of Hotel/Motel Management and became one of its youngest graduates. My mentor at Mauna Kea Beach was its Resident Manager, Jim Reed. He was my proctor for each of the Institute courses and worked with me on my hotel career progression there and with subsequent companies.

The Resort quickly became the hotel of choice for celebrities. The "Who's Who" in America and internationally flocked there. Some of the individuals I served or ran into while there included Lucille Ball, Bing Crosby, Alfred Hitchcock, Charleston Heston, Sandy Koufax, and Jacqueline Kennedy. The resort did everything in a first-class manner. All new hires went through a rigorous training program before they could serve a hotel guest. The servers' (waitresses and waiters) training was conducted by an outside expert in the field. Martha Jones was in her late thirties or early forties and, knowing her stuff, really put us through our paces. During one of our training sessions, I was on my way to the kitchen while Martha was coming from there. Shocking me, she grabbed my crotch as we passed each other. Bewildered, I just shrugged it off and went about my business.

It was also at Mauna Kea Beach Hotel that I truly learned everyone's created equal. Initially, I was intimidated somewhat in serving celebrities. However, witnessing their behavior up close with their families and friends, I quickly realized they were just like you and me. Some were nicer than perceived on screen and some were downright nasty. Alfred Hitchcock was friendly and signed his dinner check for me, unsolicited, with his famous silhouette. Lucille Ball was down to earth and a joy to be around. One evening, while working the dinner shift, I was carrying a tray full of entrees to my station and spotted from a distance a person in my station, who from the back looked familiar. Surely enough, after sitting down my tray and seeing this individual's face I realized it was Sandy Koufax, the Dodgers recent World Series MVP! Being an avid Dodger fan, I was thrilled. He gave me his autograph, which unfortunately has since been misplaced.

The highest honor bestowed on me during my Mauna Kea Beach Hotel waiter stint was to be selected to be Jackie Kennedy's personal waiter while dining at the resort. This was just a few years following JFK's 1963 assassination. Naturally, there was a vetting process preceding my distinguished assignment. Laurence Rockefeller also owned a facility called The Ranch House located approximately twelve miles away, which Jackie Kennedy, John John, Caroline, and of course her Secret Service entourage took over during her stay. However, when she and family ventured down to the resort for dinner, my responsibilities shifted into high gear. An incident comes to mind that has stuck with me all these years. During a meal service, I noticed Jackie and a gentleman exchanging glances. The next thing I knew this particular gentleman was being escorted from the resort. Later, I learned that this individual had an exchange with Jackie earlier and this time it made her feel uncomfortable so the Secret Service escorted him out of the resort and off the island.

This period of my life taught me the benefit of hard work. I wanted security for my family and saw an opportunity at the Mauna Kea Beach Resort to advance into management positions which, along with added education, would provide numerous future hotel management opportunities. With my wife holding down the household, I was able to throw myself into my managerial pursuit that included various Mauna Kea Hotel operational promotions along with obtaining a Hotel Management Educational Diploma through the Educational Hotel & Motel Institute. I was fortunate to have the hotel's resident manager, Jim Reed, take an interest in me and serve as a mentor to me while at Mauna Kea and during other periods of my hotel management career.

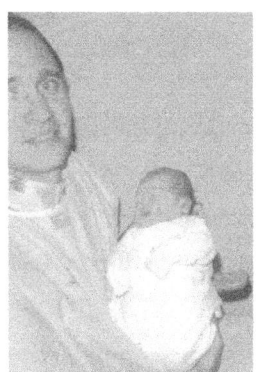

Left: Dad and Daughter Janette Dorothy Tamiko Evans.
Right: Mauna Kea Beach Hotel.

Chapter 4 | 1966–1975

This stage of my life saw progression in my hotel career, divorce from my first wife Eileen, marriage to my second wife, relocation three times to facilitate my career, and accomplishment of a rare educational feat.

A few years after my marriage to Eileen, my uncle and I got back on speaking terms again. The bridges weren't totally burnt between us. Our small family of three would visit him at his new Big Island home randomly. When Janette was around four or five, we were in his backyard conversing around the swimming pool. At that young age, Janette was naturally inquisitive. Suddenly, I heard a splash and looked over to see that Janette had fallen into the deep end of the pool. Reflexes kicked in and the next thing I knew I was in the pool to get my little girl. That incident put a scare in me that lasted quite a while.

Janette, Eileen, and I can laugh now at an incident that at the time was certainly not funny. At this stage of my life, I augmented my hotel income by working a second job at a local gas station. This necessitated us to be a two-vehicle family. Eileen and Janette met me at my gas station job one day and after a period left for home. Eileen was driving a Volkswagen Beetle, which had floorboards on each side of the car. Janette was standing on the passenger side floorboard and was talking with her mom through the rolled down window. Thinking that Janette was inside the vehicle, Eileen drove away chatting with Janette while she drove. I was following them and, noticing this potential disaster, was frantic with emotion. By flashing my lights and honking my horn, I was able to get Eileen to stop. Thank goodness Janette had held onto the Volkswagen's door during this entire episode.

A mainland trip with Eileen and Janette around 1970 to visit family in Indiana provided some fond memories. This was an opportunity for Eileen and Janette to meet my parents, siblings, and friends. My youngest sister Becky was only fourteen months older than Janette, but of course was her aunt. It was strange observing Janette, nearly the same age as my youngest sister Becky, referring to the latter as "Auntie." We made the rounds while in Indiana on Eileen's first ever mainland visit. We visited my parents, both half-sisters on my mom's side of the family, my grandparents, and both half-sisters on my bio-dad's side of the family. We also visited with my stepbrother Floyd who was recently married to his first wife, Billie, and their first child, Lee. Taking full advantage of our temporary mainland proximity we stopped in Los Angeles and visited Disneyland. It was an absolute thrill witnessing the happiness on Janette's face as we went through the park.

Anyone desiring career advancement would benefit from a mentor. For my hotel management career, I was most fortunate to have such an individual. Jim Reed was the resident manager of the Mauna Kea Beach Hotel for most of my tenure there. He took me under his wings, proctoring me through all of my Educational Institute of the Hotel & Motel Association courses while encouraging me every step of the way. A kinship developed along the way as we respected each other professionally and liked each other personally. He was the godfather to my oldest son, Shawn, and helped to guide my career for many years during and after MKB Hotel. We remained in touch through his untimely death in 2021.

To add to my food and beverage background while at Mauna Kea Beach Hotel, I completed the State of Hawaii's Professional Bartending Course. This came in handy later at MKB Hotel when I assumed the position of Beverage Manager for the resort. At the age of twenty-one while at Mauna Kea Beach Hotel, I began a hotel management curriculum offered by the Educational Institute of the American Hotel & Motel Association. My score on the accounting course earned me a National Award. Nearly three years and twelve courses later, the graduate diploma was earned along

47

with the acknowledgment that I was one of the youngest alumni ever from the program. Humbled is an understatement for having received accolades from Hawaii Congressman Sparky Matsunaga and Hawaii Senator Daniel Inouye for the accomplishment.

Early on, Hawaii was a strong union state. Its shipping center, sugar plantations, and pineapple fields, along with a steadily growing tourism industry proved to be fertile ground for union birth, growth, and nurturing. The union negotiated the best wages for agricultural workers anywhere in the world. Later, it represented benefits no agricultural worker dreamed of. It represented vacations and a myriad of other benefits. What agricultural worker at that time ever got a vacation? It represented a pension plan so good that at a certain time, when they had to eliminate thousands of workers because of mechanization, none of the workers suffered. The union was so strong that they worked out a repatriation deal, in which about 6,000 Filipinos, who came to work in the islands in 1946, went back home with severance pay, transportation, plus a lifetime pension in the Philippines. The repatriation sum was enough for almost any one of them to buy a piece of land and a home. Unions were so powerful in the fiftieth state that in 1970 Hawaii enacted the Hawaii Public Employment Relations Act (now HRS §89) to give State and County workers the right to join unions and bargain for wages and working conditions.

In October of 1970, an event occurred that would change the lives of Eileen, Janette, and me.

Mauna Kea Beach Hotel was unionized one year after its 1964 opening by the International Longshoremen's and Warehousemen's Union (ILWU). The ILWU saw its agriculture/warehousing membership base dwindling in the late fifties and branched out into tourism. The AFL-CIO union held a strong foothold on the Oahu hotels so the ILWU went after and successfully organized hotels on the outer Hawaiian Islands. They organized their first outer island hotel in 1962. To provide better wages and benefits for their membership, the ILWU went on a statewide strike.

The strike that affected over 2,000 workers on the Outer Islands began in October of 1970 and lasted 75 grueling days ending on Christmas Eve of that year. The staffing level for Mauna Kea Beach hotel was generally around 325 employees. During this strike, the MKBH was run by fifty supervisors and a few shipped in Oahu staffers. Fifty of us hotel supervisors worked seven days a week, sixteen to twenty hours a day, doing everything from making beds to pouring drinks. This arduous schedule required us to live in the hotel, which also allowed us to avoid daily picket lines. I made it through this laborious ordeal by receiving regular B-12 vitamin shots.

It was during this strike term that I met my second wife. She was part of a group flown in from Honolulu to work as strikebreakers. It was difficult if not impossible to recruit temporary employees from the local area as it was heavily union indoctrinated and sympathies lied with the employees by the local population. Thus, with minimal success some employees were recruited from Oahu and put up within the hotel once passing the picket line. My second wife was one of those individuals and worked as a waitress during the strike.

We met during one of my hectic workdays and, while not proud of the fact, I had an affair with her. We saw each other off and on during the strike and I relished the attention and freedom this relationship gave me. While not sure of my feelings for her after the strike ended, I did feel that divorce from Eileen was the right thing to do. This was a difficult decision for me and leaving my daughter at that time was one of the most heartbreaking experiences of my life.

I would be reunited on other future occasions with Janette as a custodial parent while still married to my second wife who created an impossible environment for those periods to be successful. Without getting into details, I'm ashamed to say that during the periods that Janette was with my second wife and me, I was so wrapped up with my career that I didn't know of the seriousness of the situation that my second wife placed Janette in until later on. I can say that the periods Janette was under her mom's care, I didn't miss a child support payment. There was never a question in my mind that as my daughter she was my responsibility and I wanted to provide for her in any way I could.

After divorcing Eileen, I left Hawaii and Mauna Kea Beach Hotel to pursue my then goal to become a hotel general manager and moved to the mainland. Staying at Mauna Kea would have been a prudent career move as Rock Resorts, owner of MKB, and several other luxury resort properties wanted to place me in their hotel management program. However, being the young full of "piss & vinegar" type, that, in my mind, wouldn't accomplish my goal quickly enough. So without a job prospect in hand, off to Indiana I went. I was offered a restaurant manager's position at the restaurant located at the top of Indianapolis's tallest building at the time. While verbally accepting the position, another offer came to me from Pine Mountain, Georgia, of all places. The offer was to be the manager of dining services at Callaway Gardens, which was a resort just outside of that town. So pulling a 180 turn-around, I informed the prospective Indianapolis employer that I was instead accepting a position in Georgia feeling it would be a better career move.

Thus, in January of 1971, I drove from Indianapolis, Indiana, to Pine Mountain, Georgia, to formally accept my new position. I arrived late in the afternoon and after meeting my superiors was handed a floor plan of a newly renovated all-purpose dining room located within the hotel, indicating where tables and chairs should be placed and told to have the room ready for breakfast the following morning. With busboy assistance of moving tables and chairs, we were able to have the room set according to the diagram, all condiments refilled and ready, and menus preset for the hostesses. As the manager of dining services, this was one of two dining rooms I was responsible for.

The other dining room was located within the actual gardens of Callaway. The hotel dining room served breakfast, lunch, and dinner offering a buffet for all three meals as well as menu service. The Gardens restaurant wouldn't be in full swing for a couple of months so my immediate focus was on the hotel dining room. The high-volume traffic at this dining room was an eye opener for me coming from a resort specializing in fine dining. Each and every meal was quite busy. Pure exhaustion contributed to a good night's sleep for the hours I actually slept.

Having experienced this high-volume dining room for a couple of months, I thought the Gardens restaurant would be a piece of cake. Boy was I wrong! Callaway Gardens had over 2,000 acres of beautiful foliage, hiking, bike trails, and world-class golf. Guests came from a six-state area annually to experience Callaway. The Garden Restaurant served a daily luncheon and dinner buffet with no menu service. I soon learned why the focus was on buffet service. The restaurant line began to form twenty to thirty minutes before we opened each day for lunch, and the line literally didn't end until we closed at the end of day following dinner. I had never experienced such a heavy food service volume in my early career. At times, I would go outside to see how far the line extended wondering if we'd get a break from the crush of diners. The breaks were few and far between.

Pine Mountain, Georgia, is located about eighty miles south of Atlanta. The current population is approximately 1,400. When I was there in 1971, it was much smaller. The town had one traffic light and it wasn't even a stop-light. Instead, it was a flashing caution light that few paid attention to. Due to its remote location, the resort had difficulty hiring and maintaining staff. To combat this, an innovative recruitment program was developed offering free college tuition on a semester-by-semester basis for each semester worked by students taking advantage of this opportunity. These prospective employees were provided housing and meals allowing them to save money toward their other schooling expenses. I went on one of these recruiting trips and the Human Resources Director and I drove from college to college pitching this program, staying in motels along the way.

My second wife moved to Pine Mountain that year and we were married that December. Employment for her at Callaway was simple due to employee scarcity. She was hired as a desk clerk so we would be in two different departments. Between our work schedules, we didn't see each other much. An incident occurred shortly after our marriage, which stays with me to this day. My second wife was not Caucasian. Our duplex unit didn't have laundry facilities so we had to use the one and only town laundromat. On one of these visits, a white patron asked her whether she was Black or White! Looking back on this, I realized that this occurred a scant three years following Martin Luther's King's assassination, and racism was still rampant in the deep south.

Our closest friends at that time were a black couple, Lenora and Zeke Fitzpatrick. Zeke was the banquet manager at the resort and we shared an office. We also shared a passion for professional baseball. My second wife and my hectic schedules prevented much free time, but when we could, socializing with Lenora and Zeke was a good time.

Feeling that I was in danger of being labeled with only a food and beverage background, I decided to broaden my qualifications and experience other hotel departments. My thought process was that to become a hotel General Manager I would need history in several departments. Callaway Gardens didn't provide me with such an opportunity so I returned to Indianapolis, Indiana, and assumed the position of front office manager for the Sheraton Hotel on the east side of town. The Sheraton was a 179-room property, jointly owned by a real estate executive and a Ford car dealership owner. I felt fortunate in landing this opportunity since outside of auditing I didn't have any experience in this arena.

My duties included management of the front desk, reservations, and credit functions. It was my responsibility to see that the front desk was staffed with well-qualified, trained individuals for all three eight-hour shifts. The graveyard shift assumed the additional responsibility of a night auditor function. When you think of it, hotels are a unique enterprise. They're like a city unto themselves. Hotels are open 24 hours a day, 365 days a year. If you desire a career in hotel management, you have to be a dedicated, flexible individual. There's no such thing as "a normal work week." However, at this point in time, it was possible to advance through hotel management by rolling your sleeves up and working hard. These days, advancing to a hotel general manager's position without a college diploma would be extremely rare.

Among many incidents during my Sheraton Indianapolis tenure, three stand out. The first occurred on what seemed to be a normal sunny summer day. This hotel had an outdoor pool and with the temperature being hot and the sun ever present, the pool was extremely busy. While at the hotel's front desk mid-day an excited guest came into the lobby explaining there had been an accident by the pool. Most of the staff ran out to the pool to see what was happening. There was a middle-aged male lying unconscious on the pool's apron. After several unsuccessful attempts to resuscitate him by emergency officials, he was pronounced dead. Apparently, he was in the water for quite a period unconscious, and although the pool was crowded, he went unnoticed. An investigation into the incident revealed that he was sitting on the pool's edge and attempted to launch himself into the pool by pushing off with his arms from a sitting position. His thrust wasn't strong enough to propel him all the way into the pool and he hit the back of his head just before entering the pool. This had a profound effect on me being the first and only hotel-related death I had or would experience in my hotel career.

The second incident involved an overbooking at our hotel. One of the expectations of a hotel by its owners is to maximize its room occupancy and room rate. This generally is a cooperative effort between the Director of Marketing and Reservations Manager. The average room rate is driven primarily by the Director of Marketing based upon the group business he or she places into the property. The ideal scenario is to sell out the hotel to transients (individual travelers) without the aid of group business. The individual traveler generates a higher room rate than group business would. However, it's rare that a hotel would enjoy this type of demand so transient business is nearly always augmented with group business. There are numerous group market segments that hotels cater to with the most lucrative generally being corporate groups and the least favorable falling into an "all other" category that includes political, religious, school, and military groups. A hotel has built-in fixed expenses making it advantageous to fill as many of its rooms as possible even at lower rates to offset these costs.

Maximizing a hotel's room revenue is much more sophisticated now than it was in the early 1970s. These days, most hotels have a "Rooms Revenue Agent" position that has to approve all group business and rates charged to individuals on a day-by-day basis. Couple this with current technology, and hotels can now forecast their average room rate/revenue on a day-by-day basis a couple of months out!

I being the front office manager of the Sheraton East Indianapolis, the reservation manager reported to me. She entered all reservations by hand, which is unheard of with technology advances in the modern era. While not a complete science, most hotels overbook a certain amount to allow for "No-Shows." By the way, it's a complete fallacy that hotels keep a certain number of rooms available for emergencies. If they did, this they would never be able to run 100% occupancy. Hotels do and so have I rented rooms in need of repairs to desperate individuals at discounted rates. This creates an anomaly where you can run occupancy over 100% since out-of-order rooms are not considered part of the hotel's inventory.

One day, the reservation manager came to me and explained that the hotel was significantly overbooked for the next day. I asked her definition of "significantly overbooked" only to learn that we were overbooked by more than 125 rooms! This meant that we had nearly sold each room in our hotel twice. We informed the hotel's general manager and explained our plan to handle the issue. Without exception, guests with confirmed hotel reservations will have to be "walked" meaning sent away to other hotels with availability. I knew the next day would be a very long one.

Hotels have varying policies on how oversold situations are handled. The most generous of policies would provide the walked guest with a paid confirmed reservation at a comparable or better hotel than the one he or she was walked from, transportation to that hotel if he or she didn't drive in, one or two long distance phone calls so they could notify concerned associates of their new hotel location, a welcome amenity upon their arrival along with an apology note from the responsible hotel's general manager. We were a smaller hotel with finite resources and our policy was to simply provide a list of hotels with their phone numbers known to have availability for that night.

Our plan to handle this situation was as follows:

- Get a firm grasp on the number of individuals that would have to be walked;

- Alert all Front Desk and Reservation personnel that no stay-overs of in-house guests would be allowed for the following night;

- Prioritize all incoming reservations for the next day ensuring that individuals representing critical business to the hotel wouldn't be walked;

- Call around the area to prepare a list of hotels that would have availability extending the area radius until a comfort level is reached that walked guests will have accommodation options;

- Ensure a representative from hotel management (in this case, it would be me) was present and available as a fallback position to the desk clerk presenting the inconvenienced guest with the walk scenario.

After processing these steps, it became apparent to me that we would have to start walking guests early the next day. I arrived for my long day before 7 am the following morning, wishing that we'd have an abnormal number of cancellations for that day. Unfortunately, that didn't occur, so we began the "walking" process as the earlier guests arrived. The on-duty front desk clerks talked to the guests as they arrived while I intervened when situations were subject to volatility or a manager was requested. The day stretched into evening and became a long, laborious experience. As the day moved along, the staff kept watching the time as at 12 midnight reservations that hadn't arrived could be officially cancelled as "no-shows." For the first two shifts, we had the staff overlap working an hour or two overtime for additional support.

One of our desk clerks, Levi Pence working the 3–11 p.m. shift, attended a local mortuary school. Levi was obtaining the background to eventually take over his family's mortuary business. Levi was a true gentleman with a quiet, professional demeanor. We were just about though this exhausting ordeal when around 11 pm, one of our last to be "walked" gentlemen arrived and was given the walk spiel by Levi. This fellow then reached across the desk and grabbed Levi by his tie! Levi casually released the marauder's hand from his throat while concluding the spiel as if nothing had happened. In that incident, Levi epitomized the definition of "cool under pressure." That particular scene has since been replayed over and over in my mind.

In smaller hotels like ours, it was common to have one position perform multiple functions. In addition to my Front Office Manager responsibilities, I was also the credit manager. During this period, guests skipping out on their bills were common, probably leading to current day credit procedures where in most hotels the total estimated charges of arriving guests are immediately charged against an approved credit card. The Sheraton East was particularly susceptible to "skips" as it was located just off the interstate. One of my built-in characteristics is an extreme sense of responsibility. If we were unable to track them down skipped guests, accounts would have to be written off, which I was most conscientious about.

So, it was my responsibility to reduce the bad debt write-offs the hotel incurred. Working in front of the house hotel positions for the previous eight years made me a good judge of character. When dealing with the public oftentimes that's all you have to go on, your judgment. We required identification when guests checked in but that was easily forged. Additionally, we didn't have access to the instant credit verification that currently exists. The only true defense we had to avoid skips and delinquents was to refuse their reservation at check-in. This, of course created potentially additional litigation issues.

This is where the third remembered incident occurred. I checked an individual into the hotel whom I had a negative gut feeling about. On the surface, he looked the part. He was well-dressed, well-mannered, etc. But my intuition told me to keep an eye out on his activities. Sure enough, in short order, he began running up several charges on his room account. He had numerous long-distance phone calls, bar charges, restaurant charges, etc. While he was still checked in, I saw him drive off for what I thought would be the day or at least several hours. To confirm my suspicions, I let myself into his room double locking his room behind me.

Obviously, this was something that could get me into a lot of trouble but my zeal to perform out-weighed the potential consequences. To my horror, he returned to his room as I was in it searching for anything that would confirm my distrust. My heart literally jumped through my throat as he entered his key into the door while jiggling the door handle. He yelled out "Who's in there?" as I remained frozen in silence. After hearing him walk away thinking something was wrong with his key, I quickly departed the room and never again used that credit reduction tactic. We refused further credit to this individual but never recovered the charges made beforehand.

Keeping in touch with my hotel mentor Jim Reed while my career continued on the mainland, I learned that he'd left Mauna Kea Beach Hotel for C. Brewer & Company. This company was a Honolulu-based organization, which was once part of the Big Five Companies in territorial Hawaii. The company did most of its business in agriculture. The group emerged to become one of Hawaii's Big Five companies, albeit the smallest of the Big Five. In 1959, seeing the need for further diversification, the company entered the macadamia nut industry, and in the 1990s produced the majority of the world's macadamia nuts under the name Mauna Loa Macadamia Nut Corporation.

The company undertook land development for "leisure time" endeavors in the late sixties. In 1969, Brewer directors acquired Kilauea Volcano

House, the crater-side motel-restaurant, and gave the green light to a resort development scheme for their non-cultivated Big Island lands. The resort plan launched "Seamountain-Hawaii" at Kau, an incremental development that included Punalu'u Village, golf courses, condominiums and, last but not least, a luxury resort hotel. Nearer Hilo, Brewer's Waiakea Resort Village and Marketplace with 300 rooms opened in 1972. In the 1960s and 1970s, Hilo was booming with tourists. The so-called "Maui Fence" allowed visitors to start or end their vacation in Hilo for the same round-trip airfare as a trip to Honolulu. Hilo's airport once had nine carriers and was the only Neighbor Island with direct flights to the Mainland. Hawaii's popularity has since seen the addition of direct flights into Kona, Maui, and Kauai.

Those dreams and others eventually became economic nightmares. Hilo-side tourism numbers declined, hastened ironically by the hotel I began my career in, the Mauna Kea Beach Hotel on the west side of the Big Island. Mauna Kea had a beautiful beach, better weather and—thanks to the governor and the legislature—a highway and a nearby major airport. Similar high-end hotels followed in the same area. Its rainy climate and scarcity of beaches meant Hilo would never again be the most popular visitor destination in the state.

Jim Reed presented the Punalu'u Village/Seamountain development to me as an opportunity, and in early 1974, I went to work for C. Brewer to manage this Kau development for the growth potential it offered. My candidacy was buoyed by the fact I had graduated from high school on this very island a little more than an hour away from Kau. You could say that for this opportunity like another I'll get into later, I was in the right place at the right time. My first C. Brewer title was Executive Assistant Manager for Punalu'u Village and the Volcano House. My long-term vision was to be the general manager of their proposed luxury resort as well as an area vice-president, overseeing all operations in the Kau area.

My initial focus was on the Punalu'u Village restaurant. The complex was a series of Polynesian themed huts that included separate units for the restaurant/bar, a gift shop, a museum, kitchen, and administration offices.

These huts were strategically placed behind lovely fresh water lagoons created for the concept. Fronting the lagoons was the state's only black sand beach. It was truly a tropical-postcard-like setting. My compensation package included housing and a company van.

The company rented a home for me in Pahala, a town approximately five miles away from the Punalu'u Village complex. A sugarcane plantation created Pahala, which had a 2010 population of 1,378 but was even smaller during my time there.

The area selected to house the sugar refinery had several key features:

- A flat plateau on a sloping mountainous region;
- Direct access to a water well;
- A strategic central location to sugarcane fields.

In Hawaiian, Pāhala refers to the ashes of leaves from the hala tree. Long ago, when cracks were found in the sugarcane fields, workers would stuff them with hala leaves and burn them.

My first day in my new position was unusual. Falling asleep due to a heightened level of exhaustion the previous evening, I overslept the following morning. Realizing that my new staff was awaiting arrival of their new manager, I readied myself quickly running out to the company supplied van. Tearing out of my driveway I hurried to the restaurant complex, far exceeding the speed limit. Before addressing the staff, I went into the offices to collect my thoughts. While there, a police officer came in to admonish me for speeding. He claimed that I was going so fast that he couldn't catch up with me or he would have most certainly ticketed me. I never saw him nor realized he was in pursuit. That police officer, Tommy Aiona, and I later became good friends and often laughed at how we first met.

Among my first tasks were the indoctrination and training of the raw but eager staff along with fighting off a unionization effort. The training and indoctrination were simple enough but the union contest was an entirely different challenge. Most of these employees all grew up in union households with their parents employed by the local sugar plantation. Unionization was all the local populace knew. Although we defeated the union on their first attempt, realization set in that we were just stalling the inevitable and, sure enough, the Punalu'u Village complex eventually unionized. The staff eagerly trained for their new hospitality positions of cooks, servers, bus personnel, attendants, etc. To augment this effort, being a graduate of the Educational Institute of the American Hotel and Motel Association, I taught courses within their curriculum to the staff and locals who would become part of an additional talent pool for future employment.

Hawaii has long been known for its "Hawaiian Spirit," which is reflected in the attitudes and genuine caring of the tourists they serve as well as ministering to their own "Ohana" (family, relatives, kin group). The Punalu'u Village complex offered long term employment opportunity for the area and they eagerly put their hearts and souls into the project. Successful completion of C. Brewer's master plan for this area would put the community on solid financial ground for years to come. The company got involved in the community contributing to good causes, sponsoring a basketball team that I played on, etc.

There were challenges to be sure. The area was in a remote section of the island and the restaurant was heavily dependent on tour buses stopping in as they circled the island. To some degree the restaurant competed against itself as its main competitor, the Volcano House, owned by the same company, was just thirty miles away.

We conquered the luncheon problem by offering the tour bus drivers free lunches with a distinct local flare. Our Hawaiian chef developed a special local menu served strictly to these bus tour drivers, which included local favorites of sashimi, lomi-lomi salmon, poke, poi, laulau, etc. Word quickly spread among the tour bus drivers and we were able to build a solid luncheon base from these drivers as each bus represented forty to fifty customers. This luncheon base was important as tour patterns didn't provide the same opportunity for dinner business. We had to rely on the local population and the occasional diners who would make the one-hour drive in from Hilo for the evening meal. To accommodate the volume of luncheon business, we served a lavish buffet while offering a scaled back *ala carte* menu for dinner. Between the parking lot and the restaurant/bar were the museum and the gift shop. So these busloads of tourists would pass them on the way to lunch and usually patronize them before departing.

Sometime after relocating to Pahala Hawaii for the C. Brewer assignment, my daughter Janette came to live with us. This was several years before either of my sons was born. In fact, I had a vasectomy a few years earlier and didn't have it reversed until 1976, feeling that having children of my second wife's own would temper her disciplinary handling of children. Sometime during this same year, we received a visit from the local police department following up on concerns that Janette's schoolteachers had. My second wife had been physically abusing Janette and I was too wrapped up with my job to notice. We were fortunate that my second wife's parents were able to care for Janette in Honolulu on the island of Oahu for a period.

On November 29, 1975, the largest local earthquake to strike the Hawaiian Islands since 1868 eventually led to the collapse of C. Brewer's tourism plans for the area. Actually, two earthquakes occurred. The first happened around 3:30 am with a magnitude of 5.7. The second and considerably larger earthquake occurred a little over an hour later at a magnitude of 7.2. Although earthquake damage was relatively limited, a large tsunami was generated by the second quake. A wall of water approximately 25 feet high traveling over 600 miles per hour devastated the area, causing millions of dollars in property damage along with two tragic deaths. It also triggered a small brief eruption of the Kilauea volcano.

That was a horrific event to experience. I remember that lying in bed, I was awakened by howling noises from dogs and the bleating of goats outside. Following this was the beginning of the quake where dishes in the kitchen cabinets began to fall out, medicine from the bathroom vanities fell from their shelves, and you could feel the house shaking physically. I got up but felt absolutely helpless by the events developing around me. There wasn't any one place that was necessarily safer than another. If there was one word to describe those seemingly endless hours, that would be "terrifying."

Early the following morning, I drove down to the restaurant complex to survey the damage. I parked in the parking lot, which was located more than a quarter of a mile from the ocean, only to discover debris and dead fish that the tsunami had deposited there. The same scene was apparent as I walked downhill from the lot to the restaurant complex. The individual hut structures were still standing probably due to them having large plate glass windows that gave way when the tidal wave crushed its way through. Some furniture and fixtures had been swept out to sea. The tsunami left furniture, fixtures, canned food, etc. in the lagoon situated between the restaurant complex and the ocean. It was disgusting to see that Caucasian hippie types had descended on the area and were pilfering whatever they could carry away. There was a police presence but the area was too vast for the small Pahala force to govern.

My immediate superior Jim Reed, was on the mainland for business. After first glance of surveying the damage, I made the very difficult phone call to him. Through the media, he had learned of the earthquake and tsunami events but was unaware of the degree of damage these natural disasters had caused to the facility. To the best of my ability, I described the scene and he indicated that he'd get to the restaurant complex as quickly as he could. To this point, I hadn't been to the administration offices so I decided to inspect them. I walked uphill into the hut and to where my office was, only to find my desk smashed by one of our industrial-sized refrigerators previously located in our kitchen in another structure weighing several hundred pounds! The November 29, 1975 earthquake and tsunami that hit the Punalu'u Village Complex was the beginning of the end of C. Brewers' venture into Hawaii tourism.

One of the anomalies of this catastrophic incident was that a nine-foot tall by twenty-two-foot-wide Herb Kane mural of Punalu'u Bay displayed in the museum was untouched. Kane was a celebrated artist-historian and author with a special interest in the seafaring traditions of the ancestral peoples of Hawaii. Along with volcano architect Boone Morrison, Kane designed the museum and restaurant at Punalu'u. Early after my Hawaii arrival, I'd learned to respect Hawaiian traditions as well as their superstitions. Due to the museum's location between the restaurant and parking lot, this appeared to me to be a case where a higher power protected this fabled mural from destruction.

Hawaiian culture has many beliefs and legends. I'd experienced an incident during my Hawaii residency, making me a believer of the local superstitions. One legend is that of Pele. Pele, the Goddess of Fire, is known for her fiery temperament and powerful personality. There are many stories of Pele which illustrate lovers' quarrels, epic battles with siblings, and the driving away from her native Tahiti to the Hawaiian Islands. Pele's home is believed to be Halemaumau Crater, which is located at the summit of Kilauea Volcano. Kilauea, located inside of Hawai'i Volcanoes National Park, is one of the world's most active volcanoes, and the frequent volcanic activity is believed to be Pele's longing for her true love. When lava spews from the volcano, it is believed that it is her erupting. She leaves behind pieces of "Pele's Hair" and "Pele's Tears," which are the long strands of hardened lava and small lava rocks found all over the park.

The road between Punalu'u and the volcano is an isolated, secluded lonesome drive. It's particularly eerie at night; during my tenure, there were no highway lights between these two destinations. With responsibilities at facilities in both areas, I made the thirty-minute trip frequently, both during daytime hours and at night. Late one evening, I was driving solo up from Punalu'u to the Volcano House. A surreal sensation came over me and I looked in my rear-view mirror and saw what appeared to be a beautiful middle-aged woman in a long white dress sitting in my back seat! I was absolutely petrified and after gathering myself looked again and she was gone. Was she actually there? Whether she was or not I became a believer right then and there in Hawaiian traditions and superstitions.

Punalu'u Village Restaurant before Tidal Wave disaster.

Punalu'u Village Restaurant after Tidal Wave disaster.

Chapter 5 | 1976–1985

During this ten-year period, my two sons were born, I formed a Hawaii Big Island chapter of the American Hotel & Motel Association, acquired my Hawaii Real Estate License, realized my hotel General Manager goal, earned my Associates Degree, and had what I discovered later to be a life-or-death operation.

Following the disastrous Big Island tsunami of November 1975, C. Brewer & Company shifted responsibilities in their travel and tourism division. Jim Reed informed me that in lieu of my overseeing the now closed Punalu'u Village Restaurant, I would oversee the Volcano Golf Course in addition to the Seamountain Golf course and condominiums, and report directly to him. This was a new challenge but left me with an unexplainable void. My dream of overseeing a large resort complex was in potential peril. C. Brewer and Company was obviously reviewing their future options and where tourism fell within their plans, I had no idea.

Directly after the tsunami calamity, I studied for and obtained my Hawaii Real Estate License. My thinking was that it would benefit me with my condominium responsibilities and provide a possible hedge if my hospitality career suddenly ended. It was demanding but also a rewarding undertaking while I contemplated my future. As I worked toward the real estate final exam, an idea sprung to mind, which could potentially benefit the local area while enhancing my employment goals. The enthusiasm of the now unemployed as well as the remaining employed populace made me feel a local chapter for American Hotel and Motel Association would be successful.

So in 1975, the Kau Chapter of the American Hotel and Motel Association was formed. A slate of officers was elected, making me the president of the organization; the national office located on the mainland certified the chapter. The chapter's main focus was to develop hospitality graduates while being staunch supporters of the local tourism industry. Being a program graduate qualified me to teach the hotel courses that would lead to other Big Island graduates. My hope was that C. Brewer and Company would take notice of this initiative, encouraging them to maintain their local hospitality pursuits.

The Kau Chapter of the American Hotel and Motel Association was an overwhelming success. Of the more than 100 chapters located nationwide, the Kau Chapter was ranked in the top 10, competing with elite chapters in Boston, Denver, Kansas City, Seattle, Shreveport, and Minneapolis merely after its first year of service. One of the chapter's key accomplishments was the donation of $1,000 to the Big Island's tourism promotion arm of the Hawaii Industry Visitors Industry Association (HIVIA). The $1,000 donation was the largest contribution HIVIA had ever received from a non-corporate group at that point. To raise this substantial sum, the chapter held a series of events. A golf tournament was held, in which a portion of the green fees and cart rentals were set-aside for HIVIA. Two auctions were held with handmade items by the chapter's members put up for sale. A bake sale also contributed to the donated funds. The $1,000 check presentation took place at the local Naalehu Clubhouse attended by 70 Kau residents, the President of HIVIA, members of the Kau Chapter of the American Hotel & Motel Association, and the Mayor of the Big Island of Hawaii.

To maintain a public chapter presence during the summer of 1976, we decided to enter a float in the annual Naalehu 4th of July parade. Having received an extraordinary amount of press coverage for the chapter's HIVIA project, we felt it important to maintain momentum in the public relations arena while working our way up the top ten-chapter list for the American Hotel and Motel Association. Hundreds of volunteer hours and countless donated resources culminated in the chapter winning first place out of forty-five entries for its production. However, much to our dismay, these herculean efforts did not translate into C. Brewer and Company moving forward with its initial mega hospitality development project.

During 1976, my parents along with my two half-sisters from my mother's side of the family relocated from Indianapolis, Indiana, to the island of Maui. This, in my opinion, was huge as my parents were real homebodies and for them to undertake such a move was hard to fathom. My stepfather was in ill health and had retired from his Ford Motor Company factory job so outside of family they didn't have other ties in Indiana. My uncle Jack had a place on Maui and apparently promised it to my parents if they would move out to the islands. For whatever reason, my uncle reneged on the offer, creating a temporary hostile living environment for my parents and sisters. My uncle subsequently either gave or sold this Maui property to a friend of his instead. The silver lining in the move for my parents was my stepfather's better health. There's no question in my mind that their move to Hawaii lengthened his life span.

Undeterred by events around me, I decided to continue pursuit of my goal to become a hotel General Manager. With minimal available options to me at this point, I decided to accept the position of Food & Beverage Director for the Waikiki Beachcomber Hotel in Honolulu. Amfac Resorts, a well-established Hawaii Hotel company, managed the Waikiki Beachcomber Hotel at this time. Amfac, Inc., (parent company of Amfac Resorts) formerly known as American Factors, was a land development company in Hawaii. Founded in 1849 as a retail and sugar business, it was considered one of the so-called Big Five companies in the Territory of Hawaii. Amfac Resorts was formerly known as the Fred Harvey Company managing several national park resorts, restaurants, and tourism services. In 2002, Amfac changed its corporate name to Xanterra after the bankruptcy of Amfac Hawaii. The name comes from a combination of Xanadu and terra (Earth). Xanterra specializes in tourism in U.S. national parks, and has a presence in Yellowstone and the Grand Canyon, along with a number of other national and state parks. They are contracted by the U.S.

National Park Service to provide lodging and food and beverage services in these parks.

My tenure as Food Beverage Director at the Waikiki Beachcomber Hotel was uneventful. The food & beverage offerings of the hotel were varied and included an all-purpose coffee shop, a dining room, a lounge, and a show room. The hotel was located on Waikiki's main street, Kalakaua Avenue, that provided an inordinate amount of pedestrian traffic. Unfortunately, the hotel's food and beverage facilities were located on the second floor of the building necessitating prospective non-hotel patrons to navigate a steep escalator ride for access. Given the location of its restaurants and bar, its business (with the exception of the show room) the hotel was highly dependent on in-house business and ebbed and flowed with the hotel's occupancy levels.

My first son Shawn (named after actor Sean Connery) Douglas Evans was born during this period, on May 17, 1977. Weighing slightly over seven pounds, Shawn was born at Honolulu's Kapiolani hospital at 12:55 pm. He was a handsome little guy and still is, handsome that is, not so little. I recall being so excited over his arrival that I immediately went out and bought him a full-size basketball. What propelled me to do that is a mystery, as he wouldn't be able to use it for several years. This turned out to be one of the few periods that my second wife and I had assistance from either of our parents with our children. My second wife's parents resided on Oahu and were able to assist us with our baby boy for a few months preceding my next hospitality assignment.

Hawaii presented a relaxed environment that was often referred to as Polynesian Paralysis. The best way I can describe this is that tourists visiting the islands felt so relaxed and uninhibited that their behavior was carefree. For example, tourists buying packages to visit the Aloha State would be careful to spend minimum amounts on packages that included hotel accommodations, airfare, and perhaps some meals. However, after their arrival and experiencing the tropics for a day or so, they would commonly spend more on island tours, events, and clothing than they did on their entire vacation before arrival! Separate companies were established in Hawaii to take advantage of this, setting up tour desks in most hotels. Tourists were invited to "Orientation Sessions," which featured a complimentary meal and sometimes even entertainment, where at the end of these sessions tourists would open their checkbooks to purchase numerous described Hawaiian options.

Visiting college sport teams would fall into this tropical trap. Not so much from a spending standpoint but letting their guard down when playing local collegiate teams, succumbing to Polynesian Paralysis. Chaminade's 77–72 victory over Ralph Sampson and top-ranked Virginia in 1982 is widely considered the biggest upset in college basketball history and among the greatest in any sport. Chaminade, an 800-student facility, posed no threat at all to the 8–0 Virginia Cavaliers. Virginia had just beaten half of the previous season's Final Four contenders; they had the best player in country and they were ranked the best team in the country. Chaminade, which was an NAIA school (meaning that they weren't even a part of the NCAA and were less relevant than a Division III school), defeated mighty Virginia 77–72!

Later in 1977, my hotel General-Manager goal was realized. My hotel mentor Jim Reed established himself as Area Vice-President for mainland-based Dunfey Hotels and secured an interview for me. Dunfey Hotels, headquartered in Hampton, New Hampshire, was a small New England chain with an interesting history. The chain began when five Dunfey brothers purchased Lamie's Tavern in Hampton, New Hampshire, a combination restaurant and motor inn. The Dunfeys primarily wanted the restaurant, but the owner insisted that the adjoining thirty-two-room hotel be part of the deal. The brothers adopted a theme of "Good old New England hospitality" for their hotel and touted the restaurant as a "cracker barrel lounge."

The success of the Lamie Motor Inn convinced the Dunfeys that they could make more money as innkeepers than they could by operating restaurants. They purchased their first real hotel of over 300 rooms in 1958 and founded the Dunfey Hotels Corporation. During the late 1950s and early 1960s, the brothers, under the guidance of company president Jack Dunfey, bought several other properties throughout New England. The Dunfeys became some of the first pioneers of hotel franchising in 1964 when they obtained several existing hotels and motor inns that bore the Sheraton name. With their Sheraton Inns acquisition, the Dunfey Hotels Corporation became the largest hotel franchise holder in the world with a total of fourteen inns.

By the mid-1960s, the Dunfeys had hotels and operating offices scattered throughout Massachusetts, Maine, and New Hampshire. The properties were successful partly as a result of the Dunfeys' marketing and management strategies. For example, they retained their original New England hospitality slogan and integrated the cracker barrel lounge into many of their hotels. They consolidated their acquisitions' management into the Dunfey Hotels Corporation's New England headquarters to maintain control over their growing operation. The Dunfeys also devised a strategy of targeting struggling hotels in need of renovation, which they could buy inexpensively. In 1968, for instance, they bought the financially ailing Parker House in Boston, renovated the facility, and returned it to profitability.

Dunfey Hotels flew me from Hawaii to Hampton, New Hampshire, for my interview with company executives Jim Stamas and Toni Chance. Due to the distance I traveled, they put me up at one of their hotels. The interview went well and they offered me a general manager's position. It was at their Sheraton by the Sea Hotel located on Jekyll Island, Georgia. Jekyll Island is located off the coast of Georgia in Glynn County. It is one of the Sea Islands and one of the Golden Isles of Georgia barrier islands.

Armed with a boatload of enthusiasm and the desire to prove my value as a thirty-one-year-old hotel general manager, I moved my family from Hawaii to Georgia to tackle the assignment. Dunfey Hotels housed us at the hotel and included meals as part of my compensation package. A pang of guilt came over me during the relocation process as we were leaving Hawaii just a little over a year from my parents' arrival. While they didn't make the move solely to be by me, it was difficult nonetheless.

Sheraton by the Sea was a challenging assignment partly due to logistics. The property consisted of seventeen three-story buildings spread out over fifteen acres of land. Golf carts for the housekeeping and other staff were mandatory. A weather phenomenon quickly set in with me. Stepping outside of an air-conditioned building on a summer day led to an immediate drenching in your own sweat due to the high humidity in the region. Competition in the area was fierce as Jekyll Island was surrounded by other well-known resort destinations including, but not limited to Sea Island (home of The Cloister & The Lodge, awarded five stars by Forbes Travel) and St. Simonds Island. This was my first taste of "southern hospitality" and I found the local populace to be genuinely friendly.

In relatively short order, the company moved me over 2,700 miles to San Mateo, California, to assume "Resident Manager" responsibilities. An industry outsider could perceive the move a demotion as the Resident Manager's position is number two in a hotel's hierarchy but the Dunfey San Mateo hotel was a much larger property so it was a lateral position move. Once again, my compensation package included full room and board for my family at the hotel. My son Shawn learned quickly the location of my office and would on a regular basis "drop in" to say hello on his way to breakfast. A couple of years later, while I was General Manager at another Dunfey Hotel, we were on vacation on route to Hawaii and stayed overnight at that hotel. The following morning, Shawn on his own went to where my former office used to be, thinking he'd find me there.

While living in the hotel provides tremendous fringe benefits, the downside is that you're always on call. This, of course, can lead to interesting events. Very early one morning, the phone rang in our Dunfey San Mateo hotel apartment to alert me of an incident that required my presence. Our hotel was located near a major concert venue and the headliner who was staying with us was a well-known Las Vegas personality. The alleged incident had occurred in his suite and he was requesting the presence of a hotel manager. I arrived to meet him and his manager. The story given to me was that his suite had been burglarized to the tune of $10,000.

71

Learning this, I indicated that we needed to call the police but they did everything possible to dissuade me from doing so. Fully aware of potential legal ramifications, the police were notified and I was amazed at how obstinate this celebrity and his manager were to them. Later, I learned that what truly happened was that a prostitute was invited to the suite and she managed to steal the $10,000, which our well-known guest was hoping the hotel would spring for!

On another occasion at this same hotel, the FBI approached me expressing a desire to monitor the activity of a couple of our guests. They requested a room next to their two suspects for this purpose. They claimed that the two suspects were involved in a major drug trafficking scheme. Assured that our other hotel guests wouldn't be placed in any danger and wanting to cooperate, I granted their request. Unaware of how the events unfolded, the next thing I knew was a slew of FBI agents had these two suspects lying face down on their stomachs in our lobby with guns raised, handcuffs out, and the suspects being read their rights! No one was hurt but this was not the outcome projected to me by the authorities.

The president of Dunfey Hotels, during this period, was a gentleman considered a marketing guru. Jon Canas came up with effective marketing campaigns and created a name for himself within the organization. As a general manager, his direction confounded me on a few occasions as he would change the chain's name or tagline—meaning hotels would have to discard all branded items like stationery, soaps, etc. That, depending on a particular hotel's inventory, could run into thousands of dollars. Each year, every hotel would go through an arduous planning/budgeting process to which annual staff bonus amounts were tied. Thus, each time the company would change their marketing direction, each hotel with outdated items would have to absorb those costs, making it that much more difficult to achieve bonus levels.

During this planning process, mission statements were updated and key result areas (KRAs) identified to tie objectives and budgets to the coming year. While at Dunfey San Mateo Hotel, the general manager assigned the task of overseeing this effort to me. While flattered that this important process was entrusted to me, it created an episode that has stayed with me to this day. Anxious to justify the trust placed in me for this critical assignment. I gathered the executive staff each day for several hours to identify objectives and strategies for each department that would be difference-making the following year. Finally satisfied that we had a plan that would substantially advance our hotel's gross operating profit the following year, I presented it to the general manager who also thought highly of it.

The company president required each hotel to make their presentation to him in New York before each plan could officially be adopted. Being the author of our hotel plan, I flew to New York with our general manager to make the presentation on our hotel's behalf. I reviewed and rehearsed the plan and my presentation for countless hours as this was to be my first meeting with our company president. On what I perceived to be a special day, the general manager of our hotel, our company president, several other company executives, and I sat around a board table in an elaborate boardroom in our New York Hotel for the presentation. The carefully prepared plan document was placed on the table in front of each meeting participant. The meeting wasn't more than fifteen minutes into its session when the company president admonished the plan. There was one particular phrase in the plan that he latched on to that included the words "Think Positive," which for some reason he took offense to. I believe his admonishment went something like this: "I could think snow right now but that wouldn't make it snow."

I was horrified! Here I was nearly 3,000 miles from my current home base, having spent the majority of my time in the past month on this plan and the company president was dismissing it out of hand. One of the thoughts that ran through was my mind was that this could spell the end of my brief hotel career. There really wasn't much of anything the other participants could or would do as the president had taken his stand. We were instructed to revise the plan to be more authentic for a future presentation. Fortunately for me, this wasn't the end of my Dunfey Hotels employment but the plane ride back to California was one of the longest of my life, with countless doomsday scenarios pulsating through my head.

My next assignment with Dunfey hotels was another cross-country move in 1979 to accept the position of General Manager of the Sheraton Hotel in South Portland, Maine. This time, my compensation package didn't include housing, so we purchased a home at 30 Baird Circle in South Portland. The hotel was a smaller property consisting of over 120 rooms and suites, and was circular in shape, which included tinted dark glass exterior windows. It was situated just off a major highway and, for directional purposes, was referenced as the building that looked like a large oil can. This hotel's claim to fame was that it was the hotel where Elvis Presley had the Presidential Suite reserved for the day after he died.

My youngest son, Scott David Evans, was born while we were in Maine at the Maine Medical Center. I remember being in the delivery room for his birth. The hospital required me to dress in a surgical gown inclusive of the mask that doctors wear. I was in the room before the doctor or nurse arrived. The nurse came in first and mistakenly took me for the doctor! I nearly fainted, thinking of this grievous identity error. Obviously, it all worked out and my second son and last child came into this world on October 7, 1979, at 12:51 am.

Everyone has some regrets regarding past performances. I have one from this hotel, which I would handle differently now if I were to go back in time. Each Dunfey hotel had an Executive Operating Committee (EOC) led by the general manager, which included the Rooms Division Manager, Food & Beverage Director, Executive Housekeeper, and Systems Analyst. It was this committee's responsibility to carry out the organization's policies/standards as well as to develop and execute the hotel's annual plan. This required meeting on a regular basis. I would hold the meetings later in the day to minimally interfere with hotel operations. The issue with this was that I was encroaching on the precious personal family time of the committee members with this scheduling.

The following year, I was promoted to the position of general manager of the Marquette Hotel in Minneapolis reporting to the managing director, Lawrence Jeffrey. This was my first inner-city assignment and was as inner-city as you can get. The Marquette Hotel sat directly in the middle of downtown Minneapolis. The hotel was situated within the IDS Tower complex which, once inside, is basically one covered, weather-controlled block. This was one of the better assignments I had in my hotel career. The Marquette, enjoying a very favorable city marketing position, gave me enough free time to pursue and obtain my Associates Degree with Honors from Normandale Community College in Bloomington. The Marquette Hotel at this time was the only five-star property in the Twin Cities enjoying exceptional demand from the transient non-price-sensitive markets. We realized the highest occupancy levels and highest average room rate for the twin cities. Due to our marketing position we were literally able to set the room rates for the city. The other hotels set their room rates below ours based upon their position within the marketplace. This favorable market positioning allowed me to focus almost exclusively on hotel service levels.

The luxury property had 282 guest rooms and suites, an all-purpose dining room, and a formal dining room open for lunch and dinner only. A notoriety held by the hotel was its being used for filming by the popular Mary Tyler Moore television show. The Marquette Hotel had a popular weekend package that we were able to utilize when lower occupancy levels warranted called "Pretty in Pink." This well-known weekend package famously included, among other perks, a pink negligee, a bottle of imported champagne, and room service breakfast for two.

We purchased a modest home at 1476 Independence Avenue in the St. Louis Park suburb of Minneapolis. While the hotel assignment was one of my more enjoyable ones the winter weather was an obstacle I just couldn't overcome. On my first trip into Minneapolis, I was being chauffeured from the airport to the hotel and noticed high walls along most sections of the Interstate Highway. When inquiring about these high walls, I was jokingly informed that they were for the winter snowfalls. My first

Minneapolis winter wasn't too bad, the total snowfall was only twenty-one inches. However, my second winter saw ninety-five inches of snow and my fourth ninety-eight!

Minneapolis' bitter cold weather conditions led to the birth of an above ground climate controlled "Skyway System". Sensing pressure from indoor shopping malls the city wanted to create a contained environment in Downtown Minneapolis that would offer a climate-controlled space and a way for pedestrians to move from building to building regardless of weather conditions. Two skyways, connecting the Northstar Center building to the Northwestern Bank Building and the Roanoke Building, were built in in the early 1960s. The Minneapolis Skyway System is an interlinked collection of enclosed pedestrian footbridges that connect various buildings in 80 full city blocks to over 11 miles of Downtown Minneapolis, enabling people to walk in climate-controlled comfort year-round. It is the longest continuous system in the world. Individual buildings in Minneapolis own the skyways, and as such they do not have uniform opening and closing times. The Minneapolis skyways connect the second or third floors of various office towers, hotels, banks, corporate and government offices, restaurants, and retail stores to the Nicollet Mall shopping district, the Mayo Clinic Square, and the sports facilities at Target Center, Target Field and U.S. Bank Stadium. Several condominium and apartment complexes are skyway-connected as well, allowing residents to live, work, and shop downtown without having to leave the skyway system.

The extreme cold was also something that I could never adjust to. During our first winter, one very cold evening my second wife and I went to the local Guthrie Theatre. On the way home, our vehicle would sputter and every so often die. After several such incidents, I stopped to make a call home to our sitter. I told him we would be late and explained why. He asked if we had "Heet" in our gas tank. After he explained the benefits, I put some in our gas tank and the problem was solved. Now I knew why some Minnesotans plugged their engine blocks into electricity during the winter! Notwithstanding the winters, the summers in Minneapolis were spectacular. The summer days were long lasting until 9:00 am or 9:30 pm, with near perfect comfortable temperatures.

Toward the end of 1982, the company approached me for another move. I had been with Dunfey Hotels a mere five years and was already in my fourth hotel as well as fourth state. One of the perils of hotel management during this era was the constant movement of top management. Companies moved their general managers every couple of years. This played havoc on personal lives not to mention losses incurred in buying and reselling homes after each move. There was this unwritten rule that if you didn't agree to these moves, you would be blackballed within your company, stymieing growth potential. This is not the case today as companies began opting for longer upper management stays.

This time, I was very fortunate. Dunfey Hotels was in the process of assuming management of the Northstar Hotel located just a few blocks from the Marquette Hotel within this same city. The company wanted me to oversee a multi-million-dollar renovation at the property while it continued to operate. This was a unique opportunity for me as it accomplished two objectives. First, we wouldn't have to move, meaning we'd probably have at least another two years in Minneapolis. Second, it would provide a new realm of experience for me in overseeing a major hotel renovation.

During the transitional period, working between the Marquette and Northstar hotels, a most unusual event occurred confirming a hotel saying "when you think you've seen it all, you haven't." This most note-worthy experience was expertly documented by my now long-time friend, Ron Feldman. We developed a bridge tournament, providing cash prizes to generate revenue and occupancy for the Marquette Hotel over the 1982 Thanksgiving holiday period. This event was severely challenged logistically by a larger-than-life downtown Minneapolis fire.

Below are excerpts taken directly from Ron's January/February 2020 Facebook postings which accurately reflect that accounting:

RON FELDMAN FACEBOOK BRIDGE POSTING #97

On May 4th, 1982, I received an unexpected phone call from Stephen Evans, General Manager of The Marquette Hotel in Minneapolis. Before launching into how and why this phone call was about to change my entire life (no, I am not kidding!), I need to provide some background. Growing up in Hawaii, Stephen Evans had been a Bridge Caddy as a family member in Honolulu was an avid Bridge Player.

Because Stephen Evans personally was familiar with Bridge Tournaments having been a Bridge Caddy at ACBL tournaments, he had seen on the Convention Calendar for the City of Minneapolis, Minnesota, which the American Contract Bridge League (ACBL) had scheduled its Fall North American Championships to be held at the Hyatt Hotel in Downtown Minneapolis November 19 through the 28th. So, as the Marquette Hotel was also Downtown in close proximity to the Hyatt, Stephen reached out to me to see if the Association Of Professional Bridge Players, Inc. (APBP) would be interested in having The Marquette Hotel put on a Corporate Sponsored Bridge Tournament.

Stephen Evans, as General Manager, The Marquette Hotel, wanted to see if we could structure a mutually beneficial program that would benefit the Bridge Players and The Marquette Hotel. He explained to me that the cash prizes that the hotel would put up would come out of his advertising budget. This made perfect sense. Here is why: A hotel room is a perishable commodity. Once a hotel does not sell a room on any given night, unlike a carton of milk that sits in your refrigerator and has a shelf life of a couple of weeks before it sours, a hotel room that goes unsold can never recover the revenue from any particular night.

RON FELDMAN FACEBOOK BRIDGE POSTING #98

As per my last Bridge Posting, I indicated that Stephen Evans, General Manager, the Marquette Hotel in Minneapolis, had contacted me as he wanted to use some of his advertising budget for a Corporate Sponsored Bridge Tournament that I would structure and produce in my capacity as

President of the Association Of Professional Bridge Players, Inc. (APBP), the first accredited organization for professional bridge players by the American Contract Bridge League (ACBL). For the next couple weeks, I spent all my waking hours developing a structure for this event. To me, the only way to make this work was to have the cash prizes that the Marquette Hotel would award to the participating bridge players held on three (3) non-consecutive mornings so that they would not conflict with any ACBL event being held during the Fall North American Championships, November 18–29, 1982.

Because the Marquette Hotel was located several blocks from the Hyatt Hotel where the ACBL was holding its Fall North American Championships, and because the prior year over the same calendar dates, the Minneapolis–St. Paul Airport had to close due to a winter blizzard, Stephen Evans had come up with a novel idea whereby the participants in our APBP Corporate Sponsored Bridge Tournament at the Marquette Hotel would be shuttled to and from the ACBL playing site in chauffeur-driven limousines.

More importantly, Stephen Evans and I got along famously. And that has led to a lifelong friendship. We were able to consummate a deal. And since this was the month of May, I had to scramble to put the marketing in place before the ACBL Summer Nationals, which were in Albuquerque.

RON FELDMAN FACEBOOK BRIDGE POSTING #114

Right toward the end of the Marquette Hotel Bridge Tournament, disaster struck on Thanksgiving Day in the form of one of the largest fires in Minneapolis history. At about 4 pm, Minnesota time, a fire started in an old structure called the Donaldson Building next to the IDS Center, which was directly across the street from the Marquette Hotel.

Upon hearing the fire alarms, I quickly went back up to my room and was in shock as I not only could see the flames emanating from the fire directly across the street but also because my hotel window was melting! So, I eschewed the elevators and descended floor after floor all the way down to the lower levels below the hotel lobby as the Marquette Hotel had been built originally as the seventh floor on top of a parking garage of six levels, which would accommodate both hotel guests as well as serve as a downtown parking lot. Once I had safely parked the car away from the fire, I ran into Lawrence Jeffries, who was Vice-President, Operations at the Marquette Hotel and was assisting some of the bridge players in working with the firemen to get their medications out of their rooms.

Next, I was able to locate Stephen Evans who told me that the firemen had just told him that the Marquette Hotel would have to be evacuated. He told me that all the bridge players would be relocated to the Northstar Hotel. And, the bridge tournament would be held in the ballroom of the Northstar Hotel. To that end, everything went smoothly. All the bridge players were supportive. And the Northstar Hotel, like the Marquette Hotel, was a luxury property that everyone enjoyed. The Marquette Hotel Bridge Carnival went on without any further historical calamities. Stephen Evans was the hero that night.

RON FELDMAN FACEBOOK BRIDGE POSTING #115

It is now time to begin to recognize all the efforts of Stephen Evans, the general manager of the Marquette Hotel in Minneapolis. Under the worst circumstances possible, he took the risk to sponsor a cash-prize bridge tournament in Minneapolis in the likely inclement weather of Minneapolis over Thanksgiving and the week after Thanksgiving, where the prior year the Minneapolis–St. Paul Airport was closed due to a blizzard.

Stephen Evans also relied on my efforts, knowing at that point that I had no track record in putting on the cash-prize bridge tournaments previously. This is because the organization I founded, the Association Of Professional Bridge Players, Inc. (APBP), had received accreditation by the American Contract Bridge League (ACBL); the Marquette Hotel Bridge Carnival in Minneapolis was to be our maiden voyage.

And while the Marquette Hotel Bridge Carnival was well attended and all the participants were enjoying the cash-prize bridge tournament, and being shuttled to and from the ACBL hotel by limousine day and night, on the afternoon of Thanksgiving, Stephen Evans had to evacuate the Marquette Hotel due to one of the largest fires in Minneapolis history. Yet, literally as the old hackneyed phrase goes, "and when the smoke had cleared," Stephen had a contingency plan in place to move all of us without skipping a beat, by relocating everyone to the Northstar Hotel, just blocks from the Marquette Hotel. The limousines simply shuttled all the Marquette Hotel Guests over to the Northstar Hotel. From that point, the cash-prize bridge tournament went off without a hitch for the remaining few days of the tournament. **<End of Ron Feldman's Facebook excerpts.>**

The Northstar Hotel was my second Dunfey Hotels assignment in which the company took over the hotel. This presented an additional set of challenges, as there was the need to, what I call, to "Dunfeyize" the staff, meaning Dunfey Hotels' policies and procedures needed to be implemented, indoctrinating the staff to a new culture. It was not starting from scratch but it was also not far from it. Adding to the challenge, this hotel was an older unionized property with numerous employees having more than a decade of union seniority. If a union works with an organization, it can be beneficial for both the union and the company. However, if the union's temperament lies toward extracting everything they can from the company, there's just an extra layer of management difficulty. The main issue I have with unions is their protection of individuals not suited for their position simply because they have more seniority than other more qualified applicants. That along with grievances being filed just to irritate management. However, it's a fact of life and part of the framework that when management works with the union, everyone benefits.

The Northstar Hotel was a mid-sized 226-room property. It was centrally located in downtown Minneapolis, easily accessible to the Skyway system. It had the four-star Rosewood Room restaurant, a bar, the Copper Hearth restaurant, the Bagatelle restaurant, banquet facilities, and a dinner-only restaurant called the Wine Cellar. It also had the added benefit of being located near the center of the Minneapolis Skyway System. The major challenge facing Dunfey Hotels with the Northstar in addition to the planned renovation was to improve on this hotel's occupancy and average room rate to maximize room revenues and profits. The hotel performed relatively well mid-week with corporate business but sat nearly empty on weekends.

Review of the overall business mix revealed an especially anemic weekend demand. Weekend packages accounted for only 4% of this business. This made our initial occupancy goal clear: capture a greater share of the weekend package market. The two weekend packages inherited were poor performers probably due their perceived expensive connotations. At a "think tank" session one of our participants commented on the success a sister hotel of ours enjoyed with a weekend package in New York called "The Big Apple on Sale." This rang a bell with me as I paralleled this package to a potential "Minneapple Package" assuming use of this name would be granted from the principals of the local Minneapple Company that trademarked it. Knowing one of their principals, I pursued this affiliation, which resulted in an exclusive five-year arrangement providing the Northstar Hotel the use of the Minneapple logo with our to-be-developed "Minneapple Weekend" package.

The Minneapple Weekend Package included accommodations along with a logoed Minneapple tote bag. A campaign was developed, which included advertising via radio for eight markets, television for two markets, outdoor billboards for one market, a direct mail effort that included a fresh, large juicy apple to 3,500 of our past patrons, and newspapers for nine markets. The entire radio and television campaign was financed via previously earned trade-outs (rooms, food, and beverage provided to advertising partners in exchange for their services) allowing us to stretch a $20,000 cash budget into $45,000 worth of exposure. Results of the launch of the Minneapple Weekend Special were outstanding!

We nearly doubled the total weekend package output when comparing the first ten months of 1983 with the Minneapple Weekend package to the same ten-month period of 1982. Similarly, our weekend business, as a percentage to the total mix, nearly doubled from 4.6% to 8.6%. The timing of this launch could not have been better as the hotel was under renovation during the launch and even more so needed the occupancy shot-in-the-arm.

While this was an overwhelming success, we needed the hotel to be kept in front of our marketplace so the public would know that we were open during renovations and would in fact be even better once all improvements were finalized. Having spent most of our marketing dollars to shore up the hotel's occupancy, we needed a plan that would provide maximum exposure at minimal cost. Thus, we decided to pursue these needs through the public relations vehicle. Our objective was to develop an event, which would have the potential to create a strong consumer awareness of the renovation in a sustained and creative way.

Hence, the birth of the Northstar Hotel $2,000 dinner! This was a ten-course gourmet dinner for four to be given away by us to announce our $2.4 million dollar renovation. We partnered with the Donaldson's department store and WAYL radio to assist in promoting the event. Donaldson's heavily promoted the event through all of their Twin Cities stores as well as their Rochester store. Their downtown flagship store also featured several cooking demonstrations by our hotel's Executive Chef, Andreas Sellner, who cooked a similar feast for His Imperial Majesty Pahlavi of Iran. The actual drawing to determine the winner from over 40,000 entries was held at Donaldson's Minneapolis flagship store.

WAYL Radio heavily promoted the event by mentioning the contest four to eight times daily. The radio station also provided limousine service and formal wear to the contest winners. This event tied in nicely to WAYL's targeted audience and proved to be an effective promotion.

Another effective method utilized in the promotion of the event was a Chef's Table. We invited media representatives to a pre-tasting of featured items on the $2,000 Dinner menu. Columnists, writers, and editors representing seven twin city publications attended. This also proved to be a popular strategy.

The results of this event were successful beyond description! For a $3,750 investment we received media exposure valued at over $50,000. This exposure was highlighted by a story appearing on August 18, 1983, in the national issue of *USA TODAY*. We also were featured on the local *ABC* TV affiliate, KSTP Channels 5's "GOOD COMPANY SHOW." Further benefits were realized both nationally and locally through the press and magazines.

What does a $2,000 dinner for four look like?

Here's the menu in order of service:

1. Caviar Beluga Malossol served with Stolichnaya Vodka
   Flown in from the Caspian Sea

2. Truffle Consommé "En Croute"
   Thinly sliced rare mushroom in broth

3. Grenouilles Sauce Champagne served with
   Bernkasteler Doktor 1978 Champagne
   Imported frog legs with lobster medallions

4. Caneton Terrine served with
   Clos Du Vougeot 1966 Burgundy Wine
   Fresh duck liver

5. Pink Papaya Sorbet
   Intermezzo

6. Anceau Perigourdine served with
   Grand Vin De Chateau Latour 1966 Wine
   Stuffed baby lamb

7. Autumn Salad
   Mache, radicchio, mushrooms, & chicken liver

8. English Stilton served with Vintage Port
   Baby Stilton cheese imported from England

9. Soufflé Danziger Goldwasser served with Strohwein 1970 Wine
   Soufflé with fresh seasonal fruit

10. Lindt Excellance Pralines and Truffles
    World-renowned confections

11. Sumatra Mandheling Coffee served with Louis XIII Cognac
    Full-bodied coffee

A Minneapolis painter and wallpaper hanger, Rod Thornbloom, won the contest. Mr. and Mrs. Thornbloom invited their bowling partners to be their guests for the extravagant affair. "I don't even know what truffles are," Thornbloom had told *USA TODAY* for the newspaper's story.

During my Northstar Hotel tenure, I worked closely with the University of Minnesota Men's basketball team. We were their *de-facto* hotel of choice, providing accommodations for their recruits and housing some of their out-of-town opponents. Jim Dutcher was the team's coach at the time and his assistant was "Flip" Sanders who, while at the University of Minnesota, started 101 of his 103 career contests and as a senior, teamed with the well-known National Basketball Association (NBA) professional Kevin McHale. Flip later went on to coach in the NBA. For the hotel's support, the team designated me as an honorary team manager. I treasure to this day a uniformed team photograph taken on their home court, which included me. Later, after I returned to Hawaii for another Dunfey Hotel assignment, the team played in an Oahu Island college basketball tournament. They designated my son Shawn as their official tournament ball boy, which was an absolute thrill for him.

Air Lingus Airlines owned Dunfey Hotels for a period during my tenure. The company underwent a monumental transformation in the early 1980s. In 1983, Dunfey Hotels acquired Omni International Hotels, a company that operated only three hotels in Atlanta, Norfolk, and Miami. Dunfey conducted a marketing analysis to determine the strength of the

Omni name and discovered to their surprise that the three-hotel "Omni" chain had greater brand recognition than the 20+ "Dunfey Hotels."

Upon learning this, the company decided to adopt a new business strategy. It chose to develop a hotel chain called Omni Hotels to capitalize on the Omni brand recognition. The new group of hotels would consist of more upscale properties and would be built from the existing Dunfey Classic Hotel Division holdings. To this end, the company was reorganized into two separate operating divisions: Dunfey Hotels and Omni International Hotels. Omni consisted of nine hotels. Dunfey Hotels was a conglomeration of fourteen hotels and motor inns that were operated under independent or franchise names, or under the Dunfey name. During the 1980s, the company gradually liquidated its Dunfey holdings, jettisoning its last property in 1992. The Dunfeys sold all of their interests in the company they had founded. They formed a new company, the Dunfey Brothers Capital Group, a venture capital company oriented toward socially responsible companies. Aer Lingus used cash from the sale of its Dunfey properties to fund the expansion and improvement of Omni. It opened the Baltimore Omni International Hotel in 1984 and the Omni Sagamore Resort in 1985. It also added two properties in Detroit, Michigan, and Charlottesville, Virginia. To speed up expansion, Omni's management elected to begin franchising the Omni brand to selected hoteliers in 1986.

The summer of 1984 was one for my personal history book. On a warm July summer day, I blacktopped our driveway. To accomplish this, I was bent over spreading tar on the driveway surface for several hours. Later that evening, I began experiencing back pain. It became so severe that there wasn't anything I could do to alleviate the pain. Eventually, my wife had to drive me to the emergency room. I was diagnosed to have a herniated disc.

Visiting my surgeon the following day, he explained that I had two options. One was the traditional cutting you open option and the other was called chemonucleolysis, which would result in much less down time. Chemonucleolysis is the injection of an enzyme into a bulging spinal disc, with the goal of reducing the disc's size. It uses an enzyme called chymo-papain (derived from papaya), which is injected into the disc space. Local anesthesia or general anesthesia may be used to control pain during the injection. Chymopapain speeds up the breakdown of the jellylike substance inside the disc (nucleus), releasing water. As a result, the bulging disc may shrink and relieve pressure on the nerve root. Unknown to me at the time as this was the option I chose, *due to a potentially fatal reaction to the enzyme*, the procedure was rarely done! It wasn't until the 1990s that laser discec-tomy came into vogue.

After chemonucleolysis, you may have moderate to severe back pain and spasms lasting from two to three days or longer. You can use prescrip-tion medicines to control pain during the recovery period. For at least six weeks, however, you have to avoid long periods of sitting and repetitive bending, stooping, and lifting. In addition to the potentially fatal reaction from the enzyme, an allergic reaction to the dye used to see the disc may occur. This happened to me although I'm convinced that part of the reason for this was they had me strapped to a table and tilted me upside down to ensure the dye traveled through to the disc. My reaction to this was excruciating daily migraine-like headaches. I was bedridden and worked from home for a few weeks and could literally set my clock for these head-ache occurrences. At 6:00 pm nightly, almost to the minute, the headaches would arrive, making it painful for me to even lift my head up off the pil-low. One saving grace was that the Summer Olympics were going on, pro-viding me with bed-ridden entertainment. Ironically, I was fine from when I awoke in the morning until that terrible 6:00 pm time arrived. Ultimately, the procedure proved to be highly effective. On rare occasions, I'll have some back pain but after over thirty-five years, I remain virtually free of back pain and back injury restrictions.

During 1985, it became apparent to me that the marriage to my second wife was seriously troubled. While still at the Northstar Hotel, my company obtained the management contract on their first ever-Hawai-ian endeavor. In 1985, the Shidler Group acquired the 502-room Waikiki

Hotel from United Airlines and selected Omni (Dunfey) Hotels as its management company. My wife expressed a desire to go back to Hawaii. Feeling that the move could benefit our marriage, I lobbied the company heavily for the assignment. Graduating from high school there along with several years of Hawaiian employment experience positioned me as a top candidate. It was a major investment on the company's part relocating a family of four from Minneapolis to Honolulu. However, my results to-date spoke for themselves and the company felt it a worthy investment. At this stage of my Dunfey Hotels experience, I had successfully met every provided challenge and likewise Dunfey Hotels had been very good to me. I was a loyal company soldier and would perform any task required of me by my employer.

So in early 1985, I was promoted to the position of General Manager for the Omni Waikiki Beachcomber Hotel, where I had worked a mere eight years earlier for another company as the hotel's Food & Beverage Director. On the day of the Omni takeover of the Waikiki Beachcomber Hotel, a series of informational meetings were held with the hotel's staff to assure them of the hotel's new direction and to introduce them to key Omni Hotel's staffers. There were looks of amazement on familiar faces as I was introduced as the hotel's general manager. It actually provided a sense of comfort to most, having worked with me eight years earlier. By design, minimal staffing changes were made. The Executive Operating Committee (EOC) was made up of current employees and a couple of importees. The executive assistant to my supervisor in Minneapolis, Debbie Benson, found her own way to Hawaii and she was hired as my secretary, helping me with the Omni transition.

The task in front of me was monumental because to get the Waikiki Beachcomber Hawaii Hotel contract, Omni loaned the hotel's new owners $7.5 million and promised to increase the gross operating profit four times over results from the previous year. I was unaware of the loan and didn't learn of it until discovering a *Pacific Business News* article published in December of 1986. Having accomplished company goals laid out before me since my hire, I felt confident that as long as I did my best the company would be supportive of my efforts. No pun intended but at times I truly felt on an island by myself. Omni's corporate office was over 5,000 miles away in Hampton, New Hampshire, while the new owners both lived within miles of the hotel. One of the owners spent a lot of time at the hotel.

The profit improvement goal was like running a marathon while juggling several objects. Staff needed to be indoctrinated and trained, new budgets drawn up, new job descriptions had to be written, strategic planning sessions had to be held, KRAs had to be developed, which supported profit obtainment goals, Omni (meaning me) needed to establish ourselves within the local and hotel communities. We also had to contend with a twenty-nine-day United Airlines strike that discouraged travel to Hawaii, and all this was taking place during a major $7 million dollar hotel renovation. The renovation included all 502-guest rooms, the lobby, banquet facilities, our Surfboard Lounge (Don Ho played there prior to his superstardom), and our all-purpose Veranda Coffee Shop.

Omni quickly realized that Hawaii hotel marketing differed substantiality from mainland hotel marketing. It was like being in another universe. Each Omni Hotel went through an annual hotel marketing "supply/demand" analysis that established the hotel's marketing/selling efforts for one- and five-year periods. This was obviously all the more important for a property where profitably levels had been guaranteed. At this juncture, Omni had limited resort experience in its hotel property folio. When we entered the Waikiki marketplace, there were 134 hotel competitors comprising over 33,000 hotel rooms. The Waikiki Beachcomber, due to its off-beach location, wasn't as attractive to tourists as those hotels located on the beach. The "across the street" beach location was something I struggled with mightily from a marketing perspective. I even walked the shortest distance from our front door to the beach to determine the exact number of steps for advertising purposes and while we were only a few hundred feet from the beach we may as well have been a couple of miles.

That few-hundred-foot beach location disadvantage meant that our market segment mix varied from the hotels that enjoyed the on-beach location. The market mix discrepancy also translated into a much lower average room rate for our hotel versus those on the beach. This placed additional pressure on us to run higher occupancy levels. Beachfront hotels realized an average hotel room rate anywhere from $30 to $50 higher than us. To put this in perspective applying the $50 differential to the Waikiki Beachcomber's proposed (based on the Supply/Demand Analysis), total rooms sold for 1986 would have generated an additional $7.6 million in pure profit!

Being the general manager of the Waikiki Beachcomber Hotel is when I came to realize the importance and reliance of the wholesale hotel market. Wholesale companies purchased blocks of hotel rooms at heavily discounted rates from Hawaii hotels on the spec that they could resell them at higher rates to generate a profit. When you gave rooms to wholesalers, they came out of your inventory as if they didn't exist. For individual hotels, this meant the rooms sold to Wholesalers gave them guaranteed occupancy of those rooms whether or not they were occupied but at the cost of a much lower average room rate. In some months, wholesalers drove the whole market. Pleasant Hawaiian Holidays, one of the larger Hawaii wholesalers, went as far as to purchase several of their own hotels in Hawaii.

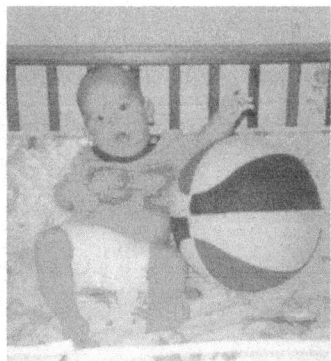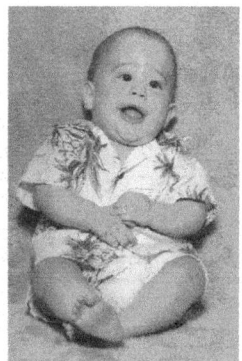

Left: Baby Shawn with Godfather Jim Reed.
Center: Baby Shawn Douglas Evans.
Right: Baby Scott David Evans.

Chapter 6 | 1986–1995

During this decade, I learned firsthand how cut-throat corporations are, changed careers after twenty-five years in the hotel industry, obtained my Bachelor of Arts college degree, was divorced from my second wife, learned the challenges of being a single parent, obtained the Meeting Professional Certification, met the love of my life, and bought my first home as a single parent.

In 1986, while at the Waikiki Beachcomber Hotel as its general manger, my second wife and I decided to purchase the home of her parents in Hawaii. Her parents were willing but wanted to be fair to their other children, so we met with each of them and came to an agreement. We took out a mortgage on the home and distributed the realized funds equally between my second wife's siblings. We promised her parents that they could live there as part of the purchase commitment.

Oahu had an annual collegiate basketball tournament that attracted top mainland colleges. For these schools, it was an alluring recruitment tool. Playing in a three- or four-day tournament in Hawaii usually meant during the winter, where at home they would be hammered with snow; however, at the tournament they would be enjoying sunshine and tropical beaches which was exciting for these players. During my Waikiki Beachcomber General Manager stint, the Minnesota Gophers played in this tournament. Having the relationship with the team from my Minneapolis stint before this Hawaii assignment, Shawn was made the official "ball boy" for them, which absolutely thrilled him. The look on his face while performing his responsibilities was priceless. I got more joy from watching him than taking in the games.

Meanwhile, at the Waikiki Beachcomber Hotel, I was trying to overcome obstacles to meet the impossible profit level promised to the owners. Having achieved success in Minneapolis with the $2,000-dinner promotion, I thought another worthy event capable of generating exposure to our hotel would put us on the path to success. The situation was similar in that we had minimal budgeted advertising dollars and the right event could generate extensive media public relations exposure.

Planning began in the first quarter of 1986 and we eventually settled on an event entitled "The World's Longest Lei." Targeting May 1 would allow us to tie the event in with Hawaii's annual "Lei Day" festivities. May 1 in Hawaii is known as Lei Day. "May Day is Lei Day in Hawaii Nei." This popular phrase in the islands prevents anyone from forgetting this special day. It was Don Blanding, a writer and poet, who first suggested that a holiday should be dedicated to the beautiful Hawaiian tradition of making and wearing leis. But it was Grace Tower Warren, also a writer, who came up with the idea that the holiday should coincide with May Day. And so since the first Lei Day on May 1, 1928, Hawaii has continued the annual celebration to this very day.

We formed promotional partnerships with Hawaii's Floral Growers and The Easter Seal Society. Floral designer Cookie Suinn oversaw the Lei's construction. Volunteers provided over 300 hours of labor to create the lei.

The event's goals were as follows:

1. Focus local consumer and business community attention on the new Waikiki Beachcomber Hotel.

2. Create a standout item to publicize in the travel trade media and thus focus travel industry attention on the new Waikiki Beachcomber Hotel.

3. Create a standout item centered on the new Waikiki Beachcomber Hotel to publicize among frequent travelers to Hawaii.

4. Create an awareness of the new Waikiki Beachcomber Hotel nationally and with the general public.

5. Focus public attention to and raise funds for the Easter Seals Society of Hawaii.

Companies and individuals donated to the Easter Seals Society as part of the event. Pledges were collected for each foot of the Lei suggesting a $5 per foot donation level. Pledge participants received a certificate commemorating their support of "The World's Longest Lei." Pledge participation was promoted through TV spots, newspaper coverage, and radio spots. Pledges were also taken by phone during a special two-day Easter Seal Telethon.

The event was an enormous success. The ceremony received coverage on the three local Honolulu TV stations, a local independent TV station, twelve radio stations, the two Honolulu newspaper dailies, neighbor island newspapers, and Waikiki tourist media, and national attention in *USA Today* as well as two wire services. A thirty-second public service announcement was carried on two TV stations. Additional post-event coverage was generated through photo and story releases sent to Hawaii-oriented consumer publications, floral trade journals, and travel trade media.

Not surprising, the exorbitant profit levels promised the owners by Omni were not materializing. A month or two after the "World's Longest Lei" event, I was asked by the Omni corporate office to prepare a report explaining budgeted profit shortfalls. To me, it was a reasonable request as they were several thousand miles away in Hampton, New Hampshire, while I was on property running the hotel. I prepared a brutally honest four-page report for my company superiors. Without going into great detail, the report explained that the renovation was behind schedule, the renovation was hampering operational efforts, and that through increasing revenues while reducing expenses wherever possible we were still able to increase profit levels two-and-half times over what it was the previous year!

Feeling the report adequately explained the profit shortfall, I continued efforts to push every dollar to the bottom line possible. A week or two later, I was called into the office of one of the hotel's owners. He began the conversation saying, "Stephen, I'm sorry you don't like working here!" Admittedly, due to this shock, the rest of the conversation was somewhat a blur to me. However, he basically chastised Omni and me personally for failing to deliver on contracted profit promises while citing almost verbatim some of the commentary from the report I prepared for my corporate office. It took me a while to piece together what had transpired. It then became apparent to me that someone from the Omni corporate office had shared the report that I thought would be kept confidential. My suspicion was that the Omni Vice President of Growth & Development was the culprit. However, I doubt he did it in Omni isolation.

After letting this incident sink in, I began to think the unthinkable to me up to that point. The company I had been loyal to for nearly ten years was using me as a scapegoat so they could keep the Hawaii Waikiki Beachcomber hotel contract! In my entire twenty-one-year hotel career, I had never been a fall-guy for an organization I worked for and was naïve enough to believe that as long as I gave 110% effort, it would never happen to me. This was my first experience of corporate viciousness. My Omni accomplishments, moves to five different states willingly, and countless hours spent day and night at the hotels I was responsible for all meant nothing at that point. To Omni, at this moment in time, I was simply a means to an end. Sure enough, a few days later, an Omni representative flew out to Hawaii to discharge me from the company. Devastation doesn't begin to describe my emotional state at that time.

Here I was in Hawaii with a wife, two sons, a mortgage, and my spouse's parents counting on me due to the mortgage on their home that we took out when purchasing it. With these responsibilities, I began an immediate employment search. My preference would have been to stay in Hawaii and on the island of Oahu where our recently purchased home was. With my pressing financial responsibilities, it was important to secure another position as soon as possible. As a side note, I'm proud to say that during my entire fifty-two-year work career, I never collected unemployment compensation. If I had more time, I may have been able to secure a Hawaii hotel general manager's position, but it wasn't meant to be.

In doing research for my autobiography, I stumbled across an article that appeared in the December 29, 1986 *Pacific Business News* publication, which exonerated me from false performance claims at the Waikiki Beachcomber Hotel. The article reported that my former company, Omni Hotels, was suing the Waikiki Beachcomber Hotel owners of the time for failing to honor the terms of the contract between the two parties. The article headline read "Omni Hotels suing Reynolds, Shidler."

Excerpts from the article follow:

"In January, 1985 Omni was given a 25-year contract with options for three additional terms of 10 years each. Reynolds & Shidler also allegedly agreed to invest almost $5.5 million for renovations to the 15-year-old building. Simultaneously, Omni offered up to $7.5 million in loans to help the hotel owners make these changes and cover some of its first mortgage debt service.

"Omni said in its suit that the hotel owners failed to honor the agreed-upon renovation schedule—causing hotel earnings to be affected, which in turn affected the amount to be paid Omni for its services—and caused the hotel's general manager, Stephen Evans, to be fired. Omni further accused the owners of dragging their feet in replacing Evans."

The story also stated that Omni had first purchase right of refusal of the hotel if it were put up for sale and that the owners had made sale overtures through a Honolulu broker without notifying Omni. The article provided absolution for me, generating in me an extreme feeling of vindication.

Meanwhile, the best opportunity for me at that time was a general manager's position at a Hilton in Skokie, Illinois. To be on equal footing with mainland applicants, I offered to relocate my family to Chicago. With that gesture, I was able to land the position. Little had I realized that this assignment would turn into a miscalculation on my part! What were the odds that I would be involved in two successive terrible negative employment experiences?

The Hilton North Shore was a privately owned/franchised over-300 room high-rise hotel. It had over 20,000 square feet of meeting/banquet space, a bar, room service, and an all-purpose restaurant. The hotel generated over $9 million dollars in revenue annually. The company with the hotel's management contract, High Country Corporation, was out of Denver, Colorado. They were my official employer while the owners were a Chicago-based company. They were a private investment firm focused on building real estate-related businesses in emerging markets. So as in Hawaii, I interacted more with the hotel's owners than with the company I worked for. My compensation package included a live-in apartment, a company vehicle, and meals.

After a brief evaluation period, my immediate objectives were to
1. Improve hotel profitability;
2. Improve hotel service levels;
3. Take the all-purpose restaurant though a scheduled renovation.

I met with the executive staff members and had each of them develop measurable departmental goals that would allow accomplishment of the hotel objectives. One area in need of improvement was the rooms' market segment mix for the hotel. We needed to increase occupancy levels of the higher rated market segments while reducing dependency on the lower rated market segments. Our operating expenses for a hotel room were the same whether the room was occupied with a high average rate or a low one. Thus, success in this area would drop the room rate differential straight to the bottom line. This was addressed in the Director of Sales and Rooms Division Manager goals.

Another area of concern that contributed to a lower overall gross operating profit level of the hotel was the profitability of the Food &

Beverage department. The overall Food & Beverage profitability on my arrival was a mere 3%. For a hotel with a high banquet business mix, this was totally unacceptable. I met with the then Food & Beverage Director and felt that with both the profitability and restaurant renovation challenges he wasn't qualified to accomplish that department's needs. So I recruited and hired a new Food & Beverage Director shortly after my arrival. I hired an individual, an Indian from Pakistan who came with sterling credentials.

Little did I realize that this specific hire would lead to a second consecutive unwarranted barbarous corporate attack on me. Shortly after his hire, hotel ownership came to me and asked that I dismiss him. No specific reasoning was given, so all I could fathom was they were prejudiced against his color and/or race. A few months into his employment, the request for me to fire him was made again. I couldn't in good conscious fire an individual who was performing outstandingly and whose only fault in ownership's eyes was his color or race.

Several months hence, the hotel was humming along. Food & Beverage profitability improved from 3% to 20%. Service levels were greatly enhanced. Renovation of the restaurant and a new concept was fully implemented. The hotel's average room rate was increased due to marketing strategies and the hotel's overall profitability significantly improved. Results were so outstanding that I was seriously considering going to ownership to request a raise.

One afternoon, I was in the outer office speaking to a couple of employees when a phone call came in for me. The secretary informed me that it was Antonio Torres, a friend of mine from our Omni days. He was the then general manager of the Hyatt St Louis. Learning who the call was from, I took the phone from the secretary to hear Antonio ask, "Amigo, are you in your office?" Antonio was Hispanic and we referred to each other as amigo. After explaining where I was, Antonio suggested I go into my office and close the door to resume the call.

I went into my office and closed the door, as Antonio suggested, and picked up the phone. The next words out of his mouth absolutely stunned me: "They're interviewing me for your position," he explained. After processing this unbelievable information, I was in total disbelief. The hotel was performing exceptionally, exceeding all expectations to the point where I was ready to request a raise and the owners were planning for my dismissal! The only task not accomplished or exceeded during my tenure was the request to fire the hotel's Food & Beverage Director.

It was obvious to me that not firing this outstanding performer was their sole rationale for firing me. Any trust I had in the ownership at that time fell by the wayside. Not knowing how much time I had before they dismissed me, I began an immediate, accelerated employment search. This resulted in good news and bad news. The good news was that I was able to obtain a position as General Manager, St. Paul Athletic Club in St. Paul, Minnesota, as they were looking for someone with hotel general manager experience. The bad news was that I didn't have adequate time to vet this new position and ended up in an unsustainable situation.

Untrusting of hotel ownership at this time, I was worried whether they would pay me the bonus I had earned along with salary due. To say I didn't trust them was an understatement. So when they eventually came to me through the management company, High Country, I explained that I planned to hold onto the company vehicle and not vacate the hotel apartment until such time as I had received the compensation I had already earned. There was an initial standoff but eventually they came to terms paying me my bonus and all accrued compensation to that point. If it wasn't for the phone call from my friend Antonio, the outcome could have been much different. Antonio didn't take the position probably leery of being undercut as I had been. By the way, we're friends to this day.

My hastily arranged next stop was the position of general manager of the St. Paul Athletic Club in St. Paul, Minnesota. Hastily, because I didn't have the time to properly vet the position. It was available and I was facing potential unemployment with two sons and a wife to support. The St. Paul Athletic Club was a St. Paul institution built in 1917. It took over a year to build it at a cost of $1 million. Today's estimated costs for that same building would be north of $80 million. The club consisted of hotel rooms, banquet facilities, meeting rooms, a bar, and restaurants. This was a severe turn-around challenge. The club was experiencing declining membership and was in desperate need of capital infusion for renovations and improvements.

We purchased a home in in the suburb of Woodbury, Minnesota, at 2484 Leyland Trail, hoping for a long-term stay. We had lived in Minneapolis in the early 1980s, so we had friends in the area. The home was a beautiful bi-level model, which we purchased for $144,000. We had some nice family outings in Minnesota. With the exception of the long winters there, the other seasons are quite nice. I remember touring one weekend with my two sons in the Stillwater, Minnesota area. It was during the fall and autumn colors were in full bloom. We did a lot of walking and exploring that day and of course stopped for treats along the way to Shawn and Scott's satisfaction.

During the first few months at the St. Paul Athletic Club, I evaluated and upgraded the management staff. Surveying the landscape and analyzing the club's historical profit and loss situation, it became apparent to me the most pressing issue would be to stop the membership drain. The club members not only contributed much needed revenue in the way of monthly membership dues, but also frequented the club's restaurants, banquet facilities, and hotel accommodations. We needed a solid membership base to support these facilities.

This stint proved to be a job and a half. I worked long days and many weekends. One weekend day, I took my two sons, Shawn and Scott, with me into the club. This was a way for me to spend time with them while trying to dig the club out of its abyss. There was a gym there, so I let the boys play there while I went to my office. The club was nearly empty, being a weekend day so sound traveled well. One of my sons let out a scream, sending me running to the area the scream came from. It turned out that both of my sons had found access to a room's ceiling and were navigating their way across the room on top of the ceiling tiles! One punctured the tiles but wasn't hurt, leaving my heart beating through my chest.

Shawn played on a little league baseball team that summer. Several of the neighborhood boys played in the same league. Going to the games was a pleasant diversion from the club's difficulties and it was welcome family time. In one particular game, Shawn got a nice hit and being fleet of foot (when Shawn first learned to crawl, he moved along the floor so quickly that I had nicknamed him "Scooter"), I thought he had the opportunity for a home run. When he got to second base in excitement, I shouted, "Go home, Shawn, go home"! Well Shawn obviously heard me and did exactly that. The only problem was he took the shortest route from second base to home, crossing the pitcher's mound for the journey versus the legal route around third base. We loved Shawn's noticeable innocence just following the request of his dad.

It was becoming more and more apparent to me that the St. Paul Athletic Club's survival was a long shot. Tiring of the twenty-four-hour pressure of the hospitality world, I longed for a career change. Not sure of what path to follow, I decided to prudently pursue direction through a three-prong approach. The first was to have a psychological analysis done, the second was to do a vocational assessment of myself, and the third was to obtain my bachelor's degree that I had been working on since my St. Paul arrival.

The psychological analysis done in July 1987 was quite revealing. For perspective, a couple of paragraphs from the summary section of this analysis performed by consulting psychologists, Inc. in Minneapolis:

"… is pragmatic and open to change (sounds like a novelty). He is a very quick learner, who picks up readily and imaginative and resourceful. Emotional organization. Has a high level of energy and intensity. Is emotionally self-controlled person. Steady and consistent in moods. Generally upbeat. Confidence is modest rather than robust. Important for him to feel accepted in that he is achieving results. Strong-willed and independent-minded.

"By nature, more introverted and quiet, yet enjoys attention and can appear to be an extrovert. More forced extrovert than a naturally gregarious person. Has ability to read what others are feeling and respond accordingly.

Goes out of his way to be agreeable and pleasant. Generally can win rapport rapidly. Is respectable and polite, and able to convey an interest in others. Likely to be viewed by others as self-assured, competent, and service-oriented. Is dominant, forceful and also a motivating individual. Comfortable with taking charge and assuming authority. Sells himself hard along with his ideas. Projects energy and knowledgeability. Tends to be somewhat 'hands-on' in management style. Not likely to be removed from subordinates."

This exercise was a real eye-opener for me. It confirmed some suspicions to me of my personality/ability traits while reinforcing my college degree objective by pointing out areas of weakness that would be improved through this pursuit. The college degree would also in itself aid in my quest to change careers.

Later in 1987, my family and I had the opportunity to attend a couple of World Series games in Minneapolis between the Minnesota Twins and St. Louis Cardinals. Tickets were made available to me through a business associate/friend. It was considered a potentially once-in-a-lifetime experience for Shawn and Scott. The action didn't disappoint as the Minnesota Twins defeated the St. Louis Cardinals in seven games. It was the first World Series to feature games played indoors. It was also the first World Series in which the home team won every game. We got to the stadium early for the first game and the air was so electric that you didn't want to leave your seats. The looks on Shawn's and Scott's faces were priceless. They really got into the game as the entire home crowd did—shouting and cheering the Twins on throughout the game. The affair was ever the more thrilling to be able to share that excitement with my two sons.

The marriage to my second wife was spiraling downward. While we had two handsome sons, a beautiful home, and our share of luxuries, there just never seemed a happy medium that could be reached. At this juncture, we were married for over fifteen years. Our relationship hit an all-time low at that point when I called the police over her abusive action toward one of our sons. She had displayed similar characteristics toward my daughter Janette, which I noticed too late and didn't want my sons to experience the same behavior. While I could not control that particular incident, I felt it important to have the incident on record to hopefully prevent future events.

The second strategy in my three-prong career change approach was to have a vocational assessment. The University of Minnesota had a respected department well renowned for performing such an assessment. They gave me a battery of tests designed to evaluate my abilities, needs, values, interests, and other work personality characteristics. Key findings from the assessment included the following:

- Client can be especially successful in a job that requires an ability to reason and make judgments.

- Client values work environments that encourage accomplishment and provides for steady employment.

- Client could be satisfied with job that provides recognition, a chance to try out some of his own ideas, and make use of his abilities.

- Client resembled others who are able to assume leadership roles, are secure and self-accepting, and who convey a sense of accomplishment.

- Client has good negotiating skills, and is sensitive to others' needs and feelings.

- Client resembles others who are very project and task oriented and who favor a hands-on approach to problem-solving.

Digesting the results and researching other occupations that would allow me to benefit from my hotel management experience made me believe that a career in Meeting/Trade Show Management would be appropriate. There were some interesting opportunities in this area, with both non-profit associations and with corporations. Wanting to avoid the corporate culture, I felt that the non-profit arena would work best. Further investigation revealed that the largest numbers of associations were in the Washington DC area followed by Chicago, Illinois.

The pursuit of my Bachelor's Degree in Business became a reality in January of 1989. The Metropolitan State University graduation ceremony was one of my proudest moments as to my knowledge my uncle was the only other immediate family member achieving such a distinction. While not the eventual recipient, I was honored as one of six students in our class nominated for "most outstanding student." The winner was a Vietnam refugee who had to, among other things, overcome the English language barrier and learn a new culture while attending college. As proud as I was of the moment an even greater hope was that my two sons would be inspired by the accomplishment to also pursue a college degree.

Meanwhile at the club, the staff and my efforts increased the food and beverage profit from 2% to 5%, reduced annual membership losses by 50%, improved the quality of the club's membership magazine while reducing its publishing costs, and improved the club's overall profitability. Unfortunately, this, in my estimation, wasn't going to be enough to save the club. Reducing membership loss wasn't enough. We needed to increase the membership base. I left the club early in 1989, realizing that the club just wasn't going to make it. Sure enough, I learned later that the club closed its doors in late 1989. It sat vacant for several years when it was purchased and renovated on several occasions, most recently reopening in 2013.

We left St. Paul, Minnesota, for Chicago for two reasons. The first was that we were familiar with the area, having lived there recently and the second was the greater employment opportunities for the larger metropolitan area. This was the first move we made that a job wasn't already secured in advance. Due to employment and family concerns I had to sell our Woodbury home at an $11,000 loss after carrying the mortgage as long as I could. Woodbury has since become one of the more affluent areas in the St. Paul suburbs and this same residence is now worth more than $300,000!

Being "burnt out" from the arduous hotel grind and wanting to avoid corporate politics, my job search focused on the new career path of

Meeting/Trade Show Management. This turned out to be a source of conflict with my second wife, as she wanted me to stay in hotel management. I could only surmise that she enjoyed the prestige of being the hotel's general manager's wife. The additional benefit of the career change would be that we wouldn't have to relocate every couple of years. Sure, there would be required travel to events but that paled in comparison to having to relocate my family so frequently. Up to the end of our marriage, my career switch was a source of conflict with my second wife.

After relocating to the Chicago area, we rented a place in Evanston, Illinois. Thus, the search for a new career began in earnest. Meeting/Trade Show Management (sometimes referred to as event management) is a field unknown to most. Wikipedia provides an adequate explanation:

"Event management is the application of project management to the creation and development of large-scale events such as festivals, conferences, ceremonies, weddings, formal parties, concerts, or conventions. It involves studying the brand, identifying its target audience, devising the event concept, and coordinating the technical aspects before actually launching the event."

The process of planning and coordinating the event is usually referred to as event planning, which can include budgeting, scheduling, site selection, acquiring necessary permits, coordinating transportation and parking, arranging for speakers or entertainers, arranging decor, event security, catering, coordinating with third party vendors, and emergency plans. Each event is different in its nature so the process of planning and execution of each event differs on the basis of type of event.

"The events industry now includes events of all sizes from the Olympics down to business breakfast meetings. Many industries, charitable organizations, and interest groups hold events to market themselves, build business relationships, raise money, or celebrate achievement."

This definition is right on with the exception of failing to include trade shows. Most associations along with a fair number of corporations participate in trade shows either as an exhibitor that secures space from the show organizer to promote their cause/company or as outright owners of the Trade Show. A Trade Show can be defined as "an exhibition at which associations/businesses in a particular industry promote their products and services.

Bank Administration Institute (BAI) was one of the first non-profit organizations I interviewed with. It originated in the early 1900s when banking executives meeting as a group realized that a national group that met in person regularly could facilitate the exchange of information. The organization became both a voice and a resource for the industry. The organization was branded BAI in the late 1960s and today serves over 8,000 member institutions.

A separate division within the organization, called SCI Limited, handled their trade shows and meetings. SCI was formed as a separate entity and had an International Air Transport Association designation (IATA #) allowing this subsidiary to collect travel agency fees on hotel bookings. This was a clever business arrangement on the association's part. BAI did over 200 meetings of various sizes, including 8 annual industry trade shows. Commissions generated from these events offset most if not all of the cost of the SCI events staff, dramatically reducing overhead for BAI.

My interview with BAI couldn't have been timelier. They were looking for someone with hotel experience for their trade show/meeting planning division. This was definitely a case of "being in the right place at the right time" or, as I firmly believe, God was looking over my shoulder. They wanted this individual to oversee the hotel contracting and felt someone coming from "that side of the fence" would be perfect. Coincidently, their other major requirement was a Bachelor's Degree, which I had just earned! BAI nearly hired me on the spot. I received their congratulatory call right after they checked my references. My twenty-four years of hotel experience, twelve as a general manager, fit perfectly.

Hotel contracting is a very critical function for trade shows/events. A third-party vendor or an individual on the event's behalf can do this. The challenge is to secure an adequate number of hotel rooms at rates attractive enough to encourage event participants to use them. An additional trial is not to over-commit room blocks with hotels, as generally there are attrition clauses in hotel contracts, making the organization financially responsible for a portion of the room block.

After organizational indoctrination, my initial responsibilities at BAI focused on hotel contracting. As the weeks went by, more responsibilities came my way. I assisted in developing food and beverage meeting specifications for hotels and convention centers. I went on site for a few smaller meetings and eventually was given a few programs of my own to manage. Once confident in my abilities, BAI gave me a couple of the larger meetings to oversee.

At this point, BAI was located in Rolling Meadows, Illinois. This was a daily commute of nearly twenty miles from Evanston, Illinois, for me, navigating all surface streets and numerous traffic signals as there wasn't a freeway route then. To avoid traffic tie-ups, I left home early, which developed into a routine of an early morning departure between 6 and 6:30 am, making me one of the first arrivals of the day.

One of my first BAI on-site conference responsibilities was in New York at the Waldorf Astoria.

BAI held numerous conferences and trade shows in New York, the financial center of the United States. Anxious to make a good first impression, I was in the General Session room an hour before the start of the 8 am conference to check out the setup. All was well, so I hung around to wait for the start of the session. Generally, there would be a decent crowd in the room within the thirty-minute-prior meeting start window. This wasn't the case this morning as we were 15 minutes from the start of the session and only a handful of the 250+ attendees were present.

Curious of the low attendance, I began exploring the Waldorf Astoria's meeting space. Being an older hotel, the meeting space was on several floors resembling a jigsaw puzzle. The meeting space was heavily used that morning, but I hadn't encountered anything out of the ordinary, until I happened onto a larger meeting room toward the rear of the hotel. Walking in, I first noticed the dimmed lights in the large room with a couple of spotlights highlighting a runway at the end of the room. Most spectators were enjoying breakfast while reveling in a negligee fashion show! Not only were the majority of our male meeting participants in attendance, but also the bulk of the hotel's staff was viewing females modeling intimate apparel.

That November in 1990, I was in New York to manage another conference. One evening, I was out walking in Manhattan when an individual ran hurriedly by me on the sidewalk. I initially brushed the incident off, but not far behind were policemen on foot and several police cars with sirens apparently pursuing this individual. Later, I learned that Meir Kahane, an Israeli Rabbi and politician, was assassinated while speaking at a nearby Marriott. The individual that ran by me was El Sayyid Nosair, the accused assassin! Nosair was not convicted of the assassination, in part due to the opposition of the victim's family members to performing an autopsy after the assassination to extract the bullets. However, he was convicted of assault, possession of an illegal firearm, and of shooting a U.S. Postal Inspection Service agent. He was sentenced to twenty-two years in prison.

To solidify my position and new career investment, I obtained the Certified Meeting Professional (CMP) designation that same year. The CMP moniker was developed by the Convention Industry Council (CIC) in 1985 to (1) enhance the knowledge and performance of meeting professionals, (2) promote the status and credibility of the meeting profession, and (3) advance uniform standards of practice. The CMP designation is recognized industry-wide. The credential lent credence to my position and I was applauded by BAI.

On the domestic front, another incident occurred that added to the marriage difficulties my second wife and I were experiencing. It happened mid-day on a weekend. My wife was napping and when she napped, I tried to keep the household as quiet as possible. One of the boys made noise that woke her up and she got up in a mini-rage. She was so upset that she dumped part of Shawn's baseball card collection in the toilet. I don't want it to appear that our eminent divorce was all one-sided. I contributed to it also, mainly by working so many hours and not being as available to my children or second wife as much I could have been. However, it was more apparent than ever to me that there was no future to our marriage.

A bright spot in my life during this time frame was Scott was playing Little League baseball. I knew the coach of his team and volunteered to be an assistant coach of the team. When Joe Putnik couldn't make it to practice or the game, I'd run the team. When we were both there together, I'd serve as the third-base coach. This gave me the opportunity to spend additional time with Scott. Scott was a natural baseball player and, in my opinion, the most talented on the team. He preferred the position of catcher but was the team's best pitcher and started as many games at that position as league rules allowed. Scott was talented enough to be recruited to a couple of all-star teams that played regional games. He was and is also quite intelligent. Scott would score in top percent of his class when tested for academics.

In another attempt to make my marriage work out in May of 1991, we purchased a home at 9258 Lincolnwood Drive in Evanston, Illinois, for $169,500. This moved us back into the same neighborhood we were in when I worked at the Hilton North Shore hotel a few years earlier. Shawn and Scott were able to get back to the same school as their friends and my second wife and I were able to reconnect with our friends in that area. This last-ditch attempt to move the marriage forward was fruitless. In late 1991, my second wife indicated that she was divorcing me.

My feelings ran along the lines of divorce for a few years now, but I hesitated to be the divorce initiator out of concern of what damage it might inflict on our sons. With such differing value systems at this time in our marriage, there was very little that we agreed on. It was obvious that divorce was the best course. One of Illinois' divorce requirements was that couples live apart from each other for six months prior to divorcing. Although we were both working, we weren't financially able to live in two separate residences, and both her attorney and mine advised against it, thinking of property settlement issues ahead. Our Evanston home had two levels, so to satisfy this requirement my second wife lived upstairs and I lived downstairs for the required six-month separation.

Upon hearing horror stories of attorneys bleeding their clients by feeding their emotional state, I began a search for an established reputable attorney. Fortunately, I came across the Chicago Divorce Association, in Itasca, Illinois. They had arrangements with a group of attorneys that handled divorces on a flat fee basis. Before agreeing to their representation, the association president suggested that I speak to a former client for a reference. He referred me to Tom Menzel who highly recommended this organization. Tom explained to me that he went to the Chicago Divorce Association after spending thousands of dollars with an attorney who failed to finalize his divorce. As Tom explained, an attorney working on a flat fee basis has no incentive to "keep the clock running." In fact, it's to their advantage to resolve each case as quickly as possible.

So I signed on with the Chicago Divorce Association, and Brigid Duffield became my attorney. I have counted my blessing numerous times since, as without the flat-fee arrangement, I'm sure the divorce proceedings would have dragged on for an exorbitant period, not to mention the potential cost of the ordeal. Brigid did an outstanding job representing me. I never once felt that she wasn't giving me her undivided representation even though she would have made out much better working the case on an hourly basis. The process took several months and it was absolutely gut-wrenching.

My marriage was in its twenty-first year as the divorce processing took place. My second wife gave me two beautiful sons and we had been through many ups and downs. Regardless of the countless adversities experienced, if you're human there are strong feelings after twenty years of marriage. Don't get me wrong, after twenty years and countless "this is the last straw" incidents, I knew we had to part but it was highly emotional to do so. By the time the divorce was legally finalized in June of 1992, I was in a highly distraught state.

Following the divorce, we were both single parents. Shawn was in my custody and Scott was in hers. With my attorney working diligently to finalize settlement terms, the process dragged on, in my opinion, longer than necessary. Wanting to finalize settlement terms, I provided two asset resolution options and told my wife that she could take her pick from these two options and I'd live with the other. Our main assets were the home in Hawaii and the home in Evanston. Of course, both had mortgages and their respective values were accounted for accordingly. She chose the option with the Hawaii residence and moved out of what was now my Evanston home but stayed in the neighborhood. Our twenty-year marriage was officially over and I thought I could continue my life in peace. I was wrong.

After she moved out, I was emotionally wiped out. It was difficult for me to make it through the day and in some instances I had to take it hour by hour. Depression became my constant companion and at times I even questioned whether life was worth living. God was definitely watching over me during this ordeal, leading me to an effective, caring counselor, and to Willow Creek Church.

Through a referral, I started seeing Willoughby Donnelan, a therapy counselor in Arlington Heights, Illinois. Willoughby was semi-retired but agreed to see me. I saw Willoughby for several months and as she felt my condition warranted, we reduced the frequency of the sessions as she worked her way into retirement. She was kind enough to see me at her home even after she gave up her office space. Willoughby even blessed my future wife and me by attending our wedding nearly ten years later.

The therapy sessions were helpful, but I felt the need for even more support. I began a search for a divorce support group that I could join. There were several in the area but none met with the frequency I felt in need of at that time. Finally, I located a group that met once to twice weekly at Willow Creek Church in Barrington, Illinois. This divorce support group was one of several "small groups" that Willow Creek Church facilitated. The church had qualified volunteer leaders that facilitated each small group as part of their community outreach programming. There was no fee for participation or pressure applied in any way.

These sessions, in addition to my therapy periods, were emotional lifesavers for me. I started attending Willow Creek Church as I just felt natural warmth while there. I befriended some individuals in the divorce small group and to this day am still in touch with one of them.

At about this time, BAI moved their offices from Rolling Meadows to downtown Chicago. It turned out that BAI moved downtown so the president could be closer to his downtown condo. Financially, this was a bad move from the beginning as it was obvious that we had more office space than needed, and office lease costs at this time were high. Sure enough, in a few months, BAI sub-leased part of their space. The BAI President at the time was a character to say the least. At one of BAI's board meetings, I witnessed him chastising the Board of Directors! He regularly belittled other staff members in my presence, making me wonder what he said about me to others when I wasn't around.

Being a single parent presented a new set of challenges. One of them was the care of Shawn while I was required to travel out of town on business. Until then, I was handling the commute downtown for work and single parenting okay but I didn't have to go out of town. A couple of months down the road I had a conference in San Francisco, which was my sole responsibility. This would take me out of town for approximately five days. There was no way I could leave my fifteen-year-old son Shawn on his own for that period. The only viable solution to me was to hire someone to stay with him during my absence. After interviewing several individuals for the job, I settled on a male who was approximately thirty years old. I arranged for him to show up two days prior to my San Francisco trip so he could become familiar with Shawn, the home and surroundings.

Well, the day came for his assignment and he didn't show up. Frantically, I tried reaching him for that whole day without success. After exhausting all options, I reached out to my brother Floyd who lived in Indianapolis, and he agreed to pick Shawn up and watch him while I was out of town. Thank goodness for Floyd, for I don't know what I would have done otherwise.

Having gone through that calamitous experience, I had to come up with a more permanent solution. After giving the problem some serious thought, I came up with the idea of renting out the lower level of my residence. Actually, there was no rent charged. Instead, the offer was free room and board in exchange for watching Shawn when I had to travel for work. When I was in town, my tenant had no responsibilities toward Shawn. This actually worked out well. The tenants were short-term for the most part but never again did I end up with the situation where I was faced with the possibility of Shawn being unsupervised during my business travels. One of these tenants was a major in the Army!

This same year, Shawn and I went to Orlando for the annual NBA all-star game festivities. One of the perks of an event planner was invitations to venues and events promoting cities and or company purveyor services. These are commonly called "FAM" trips as the purpose is for the meeting planner to become familiar with the venue and hopefully book it for a future event. For this event, we were put up at the Dolphin Hotel in Orlando, which happened to be the NBA headquarters. Shawn was absolutely fascinated with the overall experience. He would ride the elevators at all hours just to see what NBA all-star might be on it at that particular time. During our trip, he met and got pictures of Dikembe Mutombo, who played for Denver at the time, as well as of Tim Hardaway, who played for the Golden State Warriors. One of the trip highlights was a luncheon that we attended where the table centerpiece was an autographed basketball that Shawn got to have as a souvenir. One morning at breakfast after Shawn and I were seated, I glanced over at another table to see Phil Jackson, the then coach of our Chicago Bulls, having breakfast with one of his assistant coaches. The West blew out the East in this particular NBA All-Star game with Erwin "Magic" Johnson named as the MVP of the game.

In my meeting management/trade show experience, I was selective in what trips I went on, not wanting to take advantage of every offer. Over the course of each year, several attractive free trips were offered, which provided airfare, deluxe accommodations, meals, and entertainment. If I knew the organization I worked for wouldn't use that particular venue, I wouldn't take the provider up on that offer no matter how attractive it was. This in my opinion was not only fair but also ethical. It was important to me to develop an industry reputation of being reputable and honest, which I believe aided me later in my career. The industry also provided me with the good fortune to meet such dignitaries as Bill Clinton, Colin Powell, and Bob Dole.

Later that year, I met the woman who would eventually become my third wife and the love of my life. Sandra Ann Sinck (Spoula, maiden name) was facilitating a "Tough Love" group for single parents, which I'd attended for parental support. "Sandie" was a single parent; with two teenage daughters, one who was of-age and living with her father and one she was caring for. She was born and raised on the southwest side of Chicago and had never lived outside of Chicago. Our first date that October was to attend the play *Miss Saigon* at the Auditorium Theater after a reception at the recently opened new downtown Sheraton Chicago & Towers hotel. Sandie was quick-witted, had an engaging personality, and I enjoyed being with her. Having just experienced divorce along with constant antagonism from my ex, I wasn't ready for a relationship nor did I truly trust the opposite sex.

But Sandie and I had a lot in common. We were both single parents and had experienced difficult previous marriages. Although in that instance Sandie was eight years removed from marriage while my wounds were still fresh and with near daily interactions with my ex, I had little chance for immediate healing. I admired and respected Sandie for her perseverance in providing for her two daughters. Her jobs paid just enough for her to keep food on the table and pay the monthly bills of a household. For our third date, Sandie and I attended a service at the Willow Creek Community church where I was still receiving divorce group support. This was another example of the Lord working in my life. Sandie and I dated for nearly ten years before marrying and I am truly blessed that she was there for me when I was ready for the commitment. To this day, I believe that God led me to Sandie through the unfortunate events that led to the divorce from my ex.

In February of 1993, Sandie and I went on a FAM trip to Phoenix, Arizona. It was an invitation to me at BAI through Hilton Hotels. Phoenix was definitely on the radar for use by BAI, so I accepted the invite. The invitation for two included airfare, accommodations, all meals, and planned activities. This was the first real getaway that my future bride and I had together. The trip was wonderful from every aspect. Hilton rolled out the red carpet and all meals were extraordinary. Activities included everything from hang-gliding to horseback riding. The closing dinner was an extravaganza. It was one of those meals that had enough silverware, china, and glassware at each setting to accommodate a family of four. The menu was imprinted onto a mirror for each attendee. Our Hilton sales representative was Gino, a very likeable fellow. (We sadly learned sometime later that Gino perished in an airplane crash.)

That December, Shawn, Scott, and I flew to Los Angeles to spend Christmas with my daughter Janette. My ex was against Shawn and Scott having interactions with Janette, and this was one thing that was going to immediately change from my household. We stayed with Janette and her boyfriend Scott for several days and interacted with Janette's two sisters, Keturah and Sierra. It was truly gratifying seeing Shawn and Scott interact and bond with Janette. I have videos from this trip, which I still enjoy watching. As an added bonus, we visited with and had dinner with Pat Wolff (Sugai), a high school classmate of mine, and her family who lived in Huntington Beach, California.

As I closed in on my fourth year of employment with BAI work, travel was becoming more and more of a challenge. BAI promoted me on two separate occasions where I was currently the general manager of their trade shows and conferences. In effect, I was responsible for their entire travel division. This was good from a financial standpoint and career path. However, the travel required of me was too much, being a single parent.

The BAI President wanted me at every BAI trade show and major conference. To me, this was overkill as we had responsible managerial staff under me to see that everything ran well. Additionally, the president himself didn't attend every event. In fact, peculiar to me, it was the exception and not the norm that he attended these events.

To be home more often, I began another job search for a position with an organization allowing me to continue my new career path. The big advantage I had in this pursuit was in being currently employed and not having to jump at anything that came my way. Favor was once again shining down on me as I secured a position with the Institute for Interconnecting and Packaging Electronic Circuits (IPC). IPC is a non-profit, member-driven organization and leading source for industry standards, training, industry intelligence, and public policy advocacy. More than 3,000 companies around the world depend on IPC programs and services to further their competitive advantage and financial success. IPC members represent all facets of the electronics industry, including design, printed board manufacturing, electronics assembly, and testing.

One of the attractions was their location at the time. They were headquartered in Lincolnwood, Illinois, merely three miles from where I lived. IPC offered and I accepted a position with them to run their meetings/expositions department. BAI tried to talk me out of my decision to leave them but after accepting the IPC position, I felt loyalty to the new organization. Their Lincolnwood location allowed me to go home for lunch if I desired. Shawn had Maggie, a black lab, so I would go home to let her out on most days.

While dating Sandie, I learned that she had a hearing disorder. She couldn't hear well out of either ear. Years earlier, a doctor had told her it was nerve damage and nothing could be done to correct the situation. Accordingly, Sandie felt no option other than having to make the best of the condition and wore hearing aids. A friend of hers experienced something similar, which was correctable and suggested that Sandie go to her otolaryngologist. Sandie followed up on the recommendation where the otolaryngologist performed a very simple hearing test. He tapped a tuning fork on the edge of a desk and placed the tuning fork behind her ear, asking if she could hear it. She was able to hear it whereby the otolaryngologist informed her after further tests that her loss of hearing was not nerve damage but rather an issue with the stapes bone in each ear. The condition is known as otosclerosis. Long story short, after two successful ear surgeries in 1994, she regained a fair amount of her hearing. This irritated me as Sandie had to put up with inferior hearing for many years simply due to a glossed-over diagnosis.

A few months into my new IPC employment, Shawn's behavior became more and more erratic. It was an absolute struggle to get him to school on most days. He was out of the house at all hours and I'm convinced he snuck out of the house while I slept. One day, I came home from work to discover Shawn and a friend of his on our roof ripping off roof shingles and throwing them at individuals passing by! Concerned and suspicious of Shawn's conduct, I invested in a voice-activated recording device that taped our phone calls. To my dismay, I discovered Shawn's involvement in both the use of and the selling of drugs. One of the calls made me fear for Shawn's life. Digesting what I knew made me realize that for Shawn's life, he needed professional help.

My sister Sheryl had similar problems with her daughter Denise so I called her for advice. Sheryl described a program to me that Denise attended after which she was now drug-free. The name of the organization offering this program was the Pathway Family Center. The organization had a few locations. The closest location to me was in Detroit, Michigan, about a five-hour drive. Sheryl also had the good suggestion that I speak with Denise to gain her input on the program and Shawn's behavior characteristics. After getting input from Denise and others, the general feeling was that Shawn's behavior characteristics were similar to an addict's. The importance of getting help for Shawn was ever the more critical in my eyes now.

I researched the Pathway Family Center online and made phone calls to some of their counselors as well as their admissions department. There were obstacles to overcome in gaining this assistance. The first was one of logistics. One of the programs requirements was that the parent had to be an active participant in the child's recovery program. Minimally, every other weekend the parent had to attend meetings and co-host children in the program in their homes. This provided a couple of additional obstacles for me, the distance between Chicago and Detroit as well as a home to host program individuals in. The distance challenge was met when my IPC employer granted me permission to leave early on Fridays, so I could make the five-hour drive to Detroit. For this, I was and still am grateful to IPC's president at the time, Thom Dammrich, who granted this concession. The second barrier was overcome when a Detroit single dad with a son in the program said I could co-host program children with him at his home. So during the weekends I went, we co-hosted around six boys which always included each of our sons.

The second major obstacle was one of cost. With the exception of weekend hosting for kids in the program, it was a live-in situation where the program provided counseling, room, meals, and twenty-four-hour supervision. This was not inexpensive. My insurance covered a minuscule portion of the costs. There wasn't any way I could look to Shawn's mother for assistance. She made less than I did and would not agree to a program out of state. There wasn't anything in state I could find, which in my opinion would be as effective. Pathway Family Center programs costs excluding medical coverage for Shawn's tenure was in excess of $12,000. The specifics are hazy at this point, but I came up with the money between borrowing against my 401K and selling my Evanston residence. At any rate, the point was that for the sake of Shawn's life, he needed help and it had to happen.

Having made up my mind to get Shawn the help he needed and accomplishing the surrounding tasks needed to make it happen, my next step was to physically get Shawn to Detroit for the program. I knew this would be a challenge as some days it was difficult just to get him to school. By now, he was nearly my size and there were times I'd have to wrestle Shawn just to get him to school. Getting him to Detroit by myself was simply out of the question. My brother Floyd was kind enough to come up from Indianapolis and travel with Shawn and me to Detroit. The day that I told Shawn that we would be taking him to the Pathway program in Detroit was one of the most heartbreaking experiences of my life. Shawn pleaded with me not to follow through on the Pathway commitment, promising everything under the sun. In my heart, I felt then and still do that this was the only way to save Shawn's life.

Shawn's mom was totally against his being placed in Pathway even though she didn't participate financially in its costs. Truth be told, at this time I believe, his mom would have gone against anything I wanted. Divorce is painful to the children involved and even more impactful when divorced parents' actions don't take into account what's best for their children. I'm remorseful for the pain and emotional distress the divorce actions had on Shawn and Scott. I can't help but feel that some of the acting out by both Shawn and Scott was somewhat due to the divorce of their parents.

As mentioned above, to assist in financing Shawn's Pathway program, I sold my Evanston residence and purchased a condo in Vernon Hills, Illinois, at 452 Kennedy Place. This also placed an additional twenty-five miles between my ex and myself, which was probably good for both of us.

My ex was getting remarried and asked if I'd watch Scott while she and her new husband honeymooned in Hawaii. I agreed and the first week-end Scott asked if he could spend a night with a friend of his in Skokie, which was about twenty-five miles away. Taking Scott at his word, I gave my permission. Around 2 am that weekend night, I received a phone call from the Skokie police requesting my presence at Scott's mom's apartment. It turned out that Scott arranged for a party to be held at his moms' apartment and the noise got out of hand. There were beer cans, liquor bottles, and trash scattered around the premises but no permanent damage. The Monday following my ex's return from her honeymoon, I received a call at work from her new husband. As I picked up the phone, he uttered "You owe me $10,000!" He claimed there was $10,000 worth of damage done to their apartment. Looking at the phone receiver in disbelief, I simply hung up. It didn't take a genius to figure out who put him up to the call.

Scott's mom gave up on his behavior patterns and asked me to assume custody of him, which I did in April of that year. For the time being, I had custody of both of my sons. Fortunately, my new job didn't require significant travel. The hardest job in the world without exception is that of being a single parent. My heart breaks when I learn of couples divorcing, who have children. It's difficult enough being a single parent but when the divorced couple doesn't make their children a priority, the difficulty level is multiplied a hundred-fold.

Most every other week at a minimum, I traveled to Detroit to work the Pathway program with Shawn. Shawn was doing well and I was excited to see him and be part of the recovery process. Initially, Shawn's mom refused to have anything to do with the Pathway program. After several months denouncing the programs' effectiveness, she wanted to get involved. She made the case that she wanted to support Shawn's efforts and that my placing him in Detroit made it infeasible for her participation. So I ended up buying her round-trip airline tickets. She showed up a few times and befriended one of the programs parents. On one of the weekends that I didn't travel to Detroit when Shawn was staying at the home of the parent his mom befriended, he ran from the program with his mom's help.

Putting together the chain of events leading up to Shawn's planned escape, it was apparent to me that his mom, his mom's befriended parent, and Shawn planned it together. The irony of this was that I had a court order that supported his placement into the program. So I thought it would be a simple matter of bringing it back before the court to have Shawn placed back into the program. This turned out to be an exercise in futility.

To plead my case and express my feelings, I wrote the following letter to the Judge responsible for Shawn's case:

July 1, 1994

Honorable Judge Jeffrey Lawrence,
Circuit Court of Cook County,
Domestic Relations Division,
1340 S. Michigan Avenue – Room 703,
Chicago, IL 60605

Honorable Judge Jeffrey Lawrence:

I'm writing this letter on behalf of my son's case, Shawn Evans. From the very start of the unfortunate chain of events leading up to Shawn's placement at Pathway Family Center in Michigan, I have been driven by one principle: *to do what is in the best interest of Shawn*. That is why I'm writing this letter to you. If I didn't and Shawn was not returned to complete the program, I would feel that I failed on Shawn's behalf.

Your time is valuable so I will try to outline my feelings as brief as possible. My ex-wife and I were given joint custody of both of my sons, Shawn and Scott, from our divorce. I retained physical possession of Shawn and she had physical possession of Scott. Immediately preceding the divorce, Shawn and his mother got into an altercation resulting in Shawn being hospitalized for evaluation for striking his mother.

Upon Shawn's release, he started displaying behaviors indicative of an individual using drugs: school tardiness/truancy/declining grades, loss of motivation/energy, aggressive anger/hostility/irritability/family arguments, unusual mood swings, changes in friends, trouble with the law, and drug-related graphics and slogans. I worked within the Evanston school system to qualify Shawn for their special education program. Shawn's school and home performance declined to the point where he was moved from regular classes and strictly supervised special education classes to finally a placement at Forest Academy in Des Plaines, a Therapeutic Day School. All of these efforts along with working with the Skokie Juvenile Department were fruitless.

The placement of Shawn into a long-term residential-type treatment program became the primary option for Shawn especially after learning that Shawn was not only using pot and LSD heavily but also selling drugs. I investigated facilities in Illinois and could not find a long-term facility I could afford. I located a highly successful facility (Pathway Family Center) in Michigan I could afford by selling my residence in Evanston. A series of events then led this matter before you last October.

"To ensure Shawn's continued treatment, I reached an agreement with my ex-wife against the advice of my attorney. The agreement acknowledged by you and duly entered as a court order allowed Shawn to attend his mother's wedding, with a responsibility by me to get Shawn from Michigan to Illinois and back, twelve round-trip airplane tickets for my ex-wife so she would participate in Shawn's recovery, and an assumption of $1,200 of her attorney's fees. I felt confident that this would allow Shawn to fully complete the program.

"I submerged myself in Shawn's recovery program driving to and from Detroit on most weekends. If I couldn't make it one weekend, I would make it a point of going the following weekend so Shawn would not be without my visible support for more than a two-week period. I learned the required program components to serve as weekend host home parent requiring my arrival on Friday, in time for family counseling sessions followed that evening with the open meetings normally, followed by group counseling sessions. I stayed through 3–4 pm on Sundays in a loaned residence with the care of as many as six program clients entrusted to me and another dad for the weekend. I did this most every weekend.

"Even with the court order, my ex-wife fought Pathway Family Center and me most every step of the way making Shawn's complete recovery very difficult. Realizing the court order contained a provision for my ex-wife to relocate Shawn to another facility if Pathway failed to properly communicate with her, they bent over backward to accommodate her. This is well documented. Pathway finally got to the point where they were not going to let her participate in Shawn's recovery as she had become such a deterrent.

"With Shawn's mother enabling him to avoid facing his issues, Shawn's progress has been retarded. Shawn was placed into Pathway on August 8 of last year and was on the next to last level preceding graduation when he ran from the program on May 22 of this year. Shawn has taken the easy way out and ran from the program rather than face his issues. Regardless of how he came back to Illinois, the fact is that he would not have had an alternative and would have returned to the program if his mother had not supported his actions and insisted upon his return.

"Please understand that this is not a custody issue with me. It's about the life of my son, wanting him to have the opportunity to succeed in life by facing up to his issues and completing the program as he started out to and as the court so ordered and his mother and I agreed to. Shawn is now seventeen and soon will have to make it on his own. I only want him to have every tool to do just that. I've told my ex-wife from the beginning that I would not be opposed to Shawn living with her upon the completion of this program if that is what he desired.

Please allow Shawn to complete the Pathway program for his benefit. If you don't, I can't say that I understand but I will know in my heart that I've done everything in my power that I possibly can. I want a healthy relationship with a healthy son. If he doesn't complete the program and face his issues, I feel he will not make the necessary adjustments to have healthy relationships and in fact will continue pre-program behaviors including manipulation coercion, and insincerity. I'm emotionally drained and have given Shawn every ounce of energy I could during his recovery. If he's allowed to continue the program, my support will be there as it has in the past.

Sincerely,

Stephen D. Evans No. 92 D 0639,

452 Kennedy Place,

Vernon Hills Illinois, 60061

(708) 549 - 0005 Home

(708) 677 - 2850 Work

The court ruled against their own order, placing me in a state of disbelief. As I mentioned in the letter, I had given every ounce of energy I had into Shawn's recovery and determined then that if he wasn't invested in his recovery, I had to just let it go. If I ever felt any trust toward my second wife, this incident proved to me that she couldn't be trusted. I was totally disgusted with my ex for enabling Shawn, deceiving Pathway Family Center, and deceiving me. (Fast forward to 2022 and I'm elated and proud to say that Shawn has since transformed into a loving, caring husband and father to his wife Yucco and son Axel).

Meanwhile, 1994 was my first of seven years with IPC. The organization allowed me to set departmental standards and didn't require as much travel of me as BAI did. IPC was the second of three associations that I worked for in my second career. My time there provided me with further growth opportunity in my new industry. I continued educational pursuits obtaining the "Certified Association Executive" credential in 1997.

As I did at BAI, my IPC travels provided some interesting experiences. One was particularly nerve wracking. In San Jose for a series of pre-planning meetings for IPC's annual Expo and Conference, I had a dinner engagement with a couple of our purveyors. The dinner was at the Hyatt, just down the street from the Hilton I was staying at, so I decided to walk the five to six blocks. I began the walk and a middle-aged Hispanic gentleman started walking next to me. By nature, I'm a brisk walker and was walking at a rapid pace. This fellow next to me started mimicking my walk and I could smell alcohol on his breath. All of a sudden, he reached over and grabbed me by the back of my neck turning my face to his and in a cold-blooded manner made the remark, "Do you want to meet the Devil?" At that moment, my thought was, *My God! He's going to kill me.* Probably by reflex, I slowly removed his hand from my neck and backed up. Once I felt it safe to do so, I turned around and went back to my hotel. I called one of the individuals in the dinner group I was meeting and told them I'd be there but would be late. But through the rest of that evening, I felt as if his hand was around my neck.

One of my responsibilities in overlooking IPC's Annual Expo and Conference was to hire the entertainment for the big party the night before the expo opened. At this particular expo, I engaged Chubby Checker to be our headliner. Selecting entertainment for the group was always a challenge as our attendee mix was 80% male, 20% female. Our attendees were of the age that for the most part all would know Chubby Checker. There were a few acts before Chubby, so I went backstage to introduce myself and thank him for performing that night. Chubby Checker, AKA "Ernest Evans" was serenely quiet. He was so placid it was almost as if he was in a trance. I didn't know what to think. Was he high or was he just grossly past his prime? My immediate thoughts were that he was going to bomb and the evening would be a disaster. All I could do was hold my breath and wish for the best. After he was introduced on stage, he magically transformed into another person. He generated the energy of three people and was a huge hit with the audience! He joked around with me later that night calling me his cousin as we both had the same last name.

Sandie and I took a driving trip to the Florida Keys. It's said that the best way to experience a trip through the Florida Keys is via a convertible. So I rented a sporty Mitsubishi convertible for the trip. We planned to spend a few days with my sister Sheryl and her husband Jim who lived on the way in Cape Coral, Florida. I thoroughly enjoy visiting with Sheryl and due to the mileage between us just don't get to see her often enough. Sandie and I were in the early years of our relationship and Sheryl and Jim requested that we sleep in separate bedrooms, which we happily agreed to their request. The visit was great and as everyone who's met Sandie thought the world of her. Our trip was splendid as if it were out of a novel. The weather was perfect and traveling the causeways in the Florida Keys with the ocean on both sides of us was breathtaking.

Meanwhile, my parenting with Scott wasn't going as well as I would have liked. I discovered that Scott was drinking, finding a stash of alcohol in the attic recess off his room. Later that year, Scott put me through quite an escapade. Scott and a friend of his "borrowed" his friends' uncle's van and they took off out of state. When he didn't come home, I naturally became worried. I was worried enough to contact the police. A couple of days went by and I received a call from one of Scott's friends informing me that Scott was okay and that he was in Florida. A day or two after this, a call from the police notified me that Scott and his friend were picked up in North Dakota! I was fuming. Not only was I worried sick wondering where Scott was, I was also busy planning an event for work. I had to drop everything and drive to North Dakota to pick Scott up. The drive back was a long one for Scott, listening to my constant venting. Apparently, Scott's plan was to visit his sister Janette in Los Angeles and the call informing me of his Florida whereabouts was simply a smoke screen. Bill Steele, a friend of mine who lives in Minneapolis, was kind enough to let us spend the night with him on the way back to break up the trip.

That year was Scott's fifteenth birthday. He was an avid Chicago Bulls fan so I arranged to have a custom Chicago Bulls birthday cake made for the occasion. We had a mini party at our new Vernon Hills residence. Scott invited his girlfriend Sylvia and I asked Sandie to join us to mark the event. This was one of the more pleasant memories of Scott living with me in Vernon Hills. Scott ended up graduating from Libertyville High School. This, however, was no small task as it took several school meetings and the enrollment into a Special Education Center that was part of Libertyville High School, which didn't require everyday attendance. I've joked with Sandie that I'd worked as hard for Scott's High School diploma as he did.

The following year, Scott and I made a trip together that was and will always be a memorable one to me. With both of us being sports fans,

I thought a driving baseball park vacation trip would be a nice bonding experience. Initially, Scott was hesitant and not inclined to go. However, when I told him he could help me with the driving he was anxious for the trip. Our driving baseball park vacation routed us to Detroit, Toronto, Montreal, New York (for both the Yankees and the Mets), and Cleveland. We stayed in hotels for the trip beginning with a Bed and Breakfast in Toronto. When we pulled up to the Toronto Bed and Breakfast, Scott was incredulous asking, "What kind of place is this?" When we got to our accommodations, we saw that we had the whole top level of the building, and Scott was bowled over. We took in baseball games in each of these cities and saw some additional sites along the way including Ellis Island, Battery Park, the Statue of Liberty, and the Rock and Roll Hall of Fame.

That summer, my sister Becky and her husband Steve and their daughter Shelby drove up from Indianapolis for a weekend visit. Siblings visiting me was more uncommon than my driving down to Indianapolis and seeing them. Whenever a sibling visited, it was special for me. We had a grand time. Sandie joined us and we drove up to Milwaukee for the annual "Summer Fest" event.

Later in the year, Janette's half-sister, Sierra, was my guest in Vernon Hills for several days. We had a good time. While she was with me, we went to downtown Chicago and visited the famous Magnificent Mile. I knew that Janette's two half-sisters went through some rough times with their dad and I wanted to provide Sierra with a comfortable, safe place. I had in the back of my mind the kindness that my uncle had shown me back in my high school days and wanted to do as much as I could for Sierra.

This decade of my life taught me some serious life lessons. The hotel company I sacrificed eight years of my career for turned on me and made me realize that to corporations you're not necessarily human. For their purposes, you're simply an asset to be deployed in their best interests. My divorce and career change taught me that God has a plan for all of us. We may not realize it when it's happening due to our emotions but he's got our back. The importance of an education was magnified in my mind when my college degree was one of the reasons I was able to switch careers. The difficulty of single parenting was hammered home to me along with the importance of divorced parents to be united in their children's best interests during and after my divorce. No doubt about it; these ten years saw me grow tremendously as a person.

Scott's 15th Birthday with Sylvia.

Metropolitan State University Graduation.

Chapter 7 | 1996–2005

During this ten-year period, I married the love of my life, made advancements in my second career path, visited Europe for the first time, had a grandchild through my youngest son, and strengthened family relationships.

My eventual bride-to-be Sandie Sinck (Spoula) lived in Elmwood Park. During our near ten-year courtship, we never lived with one another. We'd spend some weekends and some overnights with each other but never took the next step to consolidate households. Thus, on most weekends I'd make the forty-five-minute trip from Vernon Hills to Elmwood Park for our dates. We did take many trips together, some as tag-alongs to my professional travel and others just for personal fun and family get-togethers.

In 1996, we traveled to Rosarito, Mexico, to visit my daughter Janette while she worked on the *Titanic* movie. Janette's profession since 1992 has been working in accounting positions for the movie industry. She has worked on over three dozen films during her career to-date. I'd enjoy speaking with her over the phone while she was on-site working a movie. Inevitably, the challenges of the movie she was working on would become part of the conversation. I remember speaking to her one evening while she was working on the movie, *A Time To Kill*. Midway through the conversation, she excitedly exclaimed that she needed to run, as they were about to film the burning of a house!

Sandie and I traveled to Mexico to be with Janette and visit the *Titanic* set. James Cameron wrote, directed, and produced what turned out to be a colossal hit. The main stars were Leonardo DiCaprio and Kate Winslet. The movie cost was trending significantly over budget which, of course, worried Janette and the entire accounting staff. With a production budget of $200 million, it was the most expensive film ever made at the time. Show management ordered cost cuts, which included such seemingly insignificant items as pastries for crew breaks. No one had a clue that the movie would end up being one of the highest grossing films ever. With an initial worldwide gross of over $1.84 billion, *Titanic* was the first film to reach the billion-dollar mark. A 3D version of *Titanic,* released in 2012 to commemorate the centennial of the sinking, earned it an additional $343.6 million worldwide, pushing the film's worldwide total to $2.18 billion and making it the second film to gross more than $2 billion worldwide.

We traveled along the highway from California to Rosarito, anxiously anticipating the visit to the *Titanic* movie set. As we approached the movie site, we could see the façade of the famous Titanic ship and it truly looked like the real thing. The ship's façade was made 90% to scale but once you went around the ship to its rear it was an open set. A visit to the set spotlighted the ship's staircase and other interesting film staging. A special water tank was created to simulate the ships' journey and its sinking. Oh, the magic of the movies!

We stayed with Janette for several days, enjoying the laid-back Mexican town of Rosarito. Being a cereal consumer but wanting to watch my cholesterol, we went on a quest to locate skim milk one day. After several unsuccessful attempts, we found what appeared to be the last quart of skim milk in town at a local market. I was so thrilled with this accomplishment that we took a picture of the milk carton, documenting our feat. The jubilation was short-lived however as when we returned to our accommodations and prepared our breakfast, we sadly discovered the skim milk to be sour!

Exploring the local flea markets was an adventure in itself. The poverty in the area was apparent with children constantly trying to sell us "Chiclets" chewing gum. Most of these markets inhabited by the locals sold blankets. Their main selling phrase for these blankets was "these are only for you, almost free, and better than K-Mart," which we found amusing.

At my new employer of the time, IPC, one of my current challenges was to locate and secure a suitable venue replacement for the association's annual conference and expo. IPC had outgrown the San Jose, California, Convention Center where the event was being held. When researching venues for an event, there are multiple considerations. The primary needs of IPC's annual conference and expo were exhibit space, meeting rooms, hotel accommodations, event security, event transportation, food and beverage for meals, breaks, and events' on-site temporary staffing, entertainment for the opening gala, and during the expo show, a show contractor to build and strike the expo show floor, a florist, a designated expo show freight company, and an audio–visual company. These responsibilities fell under my jurisdiction as IPC's Director of Conferences & Expositions.

Decisions made on these expo show partners can make or break the event's success. My philosophy on vendor recruitment was that they were partners in our event and should want to achieve success as much as the organization. The event's overall prosperity is measured primarily on two fronts: (1) Satisfaction of the expo show's exhibitors (considered the event's main customers) as well as the event's attendees (buyers of the exhibitor's displayed products) and (2) the exposition's profitability. Thus, service and cost are the main evaluation considerations for new vendors. Once satisfied with the service levels of a vendor it's important to systematically bid out services to be sure their pricing remains competitive. In some instances, you may be willing to pay slightly higher fees for expected greater quality levels.

On the surface, this may seem simple enough, but not so fast. Contracts are required for most of these services, which can lead to unanticipated costs. It's important to thoroughly review contract terms prior to commitment and equally important to confirm that the final invoice mirrors contractual terms. The services a general contractor provides for an exposition are numerous. My experience saw invoices up to twenty pages in length accruing over $200,000 in charges. If an invoice of this magnitude is not thoroughly scrutinized, an organization can lose thousands of dollars on their event. That can have a significant impact on an organization's bottom-line when working with a new vendor. Experience taught me to insert a performance clause into our contracts, allowing us to opt-out of multi-year agreements if we're not satisfied. It's difficult for a vendor to argue against this as they're selling us their service.

Hotel contracting is another area that places organizations in potential peril. Having worked in hotel management, I'm intimately familiar with the hotel's contractual objectives. A hotel is challenged to maximize their profitability and room sales are one of the main contributors to this success. Hotels have become very sophisticated in their marketing approach to maximize room sales. Chain and larger hotels use computerized revenue models managed by a "hotel revenue specialist" having the final say over business brought into the property by the hotel's sales force. These specialists can anticipate expected occupancy and rate levels from one to several years into the future based on the hotel's past history and an analysis of hotel business within their geographic competitive area.

Hotels cater to various market segments for their room sales and prioritize these based on their room rate potential. A hotel's goal is to fill rooms with higher rated market segments before catering to lower rated segments. Obviously, it's better to have rooms filled at a lower rate than not at all. On top of this, higher rated on the food chain are the individual transient and corporate group market segments. Conversely, some at the bottom-rated segments are religious and school groups. Political groups seem enticing from a rate standpoint but are notorious for not paying their bills. Associations (organizations I worked for while booking hotels) fall somewhere in the middle.

One of my missions when working with a hotel was to learn of their needs prior to finalizing arrangements. For instance, if a hotel's greater occupancy need was on a Thursday versus a Wednesday, the hotel may be willing to provide greater financial incentives to you for that flexibility. From my early booking experiences, I created my own boilerplate hotel contract as the starting point for negotiations. Failing that, my organization would have to begin with the hotel's contract language with terms, of course, which heavily favored the hotel. It was important to realize that once the contract was signed, all leverage was lost. If you wanted something included in the contract language, it was important to negotiate it up front, before the contract was signed.

In contracting with hotels, I viewed the arrangement on a long-term basis. There are basically two market environments when working with hotels. The first is a buyer's market, which favors the organization. The second is a seller's market, which favors the hotel. Even in a highly favorable buyer's market, I was careful not to be too demanding realizing that eventually the pendulum would swing the other way and the hotel would have you at a disadvantage. Thus, while obtaining favorable terms for the organization, it was important to be fair with the hotel to develop and nurture longstanding relationships.

Having come from a hotel background, I also understood the importance of maintaining a sterling reputation. Hotel management and sales staffs are relocated around the country for promotional and personal reasons. The hotel community is also a close-knitted one through their own conferences and networking. You can't assume that your contracting demands and hotel working relationships are kept within that one hotel. You should assume that every hotel you attempt to do business with knows of your contracting characteristics. On the buyers side, I would absolutely avoid working with hotels that had the reputation of breaking contracts with organizations in favor of a better piece of business.

IPC wanted to stay on the west coast if possible for their annual exposition and conference. The main convention centers on the west coast at that time were in San Francisco, Los Angeles, Anaheim, and San Diego. Each of these cities is considered "first tier," having larger convention centers with abundance exhibit hall space coupled with a large number of hotels. There are disadvantages in working with convention centers in "first tier" cities.

In my opinion, the preeminent disadvantage when working with a convention center in a "first tier" city is that your group tends to get lost in shuffle. With numerous exhibit halls, your event is one of several occurring simultaneously, which are probably larger. While convention centers, hotels, and vendors servicing these events concurrently will claim to provide the same level of service to all, it's just not possible under those circumstances. It can also be confusing to the event attendee. Even with adequate directional signage individuals can easily get confused with navigation efforts. Another disadvantage is overall cost for the event. Convention center space, hotel rooms, and vendor costs are all greater in the larger first tier cities.

"Second tier" cities have convention centers and hotels that cater to smaller events. Cities with convention centers catering to events in need of around 200,000 square feet of exhibit space and fewer hotel rooms are generally considered "second tier." Conversely, organizations with events occurring in "second tier" cities have the distinct advantage of being the focus of that city in lieu of a stepchild to larger organizations. In searching for a San Jose Convention Center 200,000-square-foot replacement, I was fortunate to come across an attractive "second tier" venue for IPC's 1998 annual conference and exposition.

Long Beach, California's fifth largest city, with a population of 440,000 had come a long way from its unflattering "closed shipyard" image. A few years earlier, Long Beach spent $111 million dollars to expand and upgrade the convention center. The convention center now had over 200,000 square feet of exhibition space, making it the perfect size for our exposition. The passing of this major event qualifier led me to perform a venue site inspection to determine the compatibility with our annual conference and expo.

I made arrangements through the Long Beach Convention and Visitor's Association to tour the area. The updated convention center was quite attractive. The square footage of the exhibit space and the number of meeting rooms housed in the center fit our event perfectly. There were some logistical traffic issues at the center but I felt this could be overcome with adequate signage. The hotel inventory was adequate and within walking distance of the center. Wanting to maximize my trip, I also met with the major hotels in the area and key prospective vendors. I was quite impressed with what our overall package would be and was convinced it would work well for us.

However, when working within an association (IPC in this case), you're not the sole decision-maker. Well-run associations are driven by their membership. There's an overall Board of Directors as well as numerous individual committees. In addition to my own organization's managerial structure, I had to convince the association's trade show subcommittee who, in turn, would get the Board of Directors to buy-in.

Realizing the selling challenge in front of me, I had the Long Beach Convention and Visitors Bureau arm me with area photos and statistics. The main objective I'd have to overcome was the stigma that the city of Long Beach carried as a past-its-prime, closed shipping port. Sure enough, shortly after the committee meeting began and Long Beach was surfaced as a potential site for our annual event, the committee's collective response was, "That old naval shipyard town?"

To sell the group, I first pointed out how perfectly the venue fit our event from both the convention center's space as well as the potential hotel package. In essence, the venue fit our event like a glove and would provide a warm, cozy feel. It also didn't hurt that there were ocean views from the convention center as well at several of the hotels that would be in the package. The area also enjoyed year-round good weather and the benefits afforded Los Angeles: its airport and visitor attractions without staying in LA.

This was indeed a tough sell. I remember telling the California *Wall Street Journal* in an article that "I sweated bullets" up until the favorable decision was made. The fact that we would be the city's focus during our event helped to push support for the venue over the top. IPC's trade show subcommittee approved the venue and in turn had the Board of Directors sign off on the decision. I signed a multi-year agreement after a thorough negotiation vetting process. This agreement was important as an event of this size needs to be booked several years down the road. It's delusional to think that you can pick up the phone and secure needed convention center space and hotel accommodations for an event of this size for your desired timeframe from one year to the next.

The venue change was well received by the IPC board, the IPC trade show committee, and the city of Long Beach. Long Beach rolled out the red carpet for IPC's 1998 Annual Conference and Exposition. The Long Beach Convention and Visitors Bureau put up welcome signs at the Long Beach Airport, had banners placed on street poles around the convention center, and had hotel staff wear IPC Welcome badges. The mayor, Beverly O'Neill, even showed up for a ribbon-cutting ceremony.

Our Long Beach relationship accounted for several business and personal visits to the area. On one trip, Sandie and I were invited to Long Beach to view the Long Beach Grand Prix. The Long Beach Grand Prix is the longest running major street race held in North America. It had started in 1975 as a Formula 5000 race, and became a Formula One event in 1976. The *Toyota Grand Prix of Long Beach* is an Indy-Car Series race held on a street circuit in Long Beach, California. It was the premier race on the CART/Champ Car calendar from 1996 to 2008. Since 2009, the race has been part of the unified Indy-Car Series. It is one of the longest continuously running events in Indy car racing and is considered one of the most prestigious events on the circuit. One of my favorite pictures of that trip is Sandie sitting behind the wheel of one of the Indy style racecars.

We also visited the historic RMS Queen Mary moored permanently in the harbor of Long Beach. The RMS Queen Mary is a retired British ocean liner that sailed primarily on the North Atlantic Ocean from 1936 to 1967 for the Cunard Line known as Cunard-White Star Line when the vessel entered service. Queen Mary sailed on her maiden voyage on May 27, 1936. With the outbreak of the Second World War, she was converted into a troopship and ferried Allied soldiers for the duration of the war. Following the war, Queen Mary was refitted for passenger service and commenced transatlantic passenger service. Queen Mary was officially retired from service in 1967. She left Southampton for the last time on October 31, 1967, and sailed to the port of Long Beach, California, United

States, where she remains to this day. The ship serves as a tourist attraction, featuring restaurants, a museum and a hotel. She is listed on the National Register of Historic Places. IPC used a block of rooms on the famous ship for attendees.

Toward the end of 1996, Sandie and I began an Evans family tradition. We hosted a small Evans family contingent to dinner on the Saturday following Thanksgiving. This first dinner was small, which included my Evans siblings and spouses: Floyd, Glenda, Becky, Steve, Marjie, and Rod. We ate at the now-closed Jonathan Byrd Cafeteria. This evolved into our Christmas gift for my side of the family as we spent Christmas with Sandie's side of the family. This has since expanded from the original ten-or-so attendees to thirty-five attendees at our 2017 dinner. From this event's inception until my 2016 retirement, we'd refer to this as our annual trifecta trip—we'd begin at home in Chicago and drive to Highland, IL, to visit with Sandie's sister Janice and her husband Bruce. From there, we'd journey to Indianapolis for a few days of visiting with relatives and to host our annual Christmas dinner. After the Indianapolis festivities, we'd travel back home to Chicago.

To solidify my career path and to make myself more marketable, I decided to pursue the Certified Association Executive (CAE) credential. What is the value of holding the CAE designation? Becoming a Certified Association Executive shows your commitment to the association profession. As a CAE, you commit yourself to lifelong learning and an ongoing pursuit of knowledge in the profession. Among association leaders, the CAE designation has become known and appreciated as a mark of distinction that offers a wide range of benefits. Individuals pursue the CAE for a variety of reasons, including professional development, career planning and professional pride, dedication to their career, and self-fulfillment.

The CAE credential in 1996 was one of the industry's hardest to obtain. You must first meet eligibility requirements before you can even sit for the exam. The exam is given only twice a year and once you pass you must requalify every three years to maintain the designation. After meeting the eligibility requirements and several months of group study, I obtained the credential in May of 1997 and met the renewal requirements through the rest of my employment.

One of the CAE credential maintenance requirements was to accrue over forty industry educational hours per year. To accomplish this, I would attend industry conferences and educational seminars, as time permitted. The two main conferences at that time were American Society of Association Executive (ASAE) and Professional Convention Management Association's (PCMA's) annual conferences. PCMA had a conference that year in San Antonio, which I attended.

One of my personal goals while working was to visit family and friends when my conference/business travel allowed. A cousin of mine, Marylou Zachary, and her husband Bill lived on their personally built ranch in Kerrville, Texas, which was just sixty-five miles northeast of San Antonio. They were thrilled that I wanted to visit them and drove me round trip from San Antonio for the visit. Since then Sandie and I have visited this lovely couple on a couple of occasions.

That summer produced a very special surprise. My daughter Janette was assigned to work a movie in Chicago. This was the first time in her brief film career that she worked in the same area that I lived in. The movie was *Mercury Rising,* starring Bruce Willis and Alec Baldwin. It afforded me the opportunity to spend quality time with my daughter whom I saw very seldom in years past. She was housed in downtown Chicago, so on weekends when I could, I'd drive down there from Vernon Hills to visit her. It also allowed Janette and Sandie to get to know each other better. She was on the movie for several months but time seemed to fly by. I was sorry when the movie came to an end and Janette had to leave for her next assignment.

The following year in early 1998, Janette met me between her movie assignments in Washington DC. For a few days, we toured some of the sites. We explored the Capitol, Supreme Court, and the United States Holocaust Memorial Museum. Visiting the Holocaust Museum was mesmerizing. It was relatively new having only opened in 1993. It's adjacent to the National Mall in DC and is dedicated to helping leaders and citizens of the world confront hatred, prevent genocide, promote human dignity, and strengthen democracy. The museum provides for the documentation, study, and interpretation of holocaust history. We spent the better part of the day in this fascinating replication of one of history's most sadistic schemes to irradicate a race.

Later that year, Sandie and I were privileged to travel with the IPC Board of Directors to Maui, Hawaii. Not being an IPC officer or member of the Board of Directors, I was honored to be asked to attend. The leisure trip lasted several days and apart from participating in the festivities, I was responsible for the planning and execution of the events. Everyone was housed at the Westin Maui Resort. One of the requirements in attending was participation in a golf tournament. Sandie and I knew this in advance and tried our best to prepare. Sandie had never golfed in her life and I'm a way below average golfer. Fortunately, the teams we were on weren't terribly serious and everyone had a good time. This experience allowed the IPC officers to get to know Sandie, and I learned more about the IPC Board of Directors.

Before the end of 1998, I traveled to Costa Rica to perform a site inspection at a resort property under consideration for a future IPC Board of Directors Meeting. The property was a four-star resort managed by Riu Hotels & Resorts, based in Mallorca, Spain. The area had a very different feel to it from any place I'd experienced in the United States, including Hawaii. Although not true to form, it had a third-world feel to it. Driving through the streets of the town by the resort, I witnessed a huge pig run out of the front door of a home! The resort was modern and attractively furnished. One of the key detriments was that the resort would lose power intermittently. This, in my opinion, was too much uncertainty to recommend it for the IPC Board of Directors' meeting. I just couldn't see taking the chance on the electricity going out during a critical meeting presentation or worse yet for the entire evening, leaving everyone in the dark. IPC crossed this destination off their list.

In September of 1998, Sandie's oldest daughter Olivia was getting married to Cesar Vazquez on the fourth of the month and she invited me to the wedding. Sandie and I were on a relationship hiatus then, and I really didn't know whether I should attend. I truly didn't know what to expect if I went. Would Sandie be there with someone else? Would I be genuinely welcome? I felt privileged to be invited and liked Olivia, so I went. Sandie was there without a date and invited me to sit with her. We enjoyed the festivities and I'm grateful to have been part of such a special occasion for Olivia. I drove Sandie home and we sat in her condo having a serious relationship conversation that went into the wee hours of the morning. Our relationship resumed and got stronger with each passing month.

One of the highlights from 1999 was a Florida vacation that Sandie and I went on. We visited with my sister Sheryl and her husband Jim in Cape Coral for a few days. During our visit with my sister and brother-in-law, we toured the Thomas Edison and Henry Ford Winter Estates in Fort Myers. The site included a historical museum and a twenty-one-acre botanical garden that were adjacent sites to the Edison and Ford winter homes. During this Florida excursion, Sandie and I took in Busch Gardens in Tampa and ventured to the southernmost tip of Florida and the United States.

After a seven-year tenure with IPC, I left the organization in February of 2000 to join National Marine Manufacturers Association (NMMA), headquartered in downtown Chicago. NMMA is an association comprising companies doing business within the marine industry. As the industry's largest trade association, NMMA leverages the strength of its membership to provide a strong voice of leadership for the industry, representing recreational boating to policymakers, the media and the public. NMMA membership keeps companies connected to issues vital to their business and provides information, resources, programs, and services to help them grow their business. NMMA promotes numerous benefits to its membership. One of a company member's primary benefits was a significant discount to exhibit at NMMA consumer boat shows.

NMMA is the world's leading producer of consumer boat and sport shows, managing eighteen shows in the largest cities in the U.S. NMMA boat and sport shows provide the recreational boating and outdoor sports industries with quality sales venues that engage consumers and promote the boating and outdoor lifestyles. Companies exhibiting at several of these shows would more than recoup their membership fees from realized space cost discounts.

My NMMA tenure was brought on through the resignation of IPC's President, Thom Dammrich. Thom was IPC's President for the entire seven years I was with the IPC Association. We worked well with one another and I was comfortable with his leadership. He accepted the same position with the larger NMMA Association and I wanted to continue working with him. Thom's concession of allowing me to leave work early every Friday to participate in my son Shawn's Michigan treatment program while I was at IPC made me feel a special allegiance to him.

It was difficult to leave IPC, having made many friends during my seven years there. Of course, there was also the comfort level of feeling secure, having developed a large amount of goodwill through my IPC accomplishments. On the other side of the equation, one didn't know what to expect from the impending new leadership at IPC. To provide a smooth transition, I worked for both organizations the first month of my NMMA employment.

Jokingly, I refer to my start with NMMA as the million-dollar welcome. This was due to NMMA's cancellation of their annual conference and expo then entitled "IMTEC" in Orlando, resulting in potential hotel cancellation penalties north of a million dollars to the organization, which I was challenged to address. The cancellation occurred just before my arrival and may have factored in the organization's decision to replace their outgoing president with Thom Dammrich. At any rate, I'm sure that situation factored into Thom's decision to bring me on board at NMMA.

My arrival at NMMA proved to be a unique situation. There was no meetings/expo department enabling me to develop the department from scratch. Thus, I was able to create my own job description and title along with job descriptions for the other incoming departmental positions. This was challenging but also extremely gratifying as a first-time experience. Apart from setting up my new department, I set out with the demanding task of reducing NMMA's million-dollar plus cancellation exposure. In reviewing the hotel contracts, I noticed a clause in some of them that provided some financial relief to NMMA, providing we officially cancelled six months prior to the event. Due to the timing, this wasn't possible for the year 2000, but exercising this contract clause for the year 2001 it saved NMMA $170,000.

Also in February of that year, Sandie and I attended the seventieth birthday party of my stepmom, Betty Bartlett. Betty was married to my bio dad, Paul Thayer, and while I never lived with her, I considered her my stepmom later on in life. My two half-sisters from my dad's side of the family, Sheryl Pierson (Thayer) and Sharon Ferguson (Thayer), were also in attendance with their families. It was rare to be with such a large gathering from that side of the family but most enjoyable.

This year produced one of my life's greatest surprises. Unknown to me, my daughter Janette and Sandie were colluding behind my back for a surprise visit by Janette to Chicago. Janette was living in Oregon at the time and between her work schedule and the scant time she had at her place in Oregon, an unplanned Chicago visit was the last thing I expected. Sandie worked particularly hard to have me come over to her condo for a birthday celebration. My birthday that year fell during the week, making me somewhat reluctant to celebrate it then, as the next day was a workday. Being consistent with my arrival patterns, Sandie could count on me being at her place at the time we agreed on. I arrived at her building and made my way to her front door. After knocking on the door, my daughter Janette opened it. My feelings at that particular point are difficult to describe, but I felt momentarily as if I was in a "Twilight Zone." My eyes were seeing Janette but my brain was telling me she was either at a work location or at home in Oregon. It was one of the more pleasant surprises I've had in my life. Between Janette's work schedule and her Oregon residence, we didn't see each other as often as I'd like.

Meanwhile, my new employment was going well. Between the inherited hotel contracting issues and establishing myself within a new organization, I was kept busy. NMMA then decided to develop another trade show. This was for the aftermarket segment of the marine industry. The new show was called the Marine Aftermarket Accessories Tradeshow (using the acronym MAATS). It was my responsibility to secure a venue for this new venture and the desired location was Las Vegas.

This was the beginning of a love-hate relationship I would have with Las Vegas as while MAATS ran its Las Vegas course over several years, I visited and worked there around three dozen times. Making new discoveries and incurring new experiences the initial trips were exciting. However, going there year after year, I personally saw Las Vegas transform into a moneymaking machine in every sense of the word. It wasn't that long ago that you could find reasonable Las Vegas airline and hotel deals. In fact, when you visited Las Vegas, the only thing you needed to really seriously budget for was your gambling. Then, Las Vegas provided an endless array of affordable hotels where you could eat for practically nothing. Their whole marketing position was to make their money on the gambling while breaking even or even losing money in the other areas.

Not so today. hotels, meals, laundry, events, transportation, phone calls, and any other provided services are priced for maximum profitability. I literally got to the point where I felt that someone had their hands in my pockets once the plane landed in Vegas up until I was able to leave. The incident that pushed me over the top was in the late 2000s, when a group of us dined at a hotel's steak house restaurant. The menu was pricey to begin with, but we had a successful show and wished to celebrate. I ordered a steak and thought it would be nice to have one of the restaurant's custom-made sauces for it. When the waiter indicated that the sauce would be an additional $8, I nearly fell out of my chair. My spending philosophy for organizations I worked for was to try to spend the company's money as if it were my own. Whether it was company event expenses or my expense account, to me it was just the ethical thing to do.

MAATS was initially developed with exhibitor guidelines to be fair to all of NMMA companies that chose to exhibit. By design, this allowed the smaller companies that made up NMMA's membership to be on equal footing with the larger companies. The guidelines placed reasonable restrictions on display size, height, etc. The MAATS show began reasonable in total square footage requirements allowing us to have it at an area within Cesar's Palace. Unfortunately, in relatively short order the competitiveness of these companies overtook rationale, and organizations developed larger and more extensive exhibits, forcing companies to grow their display sizes to compete. You could say that these organizations were their own worst enemies. As their displays became larger and more sophisticated, their costs ratcheted up proportionally.

The increased space demand for the growth of MAATS necessitated the move from our Cesar Palace location to another Las Vegas venue. Complicating the process of selecting a new MAATS venue was the need for approximately forty hotel suites as part of our room block. These were going to be used for one-on-one supplier/exhibitor meetings while the exhibit floor was closed during the day. After a thorough search of the city, the best fit was the then Las Vegas Hilton hotel. It had its own exhibit hall along with ample suites to accommodate our MAATS show. There were other hotels with facilities that would work but these properties were either too expensive or demanded highly restrictive performance clauses within their contracts.

We ended up hosting the MAATS trade show at the Las Vegas Hilton for several years. A multi-year agreement worked to NMMA's favor saving the organization potentially hundreds of thousands of dollars over the contracted years. The hotel's staff bent over backwards to accommodate us providing special servicing of the forty or so suites we used for meetings as well as addressing other needs as they arose.

2001 was a momentous year for me. Sandie and I had been seeing each other for nearly ten years by then. On one occasion, Sandie mentioned to me that she was okay with our arrangement the way it was, our dating but living apart if that's what I wanted. Realizing the love I had for her and the sincerity of her love for me I decided to propose to her. Everyone on my side of the family adored Sandie and couldn't understand why we weren't married. So following NMMA's annual Miami Boat Show that I worked every February, usually over Valentine's Day, I decided to propose. We would typically get together for dinner following my working an event out of town and I looked forward to being with Sandie. The proposal itself was challenging but not deliberately so.

My plan was to take Sandie to a Chinese restaurant we frequented in her neighborhood and arrange to have a special fortune cookie given to her at the conclusion of our dinner that asked her to marry me. We would normally discuss dinner options and agree on a place as a couple. During this discussion, Sandie innocently asked me where I ate while working the Miami Boat Show and I confided to her that one of the last restaurants I ate at was Chinese. Because of this, she suggested that we avoid Chinese for the evening. Not wanting to spoil the surprise, I went along with the suggestion and we ended up eating at a quaint little Italian restaurant in an adjoining neighborhood to Sandie. La Bella Pasteria is located in Oak Park, Illinois, and considered one of the better Italian restaurants in the area.

Having already secured the ring, my plan then was to place it in Sandie's coat pocket so she would discover it as we left the restaurant. However, after entering the restaurant and taking her coat, I was having difficulty placing the ring in her coat pocket. She became suspicious so I had to improvise once again. My next idea was to place the ring in the breadbasket so she would discover it during the entrée. Taking the bread-basket under the table to insert the ring once again raised Sandie's suspicions, but I was successful in planting the ring. It took some awkward coaching to get her to locate the ring while maintaining the surprise but it worked. Sandie was definitely surprised upon discovering the ring and I got out of my chair and knelt on one knee and proposed to her. The restaurant patrons applauded and the management gave us our dessert that evening. To this day, that was one of the best life decisions I've ever made. My love for Sandie grows each day and she has become my everything: friend, soul mate, lover, and companion.

In June of 2001, Sandie joined me in Las Vegas for a mini vacation at the end of that year's MAATS exposition. We took in the Las Vegas sites and planned a tour to the Grand Canyon with a local tour operator. The Grand Canyon excursion would be the first for both of us. It's a bucket list item for most people and we were excited to go. I was delighted to get out of my work clothes and had even brought a brand-new pair of white shorts for the occasion. The Grand Canyon is over four hours from Las Vegas. We were staying at Cesar's Palace and were picked up well before sunset in the early morning hours and driven to a central gathering point for the bus tour.

At this tour center, the tour operators had coffee and rolls available for tour participants. Being a heavy morning coffee drinker, I took advantage of this and even took a cup with me on the bus. We were still waking up while I placed my coffee cup on the tray that came off the back of the seat in front of me. All was well initially and then the passenger occupying the seat in front of me thrust his seat backward throwing my coffee into my lap. My brand new pristine white shorts were now soiled with ugly brown coffee stains, and I was literally sitting in the liquid with my shorts having soaked up the coffee. What a predicament! Here we were just starting out on our tour without our own transportation and I was soaked in coffee, looking an absolute mess. Somewhere along the way, I was able to purchase another pair of shorts and changed, but this incident will forever be etched in my mind.

In October of 2001, I traveled to Cape Coral Florida to visit with my sister Sheryl and her husband Jim. Their adopted son James along with their new grandson Kendall also lived in the area. It was to be a short visit as I was busy at work with contracting and planning tasks for shows. On one of the days there, my sister Sheryl and my brother-in-law Jim were expecting their son James and his son Kendall over for a visit. I liked James and was looking forward to seeing him and, of course, seeing my sister's newest grandbaby.

It was an hour or so past the time for James' arrival and my sister and brother-in-law became worried. They wanted to go out to look for James and Kendall, so I offered to stay back in the event someone phoned the house. A calamitous incident occurred that day. James and his son Kendall were involved in a traffic accident at a four-way intersection that killed both of them. My sister Sheryl and her husband Jim were absolutely heartbroken. I agonized over the incident, feeling helpless, wanting to help in any way I could. My employer allowed me to extend my vacation for a few days and I stayed to support my sister. To this day, it's difficult to believe that two young lives can be taken so quickly. You read about such incidents but it doesn't truly hit home until it happens to someone close to you.

From Sandie and my engagement in February of 2001 to our scheduled wedding date of April 14, 2002, we had fourteen months for planning purposes. This seemed like a long time but amazingly the time kept slipping away. We planned on getting married in South Haven, Michigan, so Sandie's dad Joe could attend more easily. He was having health issues and we wanted to make it as simple as possible for him to be there. We made numerous trips to South Haven to scout and secure a church, caterer, and hotel for out-of-town guests. These trips also provided an opportunity to visit with Sandie's dad and his significant other, Pat.

For a church, we discovered the relatively new Peace Lutheran Church, which was off a major highway just outside of South Haven. Unknown to us, but as an absolute bonus, the church had a magnificent kitchen and meeting room that would work perfectly for our reception following our wedding service. We met with the caterer we ended up using and sampled some of her entrées to have a comfort level with her quality. Chris was the chef at the Everyday People Café in Douglas, Michigan, a short drive from South Haven. We decided on giving our guests three entrée options of salmon, beef, and chicken. The entrées along with the entire meal were delicious. We were extremely pleased with our caterer choice.

The hotel we ended up utilizing was the Old Harbor Inn. Old Harbor Inn sits within Old Harbor Village, a collection of buildings along the historic Black River. Old Harbor Inn has four boardwalk-connected buildings nestled into South Haven's picturesque Marina District. On any given day, you may see a group of future yacht captains learning the ropes, a gaggle of geese waiting for the inevitable bread toss from above, or a flow of lazy-day boaters on their way out to the lake. Also in the Maritime District is the Harbor Walk. It stretches from one lighthouse, around the harbor, and back to the other lighthouse and provides a wonderful way to experience what made South Haven the destination it is today.

This hotel's location, character, and size fit perfectly for our out-of-town guests. With its over-40 rooms, our wedding party literally took the hotel over. Apart from marrying the love of my life, some of my fondest memories of our wedding event were from that hotel experience. Everywhere we went, we ran into relatives and friends. All family members from both Sandie's and my side were present meeting, conversing, and getting aquatinted with one another. We had 98% attendance of invited guests, making the event even more memorable.

Sandie was concerned with the weather for our special day and probably rightfully so. The average South Haven April high is 56 degrees and the average South Haven rainfall for April is 3.19 inches. I kept reassuring Sandie that it would be 72 degrees and sunny on our momentous occasion. God not only led me to Sandie but he provided a perfect weather day for it. On our wedding day of April 14, 2002, it was indeed sunny and the temperature was 72 degrees!

As a surprise to Sandie, I decided to memorize and recite my vows verbatim:

"Sandie, I don't have the words to express all I wish to promise.
Therefore, my vow to you, before God, our relatives, and our friends
Is more a vow of the spirit than of the letter;
More a promise made by my heart than one reasoned in my head.
I love you more now than the world itself.
I promise to do everything in my power to nurture that love,
So that in good times and bad, in sorrow as well as joy,
My love for you will be one thing you can count on.
Sandie, this is my promise to you today: My love for you always."

It was a beautiful ceremony followed by an outstanding dinner. Being in a church, we elected to not serve alcohol except for one champagne toast but the quality of the food more than made up for the lack of alcoholic drinks.

With his doctors' approval, Sandie's dad had put off open-heart surgery until after the wedding, so he could walk her down the aisle. The surgery was scheduled the following day, so we traveled to Grand Rapids, Michigan, to see him just before leaving on our European honeymoon. It was an early morning drive after a late night of celebrating our nuptials. We couldn't stay for the actual procedure, as we had to make the drive back to Chicago to retrieve our luggage at Sandie's condo in Elmwood Park and then get to the airport for our International honeymoon flight. Sandie did get to see her dad that morning, and he ended up having quadruple bypass heart surgery that day.

Our honeymoon plans included Paris, Prague, and Rome—in that order. Reading about the beautiful European countryside we decided to transport via train between Paris and Prague and between Prague and Rome. In preparation and planning for our honeymoon, I researched hotel and sight-seeing options. I even purchased a *Europe for Dummies* book for direction and individual city advice. We ended up settling on Marriott hotels in Paris and Prague for their known quality and consistency standards. For Rome, we decided to obtain some local flavor and opted to stay at the Hotel Campo De Fiore, a locally owned and run property rated well in my *Europe for Dummies* book. For sightseeing, we scheduled tours through American Express for Paris and Rome while opting for a personal guide in Prague.

Friends of mine who had been to Paris suggested that due to the time differential, we resist the temptation to nap or sleep on our arrival. They recommended checking into the hotel and "hit the ground running" after arriving. This advice was relayed to Sandie and that was the plan as we began our romantic European getaway. The Paris flight was timely and we planned on taking the subway from the airport to downtown. One of the warnings in my Europe book for Paris was to be wary of pickpockets especially in areas heavily trafficked by tourists. Sure enough, as we were standing on and riding the subway from the airport to downtown Paris, a group of boys worked their way to us. One of them was looking at Sandie's purse. I made eye contact with him and pantomimed the words "don't try it." Fortunately this worked and we were on our way.

Paris, France's charming capital, is a major European city and a global center for art, fashion, cuisine extraordinaire, and culture. Wide boulevards and the River Seine crisscross its nineteenth-century cityscape. The Marriott we stayed at in Paris was quite nice. We checked in and went to our room to prep for some sightseeing. We got to our room and I went into the bathroom briefly and returned to find Sandie soundly asleep happily in a comatose state of rest! After Sandie's well-deserved rest, we began our exploration of Paris.

One of our first treks was to the famed Notre Dame Cathedral. The site of the Notre Dame is the cradle of Paris and has always been the religious center of the city. The Celts had their sacred ground there; the Romans built a temple to worship Jupiter. A Christian basilica was built in the sixth century and the last religious structure before the Notre-Dame construction started was a Romanesque church. The frontal west facade features three wide portals; above the portals is the Gallery of Kings—twenty-eight statues of Judean Kings—and higher up are the famous gargoyles and grotesques. While not the largest cathedral in the world, Notre-Dame might be the most famous of all cathedrals. The Gothic masterpiece is located on the Île de la Cité, a small island in the heart of the city.

The next landmark visited was the Louvre. The Louvre Museum is one of the largest and most important museums in the world. It is housed in the expansive Louvre Palace, situated in the heart of Paris. Originally a royal palace but now the world's most famous museum, it is a must-visit for anyone with even a slight interest in art. Some of the museum's most celebrated works of art include the Mona Lisa and the Venus de Milo. The museum has a collection of over one million works of art, of which about 35,000 are on display, spread out over three wings of the former palace. The museum has a diverse collection ranging from Antiquity up to the mid-nineteenth century. The most recent addition to the Louvre was the construction of the Louvre Pyramid, which functions as the museum's main entrance. The renowned American architect I.M. Pei built the pyramid in 1989. The glass pyramid allows the sunlight to enter the underground floor. Also, while in Paris, how can anyone pass up the opportunity to see the one and only Mona Lisa?

We then took a boat tour on the Paris River Seine. While it's common knowledge that the Notre Dame Cathedral is the technical epicenter of Paris, River Seine captures the real essence of the city. For centuries, poets, painters, philosophers, novelists, architects, lovers, and finally, tourists, have understood this powerful attraction. River Seine flows right through the heart of Paris. It was no accident that the city evolved around this gigantic avenue for commerce and transportation. The river is the chief commercial waterway, and half of the water used in Paris still comes from the Seine. Being mesmerized by Paris, I was going from one end of the boat to the other, taking photos of this beautiful city.

You can't also visit Paris without taking in its most famous landmark the Eiffel Tower. Even if you do not want to visit this world-famous structure, you will see its top from all over Paris. The tower rises 984 feet tall. When it was completed at the end of the nineteenth century, it was twice as high as the Washington Monument, at the time the tallest structure in the world. The Eiffel Tower was built for the World Exhibition in 1889, held in celebration of the French Revolution in 1789. The man behind the Eiffel Tower was Gustave Eiffel, known from his revolutionary bridge building techniques, which would form the basis for the construction of the Eiffel Tower. He was also known for the construction of the Statue of Liberty's iron framework.

Our final major France site sojourn took us to the magnificent Monet's Garden located approximately one and one-half hours northwest of Paris in Giverny, France. Claude Monet, the father of Impressionism, lived and painted there for more than forty years of his life. There are two distinctly unique gardens that Monet designed and modified throughout his life. Claude Monet created his Clos Normand flower garden and his water garden. Seeing the willow trees and lake full of water lilies, you'll understand why Monet used this garden as the inspiration for over 250 of his paintings.

During our trip, we decided to take the London Underground from Heathrow Airport into downtown London for lunch. The London Underground (also known simply as the Underground, or by its nickname, the Tube) is a public rapid transit system, serving London and some parts of the adjacent counties of Buckinghamshire, Essex, and Hertfordshire in the United Kingdom. We got off at the Paddington stop and looked for a restaurant to have lunch. The first restaurant we went into, Fountains Abbey, turned out to be a bikers' bar. We quickly departed and came across a middle of the road establishment called Garfunkel's Restaurant and Coffee Shop. The lunch was enjoyable and it was our first experience of using foreign currency on the trip. Having seen some of London, including its famous black taxis and double-decker buses, we then returned to Heathrow Airport via the Tube.

The next city we visited was Prague. River Vltava bisects Prague, capital city of the Czech Republic. Nicknamed "the City of a Hundred Spires," Prague is known for its Old Town Square, the heart of its historic core, with colorful baroque buildings, Gothic churches, and the medieval

Astronomical Clock, which gives an animated hourly show. Completed in 1402, the pedestrian Charles Bridge is lined with statues of Catholic saints.

Charles Bridge crosses River Vltava in Prague; it proved an excellent vantage point for activities below. Its construction started in 1357 under the auspices of King Charles IV, and finished in the beginning of the fifteenth century. The bridge replaced the old Judith Bridge built between 1158 and 1172, which had been badly damaged by a flood. This new bridge was originally called Stone Bridge or Prague Bridge but has been "Charles Bridge" since 1870. As the only means of crossing River Vltava until 1841, Charles Bridge was the most important connection between Prague Castle and the city's Old Town and adjacent areas. This "solid-land" connection made Prague important as a trade route between Eastern and Western Europe. There's a local Prague superstition that if you touch a certain statue on the bridge, you're sure to return to this magnificent city.

Our tour guide took us to the Klementinum, which is one of the largest complexes in Europe, and is home to the Czech Republic's National Library. Situated in the romantic area of Prague's Old Town, the Klementinum dates back to the eleventh century when a chapel was erected and dedicated to St. Clement. In the middle ages, the complex became a Dominican monastery, and afterwards in 1556 a Jesuit college, and was at one point, the third largest Jesuit college in the world. The Baroque complex is the second largest complex in Prague after the magnificent Prague Castle and features beautiful architectural facades, lush courtyards with numerous sundials and attractions such as the sixty-eight meters high Astronomical Tower, which affords exquisite views over the labyrinthine city of Prague, the frescoed Baroque Library Hall, and the extraordinary Mirror Chapel.

The tour guide also took us to the Old Town Square, which draws the greatest number of visitors in Prague as it boasts meticulously preserved buildings and monuments: One building that truly dominates the square is the Old Town City Hall, which dates back to 1338. In 1410, the astronomical clock was added to the Hall with a chronometer and the zodiac below;

this clock is a worldwide attraction and was one of our signature stops on our Prague visit.

Hundreds of people gather at the start of every hour to see the elaborate installation with its centerpiece, the twelve apostles rotating inside the clock. The building was badly damaged during World War II; however, the remainder of the building was carefully restored to its former days of glory. If you climb the tower, you can enjoy truly breathtaking views of the square and see why Prague is called the city of 1,000 spires.

A must-see for Sandie, an avid Beatles fan, was the *Lennon Wall* or *John Lennon Wall*. Once a normal wall, since the 1980s, it has been filled with John Lennon–inspired graffiti and pieces of lyrics from Beatles' songs. In 1988, the wall was a source of irritation for the communist regime. Young Czechs wrote grievances on the wall, and in a report of the time, this led to a clash between hundreds of students and security police on the nearby Charles Bridge. The movement these students followed was described as "Lennonism," and Czech authorities described these people variously as alcoholics, mentally deranged, sociopathic, and agents of Western capitalism. The wall continuously undergoes changes and the original portrait of Lennon is long lost under layers of new paint. Even when some authorities repainted the wall, by the next day, it was again full of poems and flowers. Today, the wall represents a symbol of global ideals such as love and peace.

Between our many sightseeing stops, we even snapped a photo in front of the gate where Nathan Hunt from *Mission Impossible* discovered Sarah killed—Kampa Island, Prague. Our guide went out of his way to ensure we ate and drank well. We were taken to true Czech eateries, sampling the finest local fare. Of course, in Prague, no meal is complete without a genuine Czech beer as an accompaniment. I enjoyed our European trip even more so witnessing the happiness exuding from my new bride through her eyes.

We took a Euro Train between Prague and Rome to soak in the beautiful Austrian countryside. We were not disappointed. From rugged mountain peaks to the bluest of clear skies the Austrian scenery, as we zipped along in our train route, was hypnotic. Truth be told, the meals we enjoyed on our European honeymoon were all outstanding except the food on the train. We didn't go hungry on our train sightseeing expedition, but the fare didn't come close to that experienced in Paris, Prague, and Rome. Also, we did have one jarring experience during our train adventure. Very early one morning, loud persistent knocking on our sleeping car awakened us. The culprits were a couple of large surly German border guards, demanding to see our passports. We were advised ahead of time that this would occur; nonetheless, being aroused from a deep sleep to those proceedings was somewhat traumatizing.

Our last stop on our romantic adventure of a lifetime was Rome. Here, we checked into the boutique Hotel Campo De' Fiori, which was somewhat of an adventure itself. This was the one city we decided to obtain local flavor via the hotel we stayed at and chose it based on the *Europe for Dummies* book. The hotel's location was described as being in the best part of Rome, the lively and picturesque Centro Storico or Historic Center in the middle of unique shops, cobblestone streets, and the pleasing sounds of real Rome. The hotel also boasted of being just a short walk or cab ride away from the Piazza Navona, the Pantheon, Piazza Venezia, the Colosseum, the Roman Forum, Trevi Fountain, the Spanish Steps, and the Vatican City.

Arriving at the hotel, we found the described location to be true to its description but soon realized it didn't offer the same comforts of an established brand name hotel. Being on our honeymoon to three European cities sandwiched with a Euro Train expedition, we had our share of luggage. We brought them to the front desk for check-in. Our reserved room was on the top floor of this six-story boutique property for the view. We checked in, and I asked for the bellman to assist us with our luggage. "There's not a bellman," the front desk clerk announced. Somewhat disgruntled, I then asked the location of the elevator. "We don't have an elevator," mentioned the clerk. Being a gentleman, I didn't want my new bride to have to haul her luggage up six flights of stairs. So this then-fifty-six-year-old made a few trips up and down the stairs to transfer our belongings to our room.

The view from our room was worth the extra effort. It overlooked a beautiful courtyard area inclusive of an array of floral colors where markets were held on weekends. We later learned that the courtyard our hotel overlooked was the site of public executions in the 1600s!

Our room rate included breakfast each day, which was served in the lower level of the hotel. The breakfast was adequate. It was more of a convenience than anything. Thus, each day before leaving our room, we'd carefully plan our needs to avoid twelve flights of stairs; six up and six down.

One of the first sites we visited was the Trevi Fountain. The Trevi Fountain is a fountain in the Trevi District in Rome, standing 86 feet high and 161 feet wide. It is the largest Baroque fountain in the city and one of the most famous fountains in the world. The fountain has appeared in several notable films, including *La Dolce Vita*, *Three Coins in the Fountain*, and *Roman Holiday*.

Next, we stopped at the Pantheon, which was a former Roman Temple but is now a church. The building is circular with large granite columns. Almost two thousand years after it was built, the Pantheon's dome is still the world's largest unreinforced concrete dome. It is one of the best preserved of all Ancient Roman buildings, in large part because it has been in continuous use throughout its history. The Pantheon is now a state property, managed by Italy's Ministry of Cultural Heritage and Activities and Tourism. The Pantheon's large circular domed cella, with a conventional temple portico front, was unique in Roman architecture. Later, it became a standard exemplar when classical styles were revived, and has been copied many times in later years.

The Spanish Steps were a must stop for us. Following a competition in 1717, the little-known Francesco de Sanctis designed the Spanish Steps. They have been restored several times. They were restored just seven years preceding our 2002 visit. A newer restoration occurred fourteen years after our visit, in 2016. There were numerous movies filmed on or around this famous landmark but the most notable was the 1953-film *Roman Holiday*, starring Audrey Hepburn and Gregory Peck, making the Spanish Steps famous to American audiences. One of my favorite Rome photos is a picture of Sandie sitting on the landing of the steps between thousands of flowers. I call it "my flower among the flowers."

That day, we had lunch at a local Italian restaurant a couple of blocks from the famous Spanish Steps. We were on a tight schedule and needed to eat and leave within an approximate forty-five-minute time frame. We informed the staff of this need and they seemed more than willing to accommodate. However, their definition of an expeditious lunch wasn't congruent with our expectations. We made our next appointment but had to really hustle. Perhaps this is where the phrase "when in Rome do as the Romans do" materialized?

Our next stop was Vatican City via the Sistine Chapel. The Sistine Chapel is a chapel in the Apostolic Palace, the official residence of the Pope, in Vatican City. Originally known as the Cappella Magna, the chapel takes its name from Pope Sixtus IV, who restored it in the late 1400s. The Chapel features Michelangelo's stunning sixteenth-century ceilings frescoes and the monumental "The Last Judgment," which covers the apse wall. The fresco-covered ceiling is the artist's greatest work and one of the most important masterpieces in history. The Sistine Chapel serves as a glorious homage to Renaissance art and is one of the most visited sights in all of Italy.

We were privileged during this visit to witness the Pope blessing the marriages of what appeared to be a few dozen couples decked out in their best wedding attire for the ceremony. It was quite the spectacle. Leading up to and following the ceremony, we would randomly see brides decked out in their long white wedding dresses, chauffeured around by their soon-to-be husbands in formal black tuxedos. Of course, it all clicked when we saw the large crowd gathering outside the Pope's residence for the soon-to-be performed blessing.

The next destination on our site-seeing journey was the Roman Ruins. The Roman Forum is a rectangular forum surrounded by the ruins of several important ancient government buildings at the center of Rome. Citizens of the ancient city referred to this space, originally a marketplace, as the *Forum Magnum*, or simply the *Forum*. For centuries, the Forum was the center of day-to-day life in the city. It held elections, was the venue for public speeches, criminal trials, and the infamous gladiatorial matches. Here, statues and monuments commemorated the city's great men. Many of the oldest and most important structures of the ancient city were located on or near this area.

However, no visit to Rome would be complete without a visit to the Colosseum. Situated just east of the Roman Forum the Colosseum, also known as the Flavian Amphitheater, is a site to behold. Built of travertine, tuff, and brick-faced concrete, the Colosseum is the largest amphitheater ever built.

This oval-shaped outdoor auditorium once served as a stage for gladiators and public spectacles. With accommodation for 60,000 seated and 10,000 standing, all of whom could enter and leave in a matter of minutes, courtesy of 80 entrances, the Colosseum stands 157 feet high, which is only 26 feet shorter than the Leaning Tower of Pisa, and covers a total area of 6 acres. The massive arena also features a vast underground structure (catacombs) called the "hypogeum," a place where historians believe gladiators, prisoners and animals were held.

One of our last stops was to the Capitoline Museums. It's a single museum containing a group of art and archaeological museums in Piazza del Campidoglio, on top of Capitoline Hill. The history of the museums can be traced to 1471, when Pope Sixtus IV donated a collection of important ancient bronzes to the people of Rome and located them on the Capitoline Hill. Since then, the museums' collection has grown to include a large number of ancient Roman statues, inscriptions, and other artifacts; a collection of medieval and Renaissance art; and collections of jewels, coins, and other items. The museums are owned and operated by the municipality of Rome.

This proved to be an absolutely amazing trip. The experience will be one that I'll carry with me always. Paris, Prague, and Rome were incredible, and the sites we picked to visit in and around these cities were beautiful as well as historical. Traveling with my newlywed bride was most enjoyable.

I'll never forget the look in her eyes as we marveled at the various sites in these exquisite cities. My love and appreciation of this terrific partner of mine deepens each day.

Hawaii will always hold a special place in my heart. I was privileged to live there a total of twelve years starting a scant five years following its admission in the United States as our fiftieth state. I graduated from high school there while living with my uncle whom I idolized, experienced the births of my daughter Janette and first-born son Shawn, and embarked on a career in the hotel industry with the unique opportunities the environment provided.

My last year of full-time Hawaii residency was in 1983. Sandie's first Hawaiian experience was in 1998 when we attended an IPC Board of Director's as a couple. Since then, Sandie has visited Hawaii with me on more than ten occasions. However, apart from the IPC Board of Director's meeting, which was held on Maui, our trips were primarily to the island of Oahu where Honolulu is located. This was for visitation of family and loved ones as Shawn, Scott, and my grandson Deacon lived there. We'd also make treks around the island for sightseeing purposes. The opposite end of Oahu holds an entirely different feel from Honolulu. It's very rural and still exudes some of Hawaii's original Polynesian charm.

Sandie and I visited Janette in Miami in 2002 where she was working on set for the movie *2 Fast 2 Furious*. This was a time-consuming endeavor for Janette, working twelve-to-fourteen-hour days for six- and seven-day work-weeks. But Janette was able to get away for a couple of dinners with us. One dinner I remember was at the then well-known "Gaucho Room" in Miami's luxurious Loew's resort hotel. It was a nice break for Janette and a thoroughly enjoyable evening for Sandie and me. I'm extremely grateful that during my courtship of Sandie and after our wedding she and Janette always got along well.

We also traveled to Kerrville, Texas, via San Antonio to visit my cousin Mary Lou and her husband Bill. Mary Lou grew up as an only child on a farm outside of Roachdale, Indiana. She's seven years my senior and as reviewed earlier, we nearly became brother and sister. Mary Lou led a military service life as her husband Bill was in the Air Force for many years as a pilot. Bill's Air Force career led them to many different home stations and when he retired they decided on Texas for their residency, having experienced it on one of Bill's military assignments. They settled just outside of Kerrville, Texas, which is approximately an hour's drive northwest of San Antonio. Mary Lou and Bill built their own home in a ranch sub-division which suited their lifestyle perfectly. They're such down to earth good people and I'm not saying that just because Mary Lou and I are related.

Following our 2002 wedding, Sandie sold her condo and we made our home in my Vernon Hills, Illinois townhouse. I had lived there the previous nine years as a single parent to Shawn and Scott. Vernon Hills is located approximately thirty-seven miles north of Chicago and twenty-five miles north of Evanston, Illinois, my previous residence.

That year, we began a Christmas tradition where we hosted family members from both sides of our families to a Christmas feast, games, and of course the opening of gifts to the delight of the grandkids. This ritual occurred annually through 2015 as we moved to Clarksville, Tennessee, in May of 2016 following my retirement. Invitees from Sandie's side of the family included her sister Janice Kryfka, Janice's husband, Bruce Kryfka, Janice and Bruce's son, Brendon, Sandie's oldest daughter Olivia, her husband Cesar, their two children CJ and Emily, Sandie's youngest daughter Julie, her husband Kenny, their four children Amanda, Kenny Jr., Taylor, and Matt. Sandie's brother Rob was a regular attendee with his wife Barb. Invited from my side of the family were my daughter Janette when she was in town, my oldest son Shawn, and my youngest son Scott. My extended family lived in Indianapolis and Florida, making it unpractical for us to invite them. Our Christmas gift to my extended family was an annual dinner gathering the Saturday after Thanksgiving held at a restaurant in Indianapolis.

Christmas is a special season, with most being appreciative of what our Lord has provided, and there's a special empathy environment making you proud to be part of the universe. Our annual family Christmas gathering was a lot of work for Sandie, but we both thoroughly enjoyed the camaraderie and affectionate environment hopeful of creating loving family memories etched permanently for those who participated. With the exception of Sandie's sister Janice and her husband Bruce, all family members lived in the greater Chicago area. Janice and Bruce would drive up from Highland, IL, and stay with us.

Our living room in our smaller three-bedroom townhouse was converted into a dining room to accommodate our annual throng of family Christmas invitees. Card tables were placed side-by-side running the entire length of our living room. If Janette was in town and everyone showed up, we could have twenty or more holiday participants inclusive of children. After Christmas dinner, we would remove the card tables to allow ample space for the opening of gifts. These were tight quarters to say the least but the environment was full of love, peace, and happiness.

The following year in 2003, we created and added an additional family event to our calendar. Feeling that we nailed our first Christmas family gathering and established its groundwork for future years we decided to create a summer family gathering. This would provide us with a minimum of two family gatherings in our Vernon Hills residence to augment the family birthdays, baptisms, etc., which we'd travel to within the greater Chicago area. The town of Vernon Hills has a nice water park, and the Village's Park system had nearby pavilions available for rental. Thus, we decided to initiate an occasion entitled the annual Summer-Splash/BBQ. We'd pick a summer day in advance and rent a pavilion where we would hold the BBQ. This worked perfectly, where the same invitees as our Christmas get together enjoyed several hours of water park fun followed by a delicious BBQ to satisfy the appetites built up from the days' fun.

Considering my work schedule, 2003 was also a fairly busy travel year for Sandie and me. We traveled to South Haven, Michigan, in April to visit with Sandie's dad and to celebrate our first anniversary. That first year flew by! We stayed at the same hotel that had provided comfort to our wedding guests just a year earlier, the Old Harbor Inn. While there, we journeyed to Douglas, Michigan, to dine at the Everyday People Café. The chef at this fine establishment catered our wedding and the food in the restaurant was just as delicious as the fare served on our special day.

One of the first family gatherings that year was for an event involving Sandie's oldest daughter's family. Olivia and Cesar Vazquez held a baptism for their son, CJ on April 27, 2003. The baptism was well attended, with most immediate family members in attendance. Olivia and Cesar were so proud of their little guy!

In July of that year, we ventured down to Highland, Illinois, which is just about thirty miles northeast of St. Louis, to celebrate Sandie's sister Janice's birthday with her. Sandie's brother Rob and his wife Barb also made the trip, and Janice's birthday was a fun Elvis theme. One of our activities during that trip was mini-golf. After returning to the Kryfka household from the round of mini-golf, I discovered my wedding ring to be missing. Panic set in, as this is one of my most treasured possessions. Figuring that I must have lost it during min-golf, a group of us went back to look for it. The search was a success and I realized it must have slipped off from the sun-protection lotion applied earlier as it was a very hot, humid day.

The following month that year we traveled to Hawaii. August, from a temperature standpoint, is not necessarily the most desirable month to visit beautiful Hawaii, but it had to fit into my work schedule. Apart from Sandie experiencing Oahu, the other motivation for the visit was to see my younger son, Scott. At this time, Scott was dating Bernadette Dau, who lived in Mililani Town on Oahu. Sandie and I treated Scott and Berna to dinner at the Kobe Steak House in Waikiki. Berna is a delightful young lady and we were thrilled to make her acquaintance. The following year, Berna and Scott had a son, my first grandchild from my side of the family, whom they named Deacon. While on Sandie's first Oahu visit, we played tourist by visiting the Polynesian Culture Center (complete with the full luau experience), the Arizona Memorial at Pearl Harbor, and went for a sunset Catamaran sail off the beach of Waikiki.

In November of 2003, we traveled down to Cape Coral, Florida, to visit with my oldest half-sister Sheryl and her husband Jim Pierson. Of my four siblings, Sheryl lives the furthest from us, so it's a real treat whenever we get to visit with her. I have an abundance of appreciation for her character. Sheryl's experiences in her teen and early adult years could have turned her into a bitter, negative individual. However, in Sheryl's case, it's the opposite. She's a caring, thoughtful, forgiving, God-appreciating person. A pleasant surprise on this trip was to meet Sheryl and Jim's delightful neighbors, Heinz and Uda who take up winter residence in Cape Coral from their German homeland.

Wanting more knowledge and feeling that another career-related credential would be of benefit, I decided to pursue the Certified Exposition Manager (CEM) designation. The Certified in Exhibition Manager™ (CEM) designation is a globally recognized designation that demonstrates the highest professional standard throughout the exhibition and event management arena. It was first created in 1975 to raise professional standards in the event industry and it continues to be a prominent testament of professional achievement in the exhibit industry. The CEM designation accommodates short- and long-term career objectives, with education designed specifically to support the exhibition industry. The designation is obtained by completion of nine courses offered through on-location classrooms and online formats. Final exams for each course in the CEM curriculum are administered by a qualified credentialed individual within the sponsoring organization, the International Association of Exhibitions & Events (IAEE).

This effort actually began in 2003, culminating with my official graduation goal being realized on December 1, 2004. The credential ceremony occurred at the IAEE annual conference held in Atlanta, Georgia, the following year. The ceremony is an absolute honor, with recipients presented with their honor on-stage during one of the conference's general sessions. The pomp and circumstance was well deserved by all and made all the more meaningful taking place in front of our industry peers.

A major event occurred in June of 2004. My first grandchild, Deacon Hendrix Evans, on my side of the family was born June 12 in Honolulu, Hawaii. The proud parents were Berna whom we met the previous year during our Hawaii visit and my youngest son, Scott. Unfortunately, by this time, Scott and Berna were no longer together so they set up shared-parenting responsibilities. Two months later, Sandie and I made our way to Hawaii to see our newborn grandson. Having toured Oahu the previous year, our focus was on spending time with Deacon. During this visit, we met Berna's parents while visiting with Berna at her home.

Sandie and I both enjoy taking in live baseball games. I'm an avid sports fan loving baseball, football, and basketball probably in that order. My favorite professional teams are the Los Angeles Dodgers (I liked them when they were in Brooklyn even), Chicago White Sox, Minnesota Vikings (who never won a Super Bowl), and the Chicago Bulls. For college athletics, I'm a fan of Indiana University Basketball and Notre Dame Football teams. Around 2005, Sandie and I started attending Milwaukee Brewers' baseball games. Being baseball fans and simply enjoying the outing, it was easier for us living north of Chicago to drive the over-60 miles to Milwaukee than to go to either Wrigley Field or the White Sox parks in Chicago due to the city's constant heavy traffic. On one of our Milwaukee Brewers "Miller Park" visits, we were on their famous Kiss Cam, creating a fond lasting memory. A lasting reflection on 2005 will always be the Chicago White Sox winning the World Series while we lived there!

My oldest son Shawn got me into fantasy football many years ago. I enjoyed it so much that I also got into fantasy baseball and fantasy basketball. Fantasy sports developed into somewhat of a hobby for me where, depending on the sport, I'll manage anywhere from three to ten teams. Fantasy sports create daily satisfaction or disappointment depending on your teams' performances. Both of my sons are also avid sports fans, which has allowed for several shared experiences. Scott and I ventured on a baseball park tour when he was sixteen and Shawn and I have taken in numerous Major League Baseball spring-training games in Arizona.

In May of 2005, Sandie and I ventured to the city by the bay, San Francisco, California. This was part of a work-related city familiarization tour so its sponsors provided our accommodation and meals. While there we were able to visit with my daughter Janette and her sister, Sierra, who both met us there, making that trip that much more eventful. Of course, we played tourist while there visiting several key San Francisco landmarks and even walking across the Golden Gate Bridge.

Hawaii was on the docket in late October that year. Deacon had turned one year old the previous June, so we wanted to see the grandbaby. We invited Sandie's sister, Janice Kryfka, and her husband Bruce to make the trip with us. This would be Janice's first Hawaii visit while Bruce had spent some time there during his armed service years. I offered to take care of their accommodations using hotel points I'd accumulated through my job responsibilities. In Waikiki, we stayed at the Hyatt Waikiki located just across the street from the famous Duke Kahanamoku statue on the beach. To get away from the crowds we also stayed at the beautiful Marriott Ko Olina Resort located thirty-five miles from the hustle and bustle of Honolulu. "Ko Olina" means "Place of Joy." Part of an original royal land division, Ko Olina was once a sacred area for Hawaiian monarchs and leaders to rest and unwind. Today, the area is an inviting vacation destination for those seeking relaxation.

We rented a car allowing us to visit with Deacon along with his mom, Berna, and dad, Scott. We brought Deacon out to the resort for a day and spent time at the pool with me running after the active slightly-over-one-year-old around the pool. We were the consummate excursionists exploring the Dole Pineapple Plantation, Pearl Harbor, Waikiki, the Pink Palace Hotel (Royal Hawaiian), the USS Missouri and, of course, the Hawaiian beaches.

The year 2005 provided a sports fantasy for us. My favorite baseball teams are the LA Dodgers and the Chicago White Sox. Living in Chicago at the time my Chicago bride and I witnessed the Chicago White Sox win the World Series. The White Sox swept the Astros in four games, winning their third World Series championship and their first in eighty-eight seasons.

Although the series was a sweep, all four games were quite close, being decided by two runs or fewer. The series was played between October 22 and 26.

This stretch of my life span solidified my relationship with the love of my life, my wife Sandie. She met and developed rapport with my side of the family, and I did the same with hers. Our residence for the entire decade was in Vernon Hills, Illinois. I have and still do marvel at the way Sandie became an instant Evans family member. My family took to her immediately and the more time she spends with them the more endearing she becomes.

Our Wedding Vows - 2002.

Honeymoon Photo at the Rome Colosseum.

Chapter 8 | 2006–2015

T his stretch of my life comprised extensive business and personal travel, some major family birthday celebrations, baptism at my life-saving church, attending special events including the Kentucky Derby, and my last full decade of occupational endeavors.

The year 2006 marked the beginning of my sixth year of employment with NMMA. It also came close to being my last year there. Our one trade show, International Boatbuilders Exposition & Conference (IBEX) had matured to the point where it required an NMMA lead manager. The show was half-owned by NMMA and half by our partners, the *Professional Boatbuilding Magazine* publication. Our partners had a lead supervisor; thus the role of NMMA's lead would be to direct NMMA's efforts of the show in unison with our partner.

The position was created but never posted for interested applicants. I was shocked to learn of the position given to another individual in our organization, literally "under the table." Typically, a new organizational opportunity would be posted internally for company applicants to consider. This didn't happen and by the time I heard of it, the position had already been filled and announced. My responsibility for the show at that point was to oversee operations. Not only was I disappointed in the position not being posted, I also strongly felt more qualified for the position than the individual who was given the promotion.

For a period, my emotions were in a complete fog. Processing these events led me to the conclusion that I needed to make my feelings known directly to NMMA's president. Technically, I reported to the executive vice president so this would be going over my superior's head. The president accepted my meeting request and I rehearsed my thoughts over and over in my head, leading up to the encounter realizing that the discussion could lead to my departure.

The main points I made during the meeting were as follows:

- My passion is trade show management and my background is solid in that respect, having been the general manager, overseeing nine annual trade shows at a previous employer.

- The current year was the beginning of my sixth with the company and this promotion would allow continued growth for me.

- It's the area where my talents would be of greatest benefit to the organization.

- The position was not posted for internal consideration.

- I would work with and groom the individual who was given the promotion for her future growth.

Shortly after this meeting, the president and my superior, the executive vice president conceded to my argument and agreed to announce my increased responsibilities within a few weeks. The feeling of relief at that point is an understatement as I realized the decision could certainly have gone the other way. The individual whose appointment was rescinded reported to me and I was diligent in my efforts to make her feel included and to groom her for future opportunities. On the surface, she seemed to take it well, but a couple of years later when she left NMMA she made some rather disparaging comments concerning me during her exit interview. It saddened me to learn that behind her smile was such hatred and hostility.

Sandie and I celebrated our fourth anniversary in South Haven, Michigan, in April of 2006. Our wedding host hotel, the Old harbor Inn was revisited for the occasion. While there, we ambled lazily through the downtown area of South Haven browsing through storefronts enjoying the ambiance of this slower-moving resort-feel town. We even rented and rode bicycles through the town. While in the area, we visited Sandie's dad, Joe, and his significant other, Pat, in Bangor, Michigan. We didn't get to spend a lot of time with Sandie's dad as a couple but enjoyed the time we did have with him. Sandie's dad Joe was a funny, full of life individual and was pleasant to be around.

The following month, I tagged onto a business trip and journeyed up to Portland, Oregon, to visit with Janette. She lived approximately an hour outside Portland in the country close to the town of Seaside, Oregon. This was true country-living with neighbors being few and far between. Janette enjoyed country living, but it proved challenging for household upkeep. Being the distance she was from the city, it was difficult to obtain household services or even confirm delivery dates of newly bought appliances, furniture, etc. May of 2006 was one of those rare times that both Janette and I were able to meet when she wasn't working and I was in her area. She had already done a lot to her once cabin in the woods and it truly took on a homey feel.

Sandie and I ventured to Hawaii again in 2006, mainly to spend time with our two-year old grandson, Deacon. We did some sightseeing while in the fiftieth state but spent as much time as possible with Deacon, his dad Scott, and his mom Bernadette (Berna). While we saw Scott and Deacon at his apartment, we visited with Berna at her home where she lived with her parents. It was a treat meeting Berna's parents and seeing the loving home that Deacon was able to share with his mom. Berna's mom impressed Sandie with the true aloha spirit, by cutting up a whole pineapple for our enjoyment.

On November 19, 2006, Sandie and I were privileged to witness Cesar and Olivia's daughter Emily's baptism. Emily was exactly eight months old that day and looked like a little doll attired in an adorable little white dress. Smiles were plentiful that glorious day. All grandparents and close relatives including Olivia's sister Julie's full family were in attendance.

The following month, Sandie and I hosted our fifth consecutive family Christmas gathering in our small three-bedroom Vernon Hills, Illinois townhouse. There were a total of eighteen of us that year. Shawn was able to make it over with a date. Sandie's sister Janice, her husband Bruce, and their son Brendon drove up from Highland Illinois for the occasion. Also in attendance were Sandie's brother, Rob, along with his wife Barb and, of course, Sandie's two daughters, Olivia and Julie with their families.

In April of 2007, I was able to tie-in one of my Las Vegas pre-planning trips to my niece's wedding. Courtni was marrying Jeremy and the wedding was strategically held in Las Vegas to maximize family attendance. Courtni's dad, Rod, is from Hawaii and her parents lived there for several years. As they were living in Indianapolis at the time, Las Vegas was a decent halfway point for the wedding. Courtni's grandparents, along with two of her Hawaii uncles with their spouses, made it to the ceremony. Jeremy's parents and immediate family also made it to the special occasion. I was grateful to have the opportunity to witness the festivities.

That May, Janette made her way to Vernon Hills for a visit. She was between assignments, allowing time for the trip. We always enjoyed Janette's company, not knowing how long it would be before the next opportunity to spend time with her. One of our side trips took us to the quaint little town of Long Grove, IL, located a few miles from our Vernon Hills residence. They have an annual Chocolate Festival there, which Sandie and I have taken in on more than one occasion. While there, Sandie and Janette discovered the Glunz Family Wine tasting room. For a nominal fee, they were able to sample numerous wine varieties. Needless to say, we all had a good time.

Janette's visit was also timely from another event milestone. Shawn celebrated his thirtieth birthday that month. To celebrate this momentous occasion, we took in a White Sox baseball game followed by an epicurean experience in the Fairmont Hotel's gourmet restaurant. I'm sure Shawn was grateful to have Janette participate in the festivities. Due to residences and work responsibilities, it's extremely rare for me to be with more than one of my offspring at the same time making this all the more special to me.

May of 2007 was momentous from the standpoint of Sandie graduating from the College of Lake County, earning her associates degree. She was a model student, taking her studies seriously, earning high honors for her efforts. To celebrate her tremendous accomplishment, I arranged a surprise party for her at the Vernon Hills Portillo's restaurant. I was able to reserve a separate room at the facility and was overjoyed at the attendance. With the exception of Sandie's older brother, Mickey, her entire family was there with their families. Janette, Shawn along with Marjie, Rod, and Jasmine also made it to acknowledge Sandie's extraordinary achievement. Adding to the fun, I was able to secure the services of a clown who doubled as a face-painter, who was a great hit.

In June of 2007, another first in my life occurred. I entered a sweepstakes with the grand prize being an all-expenses paid to Atlanta, Georgia. To that point, my largest prize entry winning was a TV console years ago while living in Hawaii. Much to my surprise, I won! The prize included airfare to and from Atlanta, accommodations at the Westin hotel in downtown Atlanta, and some tours. We had a good time visiting Atlanta's world-renowned aquarium, dining, and sightseeing. We decided to try a Segway tour, which didn't turn out well. I zigged when I should have zagged on the two-wheeled self-propelled scooter and ended up falling off, which did some damages to my leg. This put somewhat of a damper on what was left of our trip, but it certainly provided a memory permanently etched into my mind.

The Evans Family Reunion is always held the first Sunday in August in the Indianapolis, Indiana area. We try to make it each year and were fortunate to attend this year. Attendance was okay but in obvious decline. Having fond memories of large gatherings in years past, I'm hopeful that they continue. The generation below mine needs to step up to ensure the survival of the annual Evans Reunion. That same month, Sandie and I were invitees of the Hyatt McCormick Place to attend Chicago's Annual Air and Water show. NMMA's Chicago Boat Show is a customer of this Hyatt property, and this was one of their good-customer events. The Hyatt put us up and provided excellent reserved seating for the event. The day was overcast but the show, as usual, was spectacular.

Christmas of 2007 was a bit different from other Christmases. Sandie's father, Joe, was suffering from pancreatic cancer and dementia so Sandie drove to Bangor, Michigan to be with him and her stepmother, Pat, for a period of time at Christmastime that year. Her brother, Robert, came out to Michigan on Christmas Day and celebrated the holiday with Sandie, Joe, Pat, and Pat's son, John. (Sadly, this was to be Joe's last Christmas as he passed away on February 16, 2008.) Due to these circumstances, the Christmas holiday with the family was celebrated in early January that year and, although not on the exact holiday date, the Christmas spirit was abundant anyway. While Shawn couldn't stay the entire evening, he and a date did make it over to visit for a while. Sandie's sister Janice and husband Bruce were unable to make it up probably due to inclement weather between Highland, Illinois, and Vernon Hills. Sandie's two daughters, Olivia and Julie, were in attendance along with their families. Sandie's younger brother Rob along with his wife Barb also made it.

Having followed the Dodgers from their days in Brooklyn, New York, to their move to Los Angeles, I had to see the famous Dodger town facility located in Vero Beach Florida before its 2009-closure. Thus, in the spring of 2008, I was able to make it down to the historic site and even take in a couple of spring training games. The excursion must have been an add-on to a business trip as my beautiful bride Sandie wasn't with me. One couldn't help but feel nostalgic walking through a facility that was the spring training home of the Brooklyn/Los Angeles Dodgers for fifty-five years. Realizing that Dodger greats Jackie Robinson, Sandy Koufax, and countless other classics worked out and played here gave me the goose bumps. 2008 was the last year the Dodgers held spring training at this famous landmark. It's since been designated a Florida Heritage Landmark. Joe Torre who is a legend himself, more associated with the New York Yankees, was the current Dodger manager. Being more of a Dodger purist, my favorite Dodger managers are Walter Alston and Tommy Lasorda.

In March of the following year, 2008, I journeyed to Indianapolis to participate in my brother Floyd's surprise sixtieth birthday celebration. My sister-in-law Glenda made the arrangements, informing us of the location. Floyd was pleasantly surprised and the special event was well attended. Floyd's two sons Lee and David were there with their families as was Glenda's daughter Kym. The two girls Floyd and Glenda later adopted, Skyla and Haley, were mere toddlers at the time. Our sister Becky and her family were also in attendance. Being a huge Indianapolis Colts football fan and liking their center Jeff Saturday, a jersey of his was the perfect gift for Floyd. Lori and David's youngest child, Abby, was just a baby at the time.

This year accounted for a major milestone. Sandie graduated from Roosevelt University earning her Bachelor's degree. Sandie's dedication to the obtainment of her Bachelor's degree never wavered. Many an evening, she would be up through the wee hours of the morning poring over her studies. The hard work paid off for her as she made the Dean's list. My heart thumped and I was and still am so proud of her as she walked across the stage to pick up her hard-earned Bachelor's diploma during the graduation ceremony.

Sandie and I were able to fly out to Los Angles to visit with Janette that year. While visiting, Sandie and I toured the Hollywood Walk of Fame, Universal Studios, and the Kodak Theater. The Hollywood Walk of Fame comprises more than 2,600 five-pointed terrazzo and brass stars embedded in the sidewalks along 15 blocks of Hollywood Boulevard and three blocks of Vine Street in Hollywood, California. It was a thrill witnessing the stars belonging to John Wayne, Marilyn Monroe, Red Skelton, and Humphrey Bogart.

Universal Studios Hollywood is a film studio and theme park in the San Fernando Valley area of Los Angeles County, California. About 70% of the studio lies within the unincorporated county island known as Universal City while the rest lies within the city limits of Los Angeles, California. It was surreal visiting recognizable movie sets. It's truly amazing what can be produced on those sets resulting in larger-than-life adventures, romance, and comedy.

The Dolby Theatre (formerly known as the Kodak Theatre) is a live-performance auditorium in the Hollywood and Highland Center shopping mall. Since the theater's opening on November 9, 2001, the theater has annually hosted the Academy Awards ceremony. It's adjacent to the Grauman's Chinese Theatre. The theater is rented to the Academy of Motion Picture Arts and Sciences for weeks before the Oscar night. Having hosted the awards ceremony annually since 2002, the theater is best known for this event. During the rest of the year, it hosts numerous live concerts, awards shows, symphony performances, and other events.

The theater was sponsored, until February 2012, by the Eastman Kodak Company, which paid $75 million for the sponsorship. In early 2012, Eastman Kodak filed for bankruptcy protection, thus ending its naming-rights deal. On May 1, 2012, it was announced that the venue would be renamed the Dolby Theatre, after Dolby Laboratories signed a twenty-year sponsorship agreement. Dolby updated the sound system and plans to continue updating the auditorium with newer technologies as they become available.

That August, Sandie and I ventured to her youngest daughter's home for her son Matt's first birthday party. The event was well attended and while he was not sure what was going on, Matt seemed to enjoy being the center of attention. In December of 2008, we ventured to Hawaii to visit with the first grandson on my side of the family. Deacon Hendrix Evans was four-and-half years old. We stayed at the Courtyard Marriott in Waikiki and hosted Deacon to fun at the swimming pool.

One of my funniest Deacon-childhood memories that Sandie and I both chuckle at happened that December. Looking for a non-video game activity to entertain Deacon, being in December, we decided to take Deacon to the annual "Honolulu City Lights" festivities. Then in its twenty-third year, the eagerly anticipated event, presented each year by the City and County of Honolulu and the Friends of Honolulu City Lights, is an island tradition for thousands of residents and visitors, marking the start of the holiday season. The event includes a Christmas electric parade, the lighting of a fifty-foot Christmas tree, arts, crafts, food vendors, and just good wholesome fun. We presented the suggestion to Deacon as "going to a fair." We drove to the venue, and got out of the car. At first sight, Deacon was thoroughly unimpressed and proclaimed, "You call this a fair?!?" Obviously, Deacon expected carnival rides and games, etc. However, there were activities for children that we got Deacon involved in. One was building a gingerbread house. Initially, he was reluctant but once he got into the program, he thoroughly enjoyed it. He was very proud of his finished gingerbread house along with his snowman puppet creations. While Deacon's day started with snarled expressions, it ended with smiles a-plenty. To this day, Sandie and I recreate Deacon's famous "You call this a fair?" line when passing anything resembling a similar event.

The summer of 2009 was the first of six consecutive years of our newly developed annual family gathering. Living the distance we did from both of Sandie's daughters, we created a BBQ–Summer Splash event so we could have the entire family together for two annual events versus the singular Christmas celebration. Vernon Hills had a good park system that provided an upscale waterpark along with the ability to rent in a separate location a pavilion that had grills and overhead protection in the event of inclement weather. We would invite our extended families up to Vernon Hills, pay their way into the water park and, after soaking up sunshine and enjoying the water park amenities, would venture over to our private rented pavilion for a cookout.

That August, we drove to Oak Lawn to celebrate CJ's seventh birthday with his family, friends, and relatives. It was held at Olivia and Cesar's apartment on Minick, with an excellent turnout. It was a pirate-themed party with CJ wearing a pirate's hat for the occasion. There was a piñata stuffed with candy and goodies for the kids to take turns swatting at. However, the hit of the party was a game where the kids took plates of whipped cream and tossed them on each other. There were some sticky children at the end but all had a great time.

The year 2009 was very productive for me at work. I had to relocate IBEX, our large trade show, out of Miami. After a comprehensive geographic search that satisfied our space, hotels, costs, and vendor availability, we settled on Louisville. Unbeknownst to me at that time, the Louisville Convention Center, by their airport, was one of the largest in the United States. I was able to negotiate through the city's Convention & Visitors Bureau a three-year agreement that assuming certain hotel occupancy criteria were met would save my organization, NMMA, over $500,000 in lease costs. The key was an innovative agreement where our lease costs were predicated on a hotel room pick-up based on an established sliding scale. To ensure proper hotel pickup crediting, I was able to work out with our registration contractor a system that would capture hotel stays when each event participant picked up his or her required name badge. Included in our agreement with the Louisville Convention & Visitors Bureau was the stipulation that NMMA would receive credit for all captured room nights even if they were not part of our contracted room blocks with participating hotels. To my knowledge this was the only agreement of its type in the industry at the time making me extremely proud of the accomplishment.

On another 2009 work note, I traveled internationally to Amsterdam to manage operations of NMMA's pavilion at Marine Equipment Trade Show (METS). Amsterdam is the Netherlands' capital, known for its artistic heritage, elaborate canal system, and narrow houses with gabled facades, legacies of the city's seventeenth-century Golden Age. Its Museum District houses the Van Gogh Museum, and works by Rembrandt and Vermeer at the Rijksmuseum. Cycling is the key to the city's character, and there are numerous bike paths.

But my trip got off on the wrong foot. I was travelling with our organization's president and a key member of our trade show planning committee. We changed planes at London's Heathrow airport. Half asleep, reentering airport security for the last leg of our trip, I inadvertently left my laptop. I didn't realize this error until after arriving in Amsterdam. My immediate reaction was one of panic and dismay. Panic because it was company equipment entrusted to me and dismay due to my heavy reliance on it while working an event. Calling security at Heathrow Airport in London, I learned with much appreciation that my laptop was secured in their lost and found room and I'd be able to pick it up on my return through there to the United States.

Working an international trade show was educational from both a professional as well as on a personal level. It was professional due to the different rules and regulations used on their trade shows, and educational through experiencing the local community. I was extremely busy working long hours at the show but was determined to visit the famous Anne Frank house located at Prinsengracht 263. My visit to there was not disappointing. For two years during the Second World War, the Secret Annex served as a hiding place for Anne Frank and the other people there. After the war, it fell into disrepair. The Anne Frank House was established in 1957 and its main purpose was to preserve the hiding place. Having undergone a recent renovation the experience was surreal. You actually could feel and picture Anne Frank and her family's daily fear of being captured. Enamored with this experience and horrendous story, below is a synopsis for your review:

In July of 1942, Anne Frank went into hiding with her family in the building's Secret Annex. Having already known each other, the Van Pels family followed a week later. Herman Van Pel worked for Anne's father's company. Four months later, Fritz Pfeffer, an acquaintance of the Frank family, joined them. Anne Frank, her family, and acquaintances spent 761 days in the Secret Annex. Although each day was different from the last, there was a certain rhythm to life in the Secret Annex.

Based on Anne's diary and a few of her short stories, a typical day in the Secret Annex could be reconstructed:

A TYPICAL DAY IN THE SECRET ANNEX

IN THE MORNING

At 6:45 am, the alarm of Mr. and Mrs. Van Pels went off. Hermann van Pels got up, put the kettle on, and went to the bathroom. After fifteen minutes, the bathroom was free again and it was Fritz Pfeffer's turn. Anne got up and removed the blackout screens from the windows.

The people in hiding took turns using the bathroom. At 8:30 am, a risky half hour started. The men in the warehouse started their working day, while the office helpers had not yet arrived. Any noise from the people hiding was dangerous, as the warehouse was located below the hiding place and the warehouse staff was unaware of the people in hiding.

At 9:00 am, the helpers started working in the office above the warehouse. The people in hiding walked around in socks and still had to be quiet, but sounds from above now caused less suspicion. The rest of the morning was devoted to reading, studying, and preparing for their lunch break.

THE LUNCH BREAK

At 12:30 pm, the warehouse workers went home for lunch, and the helpers and people in hiding had the place to themselves for a while. At 12:45 pm, a few of the helpers, usually Johannes Kleiman, Victor Kugler, and Bep Voskuijl, came up to the Secret Annex to have lunch. In the beginning, Johan Voskuijl (Bep's father) often came up, too. Jan Gies (Miep's husband) frequently joined them as well, although he worked elsewhere. Miep Gies usually stayed in the office to keep an eye on things. For the people in hiding, it was nice to see other people and to hear the latest news. At 1 pm, the radio switched on for the BBC news. At 1:15 pm, they had lunch and at 1:45 pm, the helpers went back to work.

IN THE AFTERNOON

After the people in hiding had cleared everything away, most of them took an afternoon nap. Anne used that time for studying or writing. Around four o'clock, they had coffee and then started on the preparations for dinner. At 5:30 pm, the warehouse workers went home. Helper Bep Voskuijl usually came by to see if the people in hiding needed anything. After she had gone home at a quarter to six, the people in hiding were no longer restricted to the Secret Annex and they spread out through the building.

IN THE EVENING

Hermann van Pels looked at the day's post, Peter van Pels fetched the bread that had been left for them in the office, Otto Frank wrote business letters on the typewriter, Margot and Anne did administrative chores and Auguste van Pels and Edith Frank cooked dinner. After dinner, they read, talked, or listened to the radio. Around 9 pm, they started preparing for the night. Pieces of furniture had to be moved, for instance in the room of Hermann and Auguste van Pels. Just like in the morning, they took turns using the bathroom. Every day when the sun went down, the windows had to be blacked out. After that, the Secret Annex went quiet. With the exception of weekends, the next morning the alarm went off at 6:45 am again.

SECRET ANNEX INHABITANTS CAPTURED BY THE NAZIS

In August 1944, after over two years in hiding, Anne Frank and the seven others hiding in the Secret Annex were discovered by the Gestapo Nazis, who had learned about the hiding place from a tipster who has never been definitively identified.

After their arrest, they were sent to Westerbork, a holding camp in the northern Netherlands. From there, they were transported by freight train to the Auschwitz–Birkenau extermination and concentration camp complex in German-occupied Poland. Anne and Margot Frank were spared immediate death in the Auschwitz gas chambers and instead were sent to Bergen-Belsen, a concentration camp in northern Germany, where they died of typhus; their bodies were thrown into a mass grave. Several weeks later, in April of 1945, British forces liberated the camp. All Secret Annex captives with the exception of Anne Frank's father, Otto, perished in these camps.

ANNE FRANK'S DIARY

When Otto Frank returned to Amsterdam following his release from Auschwitz, Miep Gies gave him 5 notebooks and some 300 loose papers containing Anne's writings. Gies had recovered the materials from the Secret Annex shortly after the Franks' arrest by the Nazis and had hidden them in her desk. Otto Frank knew that Anne wanted to become an author or journalist, and had hoped her wartime writings would one day be published.

After his daughter's writings were returned to him, Otto Frank helped compile them into a manuscript, which was published in the Netherlands in 1947 under the title "Het Acheterhuis" ("Rear Annex"). Although U.S. publishers initially rejected the work as too depressing and dull, it was eventually published in America in 1952 as "The Diary of a Young Girl." *The book, which went on to sell tens of millions of copies worldwide, has been labeled a testament to the indestructible nature of the human spirit."*

Frank Rettig, our international freight forwarder for the METS trade show, and I went out to a local café for dinner one evening. Once settled into this bustling establishment, I noticed a particular smell. While not ever personally experiencing marijuana I was able to distinguish its smell. Sure enough, several of the restaurant's patrons were smoking it. The smoking of drugs like cannabis and hash is not legal, but tolerated in Amsterdam. You can freely buy and smoke up to five grams of hash, weed, pot, cannabis and marijuana in special hash bars, known as coffee shops, and smoke cannabis openly in the streets in Amsterdam. We were in such an establishment where the smoking of marijuana was completely legal.

Sandie and I journeyed to Hawaii again in 2009 to visit with our five-year-old grandson Deacon and to take in the Oahu sites. While there, we stayed at the Marriott Ko Olina Resort. Located over twenty-five miles from hectic Waikiki, it offered a relaxing get-away-from-it-all atmosphere. Deacon loved the swimming pool and enjoyed the hotel. We also visited Diamond Head crater, Honolulu's China Town, Manoa Falls, and 'Iolani Palace.

Diamond Head is one of the most famous landmarks on Oahu and the entire state of Hawaii. It had once been an active volcano but hasn't spewed any ashes for more than 150,000 years. The extinct crater and lookout point at the peak of it is a popular hiking destination for many. Diamond Head State Monument offers breathtaking views overlooking the Pacific Ocean and Honolulu. In fact, the view is so good, it was used by the US military as a post for preventing attacks against Honolulu. After the attack on Pearl Harbor in 1941, further gun emplacements, pillboxes, and foxholes were built on Diamond Head to be able to better defend Oahu in the future. Many of them still remain on the crater rim and one underground facility, the Birkheimer Tunnel, houses the headquarters for the State Civil Defense Agency. Today, the entire mountain and crater is a state park known as Diamond Head State Monument. It is one of the most photographed and painted spots on the island of Oahu.

Diamond Head Crater measures 3,520 feet across and 760 feet in height. A hiking trail that Sandie and I pursued leads from the crater up to a lookout point. There are two stairs—one has ninety-nine steps and a second one has seventy-six steps. There's also a 225-foot hardly lit tunnel through which you'll have to go. The tunnel is a remnant of the former military use of the crater. It's a hike but it's definitely worth the effort once you reach the top; the view is spectacular, especially on a clear and sunny day.

Sandie and I ventured to China Town, located approximately fifteen minutes from Waikiki. On the western perimeter of Honolulu, Chinatown's historic buildings are home to a patchwork of antique dealers, temples, shops, bars, and, of course, restaurants. Honolulu's Chinatown had become a hotbed of diverse new restaurants along with the traditional Chinese fare. In the market by day, you'll find everything from exotic fruits and the freshest seafood to curiosities like "thousand-year-old egg." No visit to Chinatown is complete without partaking in its mouth-watering dim sum dishes.

We booked an actual tour to do the Manoa Falls hike. It is one of the most popular hikes in the Honolulu area, mainly because it is easily accessible from Waikiki and is classified as an easy hike. A short drive out of Waikiki towards Manoa Valley and you can be surrounded by a tropical bamboo and rainforest. Many Oahu tour operators take their guests here.

Another factor that makes the Manoa Falls trail a favorite hiking destination for many is its highlight; the 150-foot waterfall waits after a relatively easy 45-minute walk up the mountain. The waterfall is bigger if it has recently rained. During the hot and dry summer months, it is hardly more than a small dribble. The water cascades down from the mountain into a small pool. Even though it looks inviting, it is not recommended to swim in it because of the risk of rockslides, which have occurred in this area. Also, it isn't safe to drink the water because of leptospirosis contamination. But it is a beautiful spot for taking pictures.

The entire trail is about 1.6 miles out and back. It can be slippery if it is raining. It rains more often here than in Waikiki and along the coastline. The trail is in a rainforest, so even if it's dry and sunny in Waikiki, it often times is raining here as it did during our hike. We couldn't believe that one of the hikers in our group was wearing flip-flops, turning what should have been an easy trek into a dangerous one.

A couple of Hawaii's most beautiful attractions don't cost a cent. There's nothing as energizing or enthralling as a Hawaiian sunrise. Conversely, the Hawaiian sunsets are relaxing and a pure art form unto themselves. I'm an early morning riser and thoroughly enjoy that first cup of coffee in the early hours. On one of our Hawaii trips, Sandie and I stayed at the Hilton Hawaiian Village Hotel situated on one end of Waikiki Beach. I had convinced my lovely bride early one morning to venture out onto the beach. We waded into the warm Pacific Ocean to view the sunrise over Diamond Head while enjoying that first cup of coffee. While free to those there, the sunrise experience is indescribable. Hawaii's sunsets are just as captivating. One of my favorite sunset experiences occurred on Waikiki Beach where Sandie and I observed it from a Catamaran cruise.

At the end of 2009, we completed what had become an annual trip tradition officially designated the "trifecta" trip. It was labeled the trifecta trip as it began from our home in Vernon Hills, Illinois, and took us to Sandie's sister's home in Highland, Illinois, for Thanksgiving and eventually to Indianapolis, Indiana, for an Evans family Christmas dinner the

Saturday following Thanksgiving. From Indianapolis, we'd venture back home to Vernon Hills, forming the three points of a triangle. A few weeks after returning from this trip, we held our annual Christmas dinner for fourteen, consisting of Olivia's family, Julie's family, Sandie's brother Rob and his wife Barb and of course Sandie and me.

The time between Christmas and New Year's was less demanding of me at work, allowing some travel flexibility. Beginning around this time, we started exploring potential retirement destinations. I didn't retire until 2016, which gave us approximately eight years to identify a suitable retirement location. Our desired geographical retirement location would provide better weather, be easier on our expenses, provide entertainment options, and be within a day's drive of Chicago. We singled out several potential retirement locations and that particular year traveled to Clarksville, Tennessee, to check it out. Sandie's sister Janice and her husband Bruce joined us on this particular fact-finding trip. Sandie and I actually held out hope that her sister and brother-in-law would relocate with us to our eventual retirement destination. Clarksville met all of our retirement criteria and held another attractive option for Sandie's brother-in-law, Bruce. Clarksville had a large Army military post, Fort Campbell. Bruce and Janice are able to utilize military post-amenities as Bruce is ex-military.

One of our first 2010 events was attending our granddaughter Taylor's eighth birthday party. It was a cold February day, with the festivities taking place at Julie's apartment she and her family shared with her husband's Kenny's family. Right after the candles were blown and the birthday song sang, Taylor ended up, to her delight, with a face full of pink icing. Taylor had a grand time as several of her friends along with her cousins CJ and Emily made it to the celebration.

That event was followed the next month by our youngest granddaughter's fourth birthday celebration. Emily is the younger of two children from Sandie's oldest daughter Olivia. This event was held at a community center in Olivia and Cesar's community of Oak Lawn, Illinois. The Princess theme went off exceptionally well with the children attending. The blow-up house, allowing the kids into their own private roughhouse, area was a huge hit. Emily's extended family was all in attendance, including her four cousins along with her aunt Julie and her uncle Kenny.

In spring of 2010, Shawn and I traveled to Phoenix, Arizona, for Major League Baseball's Cactus League Spring Training. We stayed at the Hyatt Place in Scottsdale, which is right down the street from the San Francisco Giants spring training stadium, Oracle Park. Shawn's favorite major league team at that point was the Chicago Cubs while I held mutual admiration for the Los Angeles Dodgers and the Chicago White Sox. Fortunately for us, all three teams hold their spring training in the Phoenix area. We took in a game at the old Chicago Cubs stadium in Mesa as they played the Seattle Mariners. Shawn's favorite player at this time was Ichiro Suzuki who played in the outfield for Seattle. It was a treat for Shawn to have his picture taken at that stadium with Ichiro in the background.

In 2009, the Dodgers relocated their spring training to a brand-new park they share with the Chicago White Sox, Camelback Ranch, located in Glendale, Arizona. Obviously, we had to take in a game there. Spring training baseball parks are much more intimate than their major league counterparts. They provide an up-close experience where the players, managers, and team executives are more accessible to the average baseball fan. Shawn and I were fortunate to come across a few baseball legends while at a Dodger game: Rollie Fingers (1981 AL MVP, Cy Young Winner), Bill Buckner, and George Foster. We also saw the long-term Dodger Manager and Executive, Tommy Lasorda.

The flight back from Phoenix to Chicago left a lasting impression on Shawn since working at National Marine Manufacturers and through my travels I'd accumulated enough mileage segments to allow Shawn and me to be upgraded to first class. This aircraft was large and first-class accommodations were exuberant, to say the least, providing luxury seating that converted into full size beds.

In May of 2010, Sandie and I were privileged to be invited to the famous Kentucky Derby held annually in Louisville, Kentucky. Straight from the Derby's website: "There are few American sporting events with the history and popularity of the Kentucky Derby. Its rich traditions—sipping a mint julep, donning a beautiful hat, and joining fellow race fans in singing *My Old Kentucky Home*—transcend the Kentucky Derby from just a sporting event, making it a celebration of southern culture and a true icon of Americana. The Kentucky Derby is the longest running sporting event in the United States, dating back to 1875. The race is often referred to as "The Run for the Roses" and has continuously produced "the most exciting two minutes in sports"; uninterrupted, even when coinciding with profound historical events like The Great Depression and World Wars I & II."

Our host was the Marriott hotel in downtown Louisville. We were invited along with five or six other couples for that weekend, which included lavish accommodations and meals that could only be described as culinary masterpieces. We were astonished to see the variety of hats available for purchase for the event and at a cost that could exceed a thousand dollars! The weather wasn't very accommodating as it rained most of the day but that didn't stop Sandie and me from touring the famed facility and marveling at the headwear of Derby attendees, men and women alike. As if on cue, the sun came out for the main race to the delight of all attendees. This was an experience that will forever be etched in Sandie's and my memories.

That same year, we were pleased to have my sister Sheryl and her husband Jim spend a few days with Sandie and me at our townhouse in Vernon Hills. They were on their way to visit a couple of life-long friends in Wisconsin making us a good stop off point for an appreciative visit. That summer, we held our second Summer Splash–BBQ annual event in Vernon Hills. Sandie's sister Janice and her husband Bruce drove up from their Highland, Illinois, home for the fun. Sandie's younger brother Rob also made it along with Sandie's daughters, Olivia and Julie, with their families. We took advantage of the gathering to also celebrate summer birthdays. Julie's closest friend Jill at that time also made it to the celebration.

That December, we made an excursion to Olive Branch, Mississippi, via Memphis, Tennessee. At this juncture, we were scouting potential retirement locations and usually did this in late December for two reasons: (1) the period between Christmas and New Year's was a slower period for me at work, making it easier to get away and (2) that time of the year gave us a better understanding of the harshest weather conditions we'd have to deal with it that particular locale. Sandie's sister Janice and her husband Bruce joined us on the journey. Truth be told, Sandie and I were hopeful that wherever we ended up they would also consider relocating to.

Criteria consideration for our retirement destination included weather, cost of living, and distance from Chicago. Distance-wise Olive Branch, Mississippi, fell within location perimeters. While staying in Olive Branch, we thoroughly enjoyed the Memphis, Tennessee, stop along the way. We visited Elvis Presley's Graceland, the Loraine Motel/Museum where MLK was slain; the Peabody hotel to witness their famous walk of the ducks and even walked the famous Beale Street.

But the year 2011 got off to an unpromising start on a cold, icy Chicago January day. My life-changing event began a couple of blocks away from my employer where my feet slid out from under me as I was crossing Wacker Drive walking on Jackson in downtown Chicago. The incident occurred on my way to work on Tuesday, January 18, at approximately 6:15 am. I literally did not know what had hit me. My body came down in an awkward position on my leg, which was pointed, in the opposite direction of what it should have been in. The pain was so excruciating that I expected bones to be sticking out of my flesh by the injured ankle. What I believe was a savior was my backpack as I'm convinced that wearing it on my back prevented a potentially serious concussion by protecting me from hitting my head.

A Chicago Police Officer pulled over and directed traffic around me. At this point, I was lying in the street not sure that I could move anything. The Police Officer requested an ambulance for me and with all the pain I was in, what do you think was going through my mind? I was worried whether my work insurance would be accepted by the hospital/doctors that the ambulance took me to. The ambulance had two emergency medical attendants and between them and the police officer, they somehow

185

maneuvered me into the rear of the ambulance. Sensing the amount of pain I was in, they started me on morphine right away.

Another lesson learned—when an ambulance takes you to a hospital, you have no choice on where they take you. Standard Operating Procedure for an ambulance in these incidents is to take the victim to the *closest hospital*, which in this case was Northwestern Memorial Hospital. My assumption was that due to the "emergency" nature of the incident along with a victim's inability to request a specific hospital, the insurance carried by my employer should be responsible for care received at the hospital. Thank goodness that was the case.

After a couple of hours at the hospital, they took x-rays and determined that my leg was broken in two places: (1) just above my left ankle and (2) just below my left knee. The pain was so bad around my ankle that I didn't realize my leg was broken in an additional location. The hospital then gave me some heavy anesthesia to put me under while they "reset" my leg in preparation for required surgery due to the severity of the injuries. Following this procedure, they x-rayed my leg again to be sure it was set right only to discover that it was not. I had to go through a second reset of my leg before surgery.

Sandie, my wonderful wife, was right there beside throughout this whole process. At this point, my only thought through the unrelenting pain was to have the operation as quickly as possible. A couple of hours after this request, the hospital approached us and wanted us to go home and come back in a week or so for the operation. The hospital was over-burdened with cases similar to mine due to the icy weather conditions. I was stunned and just looked at the resident orthopedic surgeon and said, "I don't know how I can do that." There I was in so much pain (even with meds) that I couldn't think straight and the hospital was proposing that I somehow get myself into a vehicle, travel thirty-five miles north to Vernon Hills, get out of the vehicle, stay at home for a week while my broken leg healed some necessitating in all probability a third reset of my breaks in preparation of the forthcoming operation and then to reverse the process to get back downtown. The hospital eventually got me in late on Wednesday, January 19, for the operation that truthfully began the healing process.

The operation was a success. It involved inserting a titanium rod through my left leg, beginning just below my left knee and running to just above my left ankle secured by two screws at each end. Barring pain, infection, etc., the plan was to keep the titanium rod in place. In fact, my orthopedic surgeon (by the luck of the draw happened to be the Chicago Blackhawks surgeon) said I would require the rod permanently. The doctors stressed to avoid placing any more than 30 pounds of pressure on my left leg for approximately eight weeks. This meant that in addition to a Miami business trip scheduled for mid-February, Sandie and I had to cancel a Hawaii trip we'd had planned for a year. Thank goodness my employer (NMMA) eventually authorized my working from home during this period. I'm truly grateful for that.

My recovery required the need for crutches as well as physical therapy. The hospital provided lessons on crutch use. I needed to learn how to navigate stairs, get in and out of an automobile, and get in and out of a tub using crutches. Working from home as a result of the accident didn't happen instantaneously. Initially, my immediate supervisor suggested I return to work shortly after I was released from the hospital. To put this into proper perspective, my daily downtown thirty-five-mile work commute from Vernon Hills had me driving from home to the Libertyville train station, waiting on the train platform for the train, boarding the train via three to four steps, riding on the train for an hour, departing the train via those same three to four steps, accessing an escalator at the train station, and then walking three blocks to my employer. All of this was with my backpack, so I'd have the necessary work supplies. After explaining this to my immediate supervisor and offering to give it a try but feeling like it could lead to another accident, he relented and allowed me to work from home. After working from home for my entire recovery period, my immediate supervisor remarked positively on my effectiveness and eventually working from home for two to three days a week became my normal routine. I was actually more productive working from home as I gained three hours of daily commute time!

After serving on the Certified in Exhibitions Management (CEM) commission for the previous three years, I served as its chairman in 2011. It was an honor to give back to an industry that was instrumental in my growth as a professional.

On June 14 of 2011, Sandie attended Kenny Junior's eighth grade graduation at Pulaski International School of Chicago. The accomplishment was recognized at the then annual Evans Summer Splash–BBQ event in Vernon Hills. This was an extra special gathering as summer birthdays of those in attendance were also celebrated. That summer, Sandie and I also attended a reunion hosted by my step-mom's side of the family. They didn't necessarily get together every year and we weren't invited to each one, thus we made an extra effort to attend. Both of my half-sisters from my dad's side of the family would be there along with their extended families. Unfortunately, while the occasion started out as a lively event, it soon soured as my stepmom, Betty Bartlett, fell while participating in a zumba class at the reunion and had to be rushed to the hospital. All ended well despite the unfortunate incident.

The BBQ affair in 2011, which followed our Summer Splash, was a Hawaii-themed event. Leis and flowers were distributed to the ladies. One of my favorite photos of Sandie with her two daughters Olivia and Julie was taken there. Each of these three lovely ladies proudly wore their Hawaiian leis and had a flower placed in their hair. Their smiles could only be described as infectious with obvious love for one another. The grandkids Kenny Jr, CJ, Taylor, Emily, and Matt had a thoroughly enjoyable, fun day at the Vernon Hills Water Park evidenced by their sunburns visible later in the day.

Sandie's sister Janice and her husband Bruce drove up from Highland Illinois to stay with us for the 2011 family Christmas gathering. Both of Sandie's daughters, their families, and her brother Rob with his wife Barb also participated. Sandie's brother-in-law, Bruce, was fresh off a culinary school education and prepared a delicious side dish for the occasion. Sandie worked extremely hard in preparation for these family get-togethers. One of my key roles at our family Christmas gathering was to be the Bingo ringmaster. We came up with the idea to entertain the kids for a period while cleanup occurred after our satisfying dinner. The kids really looked forward to it, especially the cash prizes. While adults played, they weren't eligible for any of the cash prizes.

My older son Shawn was still residing in Chicago at this time but couldn't make it for our family dinner. Sandie and I met Shawn and his then girlfriend for a Christmas dinner instead. Our humble abode in Vernon Hills was more than maxed out, but everyone had a good time adding to our list of fond family memories.

Sandie and I started the year 2012 in Seattle, Washington. In all my travels, I hadn't made it to Seattle to that point. We actually made it the first stop on a west coast trip as we traveled from there to Los Angeles to visit with Janette. While in Seattle, we simply had to visit the world-renowned Pike Place Market. It's one of the few authentic farmers' markets in the United States, the hub of delicious scents, delectable eats, and delightful personalities, which attract over ten million visitors a year. It overlooks Elliott Bay waterfront and opened in 1907. Apart from being one of the few authentic US farmers' markets, it's one of the oldest. My recollection prior to visiting it was movie scenes where large fish were physically thrown from person to person as they were purchased. It's Seattle's most popular tourist destination and is the thirty-third most visited tourist attraction in the world.

Being a Starbucks Coffee fan and learning that the company originated in Seattle, we had to visit the store that launched this iconic global coffee giant. Founded by three partners in Seattle, Washington, in 1971 the company was originally named the Pequod by the trio after a whaling ship in Herman Melville's American classic, Moby-Dick. But the name was a peculiar one and after a series of discussions, the trio changed the name of the company to Starbuck, chief mate on the Pequod. The name Starbuck eventually morphed into the name Starbucks. As of 2018, Starbucks had over 20,000 stores in 62 countries. How was coffee discovered? It's said that an Ethiopian goat herder named Kaldi noticed that whenever his goats munched on coffee berries they became euphoric, so he decided to try some of these berries himself and as they say the rest is history.

No visit to Seattle would be complete without visiting the famous Space Needle. Built for the 1962 World Fair, it's a landmark of the Pacific Northwest and a Seattle icon. Once the tallest structure west of the Mississippi, it was built to withstand winds up to 200 mph and earthquakes of up to a 9.0 magnitude. We toured its observation deck and dined in the rotating Sky City restaurant.

Following our Seattle adventure, we ventured down to Los Angeles to visit with Janette and her then boyfriend, TK. Janette was between movie assignments that provided this stopover opportunity. We did a little touring downtown to the Farmers Market and onto the George Page Museum located in the heart of metropolitan Los Angeles. The newly named La Brea Tar Pits Museum (located in the George C. Page Museum building) displays Ice Age fossils—including saber-toothed cats, dire wolves, and mammoths—from 10,000- to 40,000-year-old asphalt deposits. We enjoyed dinner one evening with Janette and TK at TK's home in Malibu. TK's mother made it over and she was absolutely delightful. Sandie and I thoroughly enjoyed her company.

Later that January, a Las Vegas familiarization trip opportunity presented itself. My employment duties at NMMA included the scouting and, ultimately, booking of convention centers and hotels for their two trade shows at the time. Whether you call it a perk or a benefit, numerous city familiarization tour invites came across my desk. The invites were usually all-expenses-paid extravaganzas designed to impress their potential VIP guests with the flavor of the selected destination. All travel, meals, and accommodation expenses were paid by the destination where they spared no expense in going above and beyond in providing a memorable experience. Capturing just a few customers from these events could yield millions of dollars to that destination's economy.

As previously mentioned, for ethical reasoning I was very selective of the invitations I accepted. If I knew our organization wouldn't be a candidate for a particular destination, I wouldn't accept the invite. It was important in my opinion for me personally as well as the organization I represented to be viewed as having the highest moral standards. Honest, trustworthy reputations were critical in the negotiating world and once lost are difficult to recover. One of our trade shows was a definite candidate for Las Vegas, so I felt compelled to accept the invitation. The Las Vegas familiarization trip was spectacular. The city put the invitees up in suites at the MGM Grand Hotel. The meals were all culinary masterpieces and the excursions included a helicopter tour of the Grand Canyon and Hoover Dam.

In April of 2012, a Hawaii trip Sandie and I took had two purposes. We were celebrating our tenth anniversary with a Vow Renewal ceremony and we wanted to visit friends and family. We stayed at the famous Moana Surfrider Hotel in Waikiki. This glorious property was the original grand dame on Waikiki Beach. Built in 1901 as the Moana Hotel, it's grown with Waikiki's hotel industry to exceed 700 rooms but still maintains its original structure, complete with palm trees at its entrance, an unusual site on the beach side of Kalakaua Avenue. From 1935 to 1975, the Moana Surfrider hosted the "Hawaii Calls" live radio broadcast. The Moana had the first electric-powered elevator in Hawaii that is still in use today. Duke Kahanamoku, the legendary Olympic swimmer and popularizer of the sport of surfing, frequented the Moana Hotel restaurants and private beachfront. The Moana Hotel became a favorite stomping ground for Kahanamoku's famed group, dubbed the Waikiki Beach Boys.

We visited our first grandchild from my side of the family, Deacon, who was then seven years old. We met Deacon and my younger son Scott for dinner. During this visit we also spent time with his mom, Bernadette, separately. Simple geography made it difficult to maintain a relationship with Deacon. He lived over 4,000 miles from us and while we made it to

Hawaii whenever we could, the fact is that the distance simply prevented frequent visits and he rarely made it to the mainland.

For our ten-year-vow-renewal ceremony, with the help of our officiator, we chose the site of Ala Moana Beach Park. It's a beautiful, natural setting located between the hustle and bustle of Waikiki and downtown Honolulu. This 100-acre park has a wide gold-sand beach that is over a half-mile long and with beautiful mountains as a backdrop served as a perfect location for our ceremony. The park hosts special events throughout the year from fireworks shows to the Shinnyo-en Lantern Floating Festival held on Memorial Day. Researching potential presiders over our special event led me to Toni Baran on Oahu, who did an outstanding job on our behalf. Sandie is a beautiful woman and on that day she was absolutely sparkling. We had matching attire, a Hawaiian Mumu for Sandie and an Aloha shirt for me. Toni presented us both with leis, a kukui nut lei for me and a shell lei for Sandie. In the beautiful islands of Hawaii, a lei is a common symbol of love, friendship, celebration, honor, or greeting. Apart from our wedding rings, I couldn't think of a better way to celebrate our Hawaii Vow Renewal. Then at ten years of marriage, and nearly twenty years of knowing each other and every day since, I'm amazed at how time has flown by. Knowing and loving this woman is timeless.

While on this trip, I had to take Sandie to the well-known local restaurant, the Like Like Drive Inn for lunch. Locally owned and operated since its 1953 inception, the Like Like Drive Inn has become a Honolulu landmark, attracting both locals and tourists. Serving well-known local fare, the State of Hawaii has officially designated it as a place of historical interest.

A relaxing getaway on Oahu is the North Shore area. The North Shore is home to some of the world's finest beaches and bays. During the winter months (October through April), the swells at world-famous surf spots Waimea Bay, Pipeline, and Sunset Beach reach thirty feet or more. There's a series of professional surfing contests held in these areas, including the famous Pipe Masters at the infamous Banzai Pipeline. Another Oahu institution is M. Matsumoto's grocery and Shave Ice store located in Haleiwa on the North Shore. In fact, it's quite possibly the most well-known shave ice stand in the world. If you've been to Haleiwa, gateway town to Oahu's world-famous North Shore surf spots, you've seen Matsumoto Shave Ice. It's that beige, rustic storefront with the teeming, all-day crowd of visitors and residents nearly spilling out into Kamehameha Highway, Haleiwa's main drag. That's Matsumoto Shave Ice. They have more shaved ice flavors than I can feasibly list. Sandie had a large "Hawaiian," which was a mixture of banana, coconut, and pineapple flavors.

In early May, Sandie and I navigated to Kerrville, Texas, to visit with my cousin Mary Lou and her husband Bill. The distance between us prevents seeing them as often as we'd like. They're dog lovers and living on their own ranch lot has the luxury and space to accommodate four or so larger dogs; they seemed to prefer German Shepherds. In fact, as they live in the country with large acreage, the dogs serve as an additional security determent. In mid-May of the same year, Sandie celebrated Mother's Day by going to the Brookfield Zoo with her oldest daughter Olivia and her family. Previewing the lions, dolphins, stingrays, and a slew of other creatures made for a pleasurable day, watching our grandkids CJ and Emily enjoy themselves.

June 24, 2012 was my baptism date at the church, which provided me with much-needed support following the divorce from my second wife. Sandie got baptized with me at Willow Creek on that special day. I actually accepted Jesus at a service there on May 17 of 2003, making this day even more special. The baptism ceremony took place on the church grounds in one of their creeks. Willow Creek Community Church has many traditions. The one that I'm particularly fond of is held at their annual Christmas service. At the end of the service, the congregation sings *Silent Night* and time is given to family members to express their feelings to one another. It's hard for most, me included, to make it through this ritual tear-free.

In June of this year, we purchased a brand-new automobile for Sandie. She had been driving an older, proving to be unreliable, Ford Escort, so it was timely. We weren't planning to purchase that day but the preposterous offer I made on the vehicle was actually accepted. While not remembering the exact specifics, the deal kept our payments around $300 per month and the dealership made our first two payments on our behalf, making Sandie the proud owner of a new 2013 Hyundai Elantra. Over the 4th of July, Sandie and I took her new vehicle on its first road trip. We went to Minneapolis to visit my long-time friend Bill Steele.

But we had a harrowing experience that we'll never forget. We were traveling north on a three-lane interstate highway between Chicago and Minneapolis when a car shot past us on the left. We were in the middle lane and ahead, we saw this same vehicle navigate to the center lane at the same time a vehicle in the far-right lane attempted to do the same. They must not have seen each other and the two cars connected spinning the vehicle that passed us around 180 degrees, where it was coming head-on to us while we were doing around 70 miles an hour! He ended up off the road and into a ditch but not before my heart went through my throat. The whole incident occurred in a matter of seconds but my heart felt like it was a lifetime.

Our annual Summer–Splash/BBQ event was interrupted that year due to inclement weather. By necessity, we had to plan the date in advance so family could mark it on their calendars and we could reserve the park pavilion. On the planned special day, it was raining, causing Sandie and me to do some quick thinking as we didn't want to cancel the day. We ended up taking the families to an indoor activity center located the next town over from us in Mundelein, which had a little bit of everything, including go-carts. After an hour or so of fun there, the sun came out allowing us to go to the Vernon Hills water park after all, followed by the BBQ at our reserved pavilion.

That fall, we decided to get our legal papers in order. We felt it import-ant to have everything spelled out to avoid any potential future bickering. Our financial advisors, World Equity Group, recommended a Libertyville attorney who was reasonable and did good work in that arena. Thus, we had drawn up a Family Trust, our wills, and Power of Attorney for our Health Care and Property. We don't have a lot monetarily or property-wise, but we wanted to be sure to be fair to the kids. Our marriage represents my third and Sandie's second. Between Sandie and me we have a total of five children. Thus, we decided that each would be willed 20% of whatever we left, with our oldest, Janette, being the executor of our will.

Our 2012 family Christmas was extra special. Sandie's two daughters Olivia and Julie made it with their families. Her brother Rob and his wife Barb made it also and her sister Janice and brother-in-law Bruce drove up from Highland, Illinois. Janette was between work assignments, allowing her to spend the Christmas holidays with us in Vernon Hills. While Shawn and Scott didn't make it to the family dinner, they were in town and we spent time with them. This was one of the rare instances that my three kids were in the same place at the same time. My gift to Sandie that year were photo albums from our 2002 Wedding in South Haven, Michigan, and our 2012 Vow Renewal ceremony held at Ala Moana Beach state park on Oahu in Hawaii. Her surprise and obvious happiness with them were priceless.

March 17, 2013, was a triple celebration day. The main festivity was our granddaughter Emily's seventh birthday. Her dad Cesar shares the same birthdate and the commemoration took place on St Patrick's Day. Yes, there were St. Paddy's Day shirts galore spread out amongst the guests. Thus, in addition to cake, candles, gifts, and laughter, there was a sea of green. Cesar and Olivia arranged for the party to be held at their local community center to accommodate all family members and friends that attended.

Later that month, Sandie and I ventured to Florida. To satisfy one of my passions, we took in some spring-training baseball games of Major League's Grapefruit league. As major league baseball is my favorite sport, the ability to view several teams at reasonable prices on one trip was gratifying. The games are considered exhibition but have a distinct competitive edge to them as many of the players are auditioning for positions on their respective big-league clubs. The tickets are reasonable and most all seats provide excellent vantage points. We visited two parks in Fort Myers, Hammond Stadium, the spring home of the Minnesota Twins, and Jet Blue Park, the spring home of the Boston Red Sox. Jet Blue Park was patterned after Fenway, providing a comparable environment both in and out of the stadium.

We also took in a game at the New York Yankees spring training facility in Tampa, George Steinbrenner Field. It was unseasonably cold that day but enjoyable nonetheless. The highlight of the game was witnessing one of the best relief pitchers in baseball history, Marino Riviera. Wearing uniform #42 he, played 19 seasons in Major League Baseball and was an All-Star thirteen times. In his first year of eligibility, 2019, he was the first player ever to be elected unanimously into the Baseball Hall of Fame.

The two of us traveling alone in Florida also gave us the opportunity to visit my sister. Sheryl and her husband Jim lived in Cape Coral, Florida, not far from Fort Myers. It's a rare but always enjoyable treat to spend time with them. While there that winter in Florida, we also got to renew our acquaintances with their neighbors, Uda and Heinz, the absolutely delightful couple from Germany.

In early May of 2013, I was privileged to address the National Association of Consumer Shows at their annual convention. The assembly took place at the Chicago Hilton Hotel. I was asked to make a presentation on Hotel/Convention Center contracting. My presentation was entitled "Successful Hotel and Convention Center Contracting."

The session description and bio that appeared in their program read:

SESSION DESCRIPTION

Learn Hotel and Convention Center contracting strategies to maximize your bottom line. Do I really need "that" in the hotel contract? Discover what's necessary in a contract. History may be boring but it's imperative to support your room blocks and meeting space. Make sense of the "A" word in hotel contracting. Attrition language needs to be specific. Learning the departmental range of hotel profit margins provides rooms, and food & beverage attrition alternatives. The pros and cons of using a third-party housing provider will be reviewed. In the real estate arena its Location, Location, and Location. In contracting, it's about relationships and reputation while nurturing a win–win environment. Determine how to partner with your hotel and Convention Center associates. What is your show worth to the venue you're considering? Knowing your show's worth along with the Convention Center's ownership status (public or private) can help you with your negotiating efforts. This session will provide you with invaluable tips and strategies of Hotel & Convention Center contracting.

BIO

Stephen Evans, CAE, CEM, CMP, has been with National Marine Manufacturer's Association for fourteen years and is responsible for Convention Center and Hotel contracting for their twenty-one-consumer boat shows and their one trade show. Stephen held previous association positions with the Institute for Inter Connecting Packaging and Electronic Circuits as well as Bank Administration Institute, assuming Hotel and Convention Center contracting responsibilities for the shows he worked with. Prior to association work, Stephen was employed in the hotel industry advancing through various positions to become a hotel general manager. He worked in hotels from Hawaii to Maine and offers a unique contracting perspective from both sides of the fence. Stephen is a graduate of the Metropolitan State University in St Paul, Minnesota.

It was an absolute honor to be considered an expert in the area of hotel/convention center contracting. Presenting to industry colleagues was an added challenge. Not wanting to let my employer or the industry down, I put an extraordinary amount of effort into the session content. Sandie served as a sounding board for me as she patiently sat through numerous presentations, critiquing my delivery and session content. After the initial set of on-stage butterflies, I was very comfortable delivering the presentation and actually enjoyed myself.

In late May that year, Sandie and I visited Janette in Detroit on the set of *Lost River*. The film was Ryan Gosling's directorial debut and was written by him. Christina Hendricks (*Mad Men*) portrayed a single mother swept into a dark underworld while her teenage son discovers a road that leads him to a secret underwater town.

We were there for a few days and one our visit highlights was a Detroit inner-city bicycle tour. On the tour, we rode by or stopped in Ford Field, Music Hall, the Detroit Opera House, and Hitsville USA, home of the Motown Museum. A funny aside: Janette was continually lagging behind the tour group only to discover after completing the major portion of the tour that she was riding on one flat tire. Hearing so much negativity regarding Detroit, we were pleasantly surprised with the city and its sky-line. As it was during the baseball season, we seized the opportunity to take in a Detroit Tigers game at Comerica Park.

Admittedly, my city highlight was our visit to the Henry Ford Museum. Without prior knowledge of the exhibits, one would jump to the conclusion that it was all about automobiles. While there were many vehicles present, there were other unbelievable exhibits. There was a complete Civil Rights movement exhibit that included history of the KKK as well as the famous Rosa Parks bus. Actual Presidential limousines were on display from the Franklin D. Roosevelt, Dwight D. Eisenhower, John F. Kennedy, and Ronald W. Reagan administrations. The display that stopped me in my tracks was the actual chair that Lincoln sat in while John Wilkes Booth committed his heinous assassination. The plaque on the exhibit reads, "This is the actual chair in which President Lincoln was assassinated on April 14, 1865. It was originally located in the President's special box in Ford's Theatre, Washington, DC."

In July of 2013, I realized a nice birthday surprise. Janette visited Chicago between movie assignments. Shawn was still residing in Chicago so Janette, Sandie and I met him and his girlfriend for brunch. Janette took the Chicago vacation opportunity to also visit with Sandie's daughters Olivia and Julie. We traveled to their homes so Janette could see the recently purchased Vazquez and Douglas homes.

The weather was perfect that year for our annual Summer-Splash/BBQ event. Janette was in town, enabling her to attend with Olivia and

Julie's families. We added a "Bag-Toss" game to the extra-curricular activities. Amanda was unable to make it that year probably due to a work assignment. One of the more memorable photos from the BBQ was of the five present grandkids all wearing glasses we brought that had pop-out eyeballs.

On the 24th of August, Sandie and I drove down to Indianapolis from our Vernon Hills home to attend the wedding of my niece Courtni who was marrying Randy Couch. It proved to be a hectic afternoon for Marjie and Rod as they were still decorating for the ceremony after most of the guests were already seated. My Evans family siblings were all present with their spouses as Floyd, Marjie (mother of the bride), and Becky attended allowing Sandie and me to catch up with them on current events. The wedding turned out fine. Courtni was dressed in an attractive white wedding dress and looked beautiful. Natalie, Courtni's daughter from her first marriage, served as a flower girl and was cute as the dickens. Randy, the groom, and his groomsmen were dressed in Hawaiian aloha shirts, adding to the festivities.

We did our customary trifecta Highland, Illinois, Indianapolis, Indiana, and back to Vernon Hills trip for Thanksgiving 2013. On November 28, the Thanksgiving Day, we enjoyed a heavenly feast well prepared by Sandie's sister Janice, her husband Bruce, and their son, Brendon. The Kryfkas were sterling hosts for a meal of the ages featuring, of course, turkey, loaded mashed potatoes, sweet potatoes, and other dishes too numerous to mention.

Following a few days in Highland, Illinois, we drove up to Indianapolis for the annual Evans Christmas dinner hosted by Sandie and me on the Saturday following Thanksgiving. We call it a Christmas dinner as while it affords us the opportunity to catch up with Indiana relatives it's also our Christmas gift to the family as we typically spend Christmas day with Sandie's side of the family in Vernon Hills. We had a grand turnout for the occasion with thirty-four family members showing up. Included in the group was my niece Shelby (flower girl at our wedding) with her newborn, Noah. Also in attendance was Rick, my nephew, with his son Tanner. Tanner was about five at this dinner and was an absolute spitting image of his dad.

My step-mom and her husband also made it to the dinner, which was very much appreciated considering they were over eighty years old at the time.

One of Sandie and my "mini customs" was to spend a night or two preceding Christmas in downtown Chicago. We would typically walk down Michigan Avenue enjoying the Christmas decorations and stopping in some stores along the way. Between the well-known Water Tower shopping high-rise and the countless upper end stores on Michigan Avenue, we had a lot to choose from. This year through one of my industry contacts, we stayed in the Presidential Suite of the Sheraton Grand Hotel. It was amazing! With a kitchen, dining room (seating for twelve), card playing area, gaming/TV area, two bathrooms, large foyer, living room area with a fireplace, a smaller TV area, and even a separate office area with a giant iMac. The suite was so large, we had to elevate our voices to communicate if we weren't in the same room.

The 2013 Christmas dinner at our place in Vernon Hills went well. Olivia's family, Julie's family, and Sandie's brother Rob with his wife Barb, all took part. Our grandson CJ was a year or two into playing the trumpet. He brought his horn and played a few numbers for the group. Sandie, as usual, prepared a scrumptious meal and between the conversation, gift opening, and games, everyone thoroughly enjoyed themselves.

In April of 2014, Sandie and I journeyed to New Orleans. Janette was working on a movie project there, so we seized upon the opportunity to visit her and to experience New Orleans. Playing tourist, we did the Natchez Steamboat Harbor tour. The Port of New Orleans is one of the biggest and busiest ports in the world and the center of a busy maritime community. It is a fundamental transportation and distribution hub for water-borne commerce with many shipping, shipbuilding, freight forwarding, logistics, and commodity brokerage companies either headquartered in or otherwise located in the Port of New Orleans. The Port of New Orleans region accounts for much of the country's oil refining and petrochemical production. In 2005, Hurricane Katrina devastated the Port of New Orleans when the city's levees were breached and much of the city was flooded, killing hundreds and forcing an evacuation of the city. Called by some the "worst civil engineering disaster in US history," the hurricane flooded as much as 80% of the Port of New Orleans. While the city was not destroyed, it was hit hard. Historians think it may be the worst disaster in the United States since the 1906 earthquake in San Francisco. Fortunately for visitors to the Port of New Orleans, the city's historic, cultural, and business districts are on slightly higher ground and fared relatively well in the storm. In 2009, tourism returned to the Port of New Orleans.

One of the sites from the famous Steamboat was the Domino Sugar refinery. Unbeknownst to me, the Domino Chalmette refinery has more than a 100-year history in this location. The refinery was recognized as the first domestic sugar refinery to process one million tons in a single year. The business processes about 60% of the raw sugar produced by Louisiana's sugar cane farmers. The Chalmette refinery typically produces about two billion pounds annually, or about seven million pounds a day. That generally accounts for about 19% of the country's cane sugar.

Of course we had to traverse Bourbon Street while in New Orleans. The city is full of energy, as you can't walk more than block or two before coming across some type of street entertainment. Ironically, the drink that New Orleans is most famous for is the Hurricane. Pat O'Brien's Pub has been heralded as serving the best Hurricane in the city. Being in New Orleans over Easter, we decided to have brunch at the famous Antoine's restaurant.

Established in 1840, Antoine's is the country's oldest family-run restaurant. This icon of a restaurant was created by Antoine Alciatore. A New Orleans institution, it is notable for being the birthplace of several famous dishes including Oysters Rockefeller. It has an over-175-year-old legacy and is still owned and operated by fifth generation relatives of its original founder. The world-renowned French-Creole cuisine, impeccable service and unique atmosphere have combined to create an unmatched dining experience in New Orleans since 1840. Janette dropped us off as due to a parade, parking was at a premium that day. We went into the restaurant while she located suitable parking. The meal was good but, unfortunately, we discovered following the meal that Janette's auto had been towed, leading us on a chase to locate it.

We were told that no visit to New Orleans would be complete without a stop at the famous Café Du Monde. The original coffee stand was established in 1862 in the New Orleans French Market. The Café is open twenty-four hours a day, seven days a week. It closes only on Christmas Day and on the day an occasional hurricane passes too close to New Orleans. We went during what we thought would be an "off" time and the café was packed. We had their highly acclaimed beignets with coffee and were not disappointed.

The year 2014 was a disturbing employment year for me. My employer directed me to break our contracted lease in Louisville and book our IBEX event into Tampa. It seemed that following every show at our exhibitor wrap-up meeting, inevitability some of the group felt a move to another city was warranted. I would cringe at these comments, knowing full well that these same sentiments would be expressed regardless of where we held the event. This time, the voices well connected to NMMA board and committee members were forcing me to rebook the event. It was difficult for me as I felt it tarnished the reputations of both the organization I worked for and me. After drawn out negotiations, I was able to convince NMMA and the Kentucky Exposition Center that we'd return to the convention center a few years down the road in exchange for their waving cancellation fees. This saved NMMA $250,000 in cancellation fees at the time. However, it couldn't help but place a blemish on my employer, NMMA, as well as me. It was the year my sixty-eighth birthday was realized and the thought of retirement weighed heavy on my mind.

The summer of 2014 was a gratifying, meaningful one. The day before Mother's Day, Sandie and I went with Olivia, Cesar, and the grandkids (Emily and CJ) to Brookfield Zoo. It was a thoughtful, fun way to celebrate Mother's Day. It was thoroughly enjoyable seeing the smiles on Emily and CJ's face as they witnessed the kangaroos, baboons, and penguins. That 4th of July, Sandie and I drove up to Milwaukee to take in the

Milwaukee's Summerfest. The event is billed as the world's largest music festival. Walking from stage to stage, I had to agree. Each stage/pavilion had a sponsor and Harley Davidson sponsored the largest pavilion. Being that Harley Davidson was originally founded in Milwaukee in 1903, this seemed appropriate.

The weather was perfect once again for our annual Summer-Splash/BBQ event. Sandie's sister and brother-in-law drove up for the event and stayed with us for a few days. The grandkids thoroughly enjoyed the Vernon Hills aquatic park but still had plenty of energy left for the BBQ. The bean-bag toss was a hit from the previous year so we brought that along. Sandie, at this point, had become somewhat of a ringer, routing most challengers. We also played some baseball with a plastic bat and ball. Most everyone seemed to get into the spirit of the day. Sandie's brother Rob made it over for the BBQ.

The year 2014 was a challenging but at the same time pleasing year regarding work accomplishments for my employer, NMMA. It was an especially active period. Here are some of the achievements I was most proud of:

- Arranged a three-year lease agreement for our IBEX show with the Tampa Bay Convention Center, inclusive of a contingency clause allowing NMMA cancellation privileges if NMMA didn't deem the event to have a sufficient number of attendees and exhibitors. This basically provided NMMA with a risk-free venue test.

- In spite of Tampa Bay's significantly higher average room rate as compared to that of Louisville, I was able to negotiate Tampa hotel contracts for IBEX, which were similar to Louisville room rates and without attrition provisions.

- Renegotiated the Miami Boat Show 2016 lease, which significantly reduced NMMA's overall financial exposure.

- Served on the Certified Exposition Managers Appeals Commission for the International Association of Exposition Managers (IAEE).

On March 2, 2015, Sandie and I lost our cat buddy, Max. Sandie had Max before our marriage and brought him into our new household to befriend my cat, Wookie. Wookie had passed a few years earlier so at that point Max was our only pet. It's absolutely true what they say about pets becoming part of your family. Max was very social and visible at our family gatherings. He had developed kidney disease and it finally got to the point where even with medication and a prescription diet the best thing for him was to be put down. The day before, he went without eating the whole day, which was highly unusual for him. Max would have been twenty years old the next month so he lived a long, healthy, good life. He used to follow me up the stairs each night after work for playtime. He had a lot of energy and missed playtime if it didn't occur. One of our favorite games was "Matador," where I would place my shirt in front of him and he would dip his head and move to the other side of the bed. As Sandie described on many occasions, Max was a good pet. He was present without making a nuisance of himself and he enjoyed being around people in general. We miss and think of him to this day.

The following month was much lighter as we anxiously awaited a planned Disney World road trip with Sandie's youngest daughter, Julie, and her family. We had announced the trip several months earlier and the Douglas family of Julie, Kenny, Kenny Junior, Taylor, and Matt could hardly wait. Not only had they never experienced any of the Disney parks, they had not even visited Florida. Sandie also had not had the opportunity to visit a Disney theme park. We rented a Chrysler mini-van and dubbed it the "Mousemobile" for the journey to and from Orlando, Florida, the last week in April. The planning process even included confirming that the luggage we'd all be taking would fit into the Mousemobile.

We spent two hotel nights on the road trip down and two hotel nights on the road trip back to enjoy the adventure. Janette was working a movie in Atlanta so as an added bonus, we were able to visit with her on the way down to Disney as well as on the way back home. While at Disney World, we all stayed in a beautiful time-share condo near Disney at a great rate in exchange for Sandie and I sitting through a time-share presentation. With the exception of the time-share presentation the Disney experience in Orlando was phenomenal. We thought the time-share presentation would be a max of two hours sitting in a room with twenty to thirty other invitees. It ended up being a one-to-one sales presentation and tour. As we were not willing to commit on the spot, we kept getting turned over to sales individuals in higher positions with each of them presenting a "better offer." We finally left after they realized that a sale was not going to be made to us that day. The presentation cost us a whole afternoon and Sandie and I missed the Animal Kingdom Park because of it. Julie and her family didn't miss the Animal Kingdom Park as we'd arranged to meet them there since they didn't have to sit through the presentation.

It rained on our first day at Disney World. This had both positive and negative connotations. The negative impact was the fact that we weren't prepared for the rain and had to purchase rain ponchos at the park. On the positive side, due to the rain, we were able to access rides at a speed that would have been impossible if the rain wasn't keeping park patrons at bay. It really did my heart well to see the smiles on the faces of our grandkids, Kenny Junior, Taylor, and Matt, as we made our way through the park rides, meeting with Disney characters, and stopping for pictures along the way. This was an experience that would forever be etched into their memories and I was elated to be part of it.

From our Vernon Hills, Illinois residence, to Disney World in Orlando and back, we traveled in excess of 2,500 miles. Breaking the trip up into three days of travel each way kept the grandkids refreshed and enthused as the hotels we stayed in had indoor swimming pools that provided energy release and fun. The only misadventure we experienced was a GPS hiccup on the way back home from Orlando. We set the GPS for an address for a hotel we had reservations for in Horse Cave, Kentucky. The GPS took us into the middle of a forest, announcing, "You have arrived!" This was funny to all of us and thankfully the sun hadn't fully settled and we able to make it to our destination before dark. The nine-day journey was hugely successful and a great family bonding experience.

The following month, my two sons Shawn and Scott as well as my grandson, Deacon, were all in Chicago. It's rare to have the three of them together in the same place. We took advantage of the opportunity to meet at Wrigley Field in Chicago to take in a baseball game between the Chicago Cubs and Los Angeles Dodgers. Eleven-year-old Deacon was all decked out in a Chicago Cubs jersey and Cubs logos painted below his eyes. We had great seats along the right field line. Tommy Lasorda, the longtime Dodger manager that bleeds Dodger blue, was in attendance and we got our picture taken with him. A new dad sitting a couple of rows in front of us with his baby in his arm made an incredible catch of a foul ball with his free hand, which played several times on local and national TV stations. Deacon left a happy camper that night as he ended up with not one but two souvenir baseballs.

Sandie and I made what had become somewhat of a routine by taking in a Milwaukee Brewers game in Milwaukee that June. We both enjoy taking in baseball games and discovered that getting to and from Miller Park in Milwaukee was easier that fighting the Chicago traffic to either the Cubs or White Sox stadiums. The park was completed in 2001, replacing Milwaukee County Stadium and is located just off of Interstate 94 outside the city.

In July of 2015, we traveled back into Milwaukee to once again take in their annual Summerfest event. There's plenty to do there in addition to the music available on the numerous stages. We rented a leg-powered paddleboat and paddled around a little bay just off of Lake Michigan. Later that month we drove over to Moline, Illinois, located about three hours west of Chicago to attend a concert. We're both Shania Twain fans and even featured her *You're Still the One* song at our wedding. She was performing at the Wireless Center in Moline at her "Rock This Country Tour." The tour was her first in eleven years and advertised as her farewell tour.

At this stage of my life, I had been contemplating retirement for several years. I was sixty-nine on my last birthday and the fear of living on a "fixed income" coupled with the desire to cover my younger bride by nine years, Sandie, under my work medical plan had kept me working. We visited several potential retirement locations including Henderson/Kentucky, Evansville/Indiana, Louisville/Kentucky, Hendersonville/Tennessee, and Clarksville/Tennessee. Our move parameters were to achieve a lower cost of living, better weather, and be within a day's drive of Chicago for family visitations. I had also done extensive research on each of these cities to aid in our decision-making process.

My employer, NMMA, was going through some difficult financial times due to the forced relocation of our largest show, the Miami International Boat Show. Being our organization's largest show, it also provided significant revenue in support of the company. Its past home, the Miami Beach Convention Center, was undergoing an extensive renovation preventing our use of that facility for a two-year period. Being absent from the marketplace for that period was unthinkable, as a competitor would have come in and filled that void. Thus, the show was moved to Miami Marine Stadium Park & Basin, Virginia Key. While the location was ideally situated near the ocean for the in-water boat displays, there was absolutely no infrastructure built-in for the show. This required the expenditure of millions of dollars in infrastructure costs by NMMA to accommodate utilities and facilities needed for the event. While this cost could be amortized over a period of several years, it required an upfront investment that would have far-reaching effects for my employer. The financial strain was so great that NMMA had to eventually sell off their West Coast shows, eliminating all affiliated employees in the process.

Hence, the conditions my employer was facing coupled with my advanced retirement planning provided an opportunity for me to suggest a retirement package to them in exchange for my leaving. The timing of such a proposal was important and realizing the need for all hands on deck for the Miami Boat show in a few months I thought it best not to bring it up until the end of February, after the 2016 show. At this point, NMMA's annual review process was held during the October–November timeframe. Disappointment and exultation descended upon me at my annual review this year.

During my review, I was informed that my position would be eliminated on July 31, 2016. Knowing the financial situation of the company, this wasn't a total shock. In fact, I was sure others would be phased out also. I was approaching seventy and my annual salary had escalated to $108,000 without benefits, which at my salary level would add another 40% or so to the cost burden. Instead of viewing this from a victim's standpoint, my perspective was to see it as an opportunity to leave in good standing with a solid "retirement package." Thus, I offered to make my retirement date March 1, 2016, saving my organization five months of salary and benefits in exchange for three months of salary and Sandie's continued medical coverage for an additional eighteen months. So, the exultation was my ability to negotiate a nice retirement package.

The disappointment was in the way the elimination of my job was presented to me. I felt a unique friendship and closeness to NMMA's President Thom Dammrich. I worked with Thom at our previous association, IPC, for seven years and was nearing sixteen years of employment at NMMA, totaling twenty-three years of working with one another. Thom was not a strict "Chain of Command" leader. On occasion after occasion, Thom would go directly to employees one to three levels below him on the organization chart to discuss NMMA policies, strategies, and give operational direction. Thom came directly to me on numerous occasions initiating workflow specifics. He came to our wedding and delivered a speech. Sandie and I journeyed to Hawaii with Thom and his wife Carol for an American Society of Association Executives conference. After twenty-three years of a personal and professional relationship with Thom, and while I was still an admirer of his leadership skills, I was absolutely befuddled and extremely disappointed that he never came to me personally to discuss my employment situation firsthand. A friendship that I thought existed obviously didn't. For one of the most important impacts to my career, it turned out to be a pure cold-hearted numbers decision initiated by NMMA due to my age and salary burden to the organization. It didn't have to be this way. I certainly would have and, in fact, did understand NMMA's financial predicament.

Christmas of 2015 was a mixed bag of emotions for us. The annual Evans Christmas dinner in Indianapolis went well. We had twenty-nine in attendance, allowing Sandie and me to connect with our Indiana family in a group setting. The mixed bag of emotions was derived from a conflict that occurred back in February of 2015. We were at Sandie's youngest daughter's house, Julie, celebrating her daughter's Taylor's birthday. An altercation occurred to Olivia's daughter Emily, which according to Olivia and Cesar, wasn't properly handled, causing them to leave the party. That event was the start of an unfortunate split of Sandie's two daughters, and them not speaking to each other. Regrettably, that was the case until April of 2020. The only way we saw to handle Christmas that year was to have two separate Christmas celebrations, inviting each of Sandie's daughters with their families separately. Logistically, it worked out fine but was an awful lot of extra work for Sandie. Sandie's sister, Janice, along with her husband Bruce drove up from Highland, Illinois, and stayed with us for both celebrations. Sandie's younger brother and his wife Barb lived in a nearby suburb and drove over both times.

Earlier in the year, we had taken Sandie's youngest daughter Julie and her family to Disney World. We planned a comparable trip the following spring with Olivia's family. With Olivia and Cesar's previous knowledge of our intentions, Sandie and I decided to make this special announcement to CJ and Emily at our Christmas gathering. One of the gifts they received from us included cards that read: "You've won a trip to Disney World with Grandma, Stephen, Mom, and Dad." There were smiles aplenty when the magnitude of the trip sank in.

That decade provided several up and downs. The downs were associated mostly with my employment. The ups experienced during my career included a promotion, some international travel, and the value I brought to NMMA through careful marshaling of their resources. The descents included a near exit from the organization early in the decade, having to cancel contracted leases, damaging the reputation of NMMA as well as myself, and the way my employment cessation was communicated to me. Another high was Sandie and I being baptized at Willow Creek Community Church. Family connections were euphoric, including witnessing Sandie's educational growth earning both her Associates and Bachelor's college degrees, traveling to Disney World with Sandie's youngest daughter's family, committing to a Disney World trip with Sandie's oldest daughter's family, and meeting my son Shawn in Phoenix, Arizona, for some spring training baseball games.

Anne Frank Home 2009.

Kentucky Derby 2010.

Chapter 9 | 2016–2017

S andie and I both looked forward to this next chapter of our lives as I
was positioned to retire early in 2016. We looked forward to moving
from Illinois, and we planned to enjoy retirement primarily though traveling. We purchased our dream home in our desired geographical location
together, following eight years of research and numerous locale site visits
coupled with home inspections.

Toward the end of January 2016, Sandie and I flew to Tampa to
attend the annual Gasparilla Pirate Festival. The Gasparilla Pirate Festival
is a large parade with a host of related community events held in the city
almost every year since 1904. The theme of the festivities is the legend of
José Gaspar (also known as Gasparilla), a mythical Spanish pirate who
supposedly operated in Southwest Florida from the late 1700s until the
early 1800s. The main event of the festival is the Parade of Pirates, which is
organized by the city of Tampa along with Ye Mystic Krewe of Gasparilla
(YMKG), an organization modeled after the "krewes," which participate in
Mardi Gras in New Orleans.

Tampa's Gasparilla parade began as a one-day event, which was held
in conjunction with other community celebrations. It became a stand-alone
event in 1913 and has expanded over the years into a "Gasparilla season,"
which runs from approximately mid-January to mid-March and features
three large parades plus many other activities. The focal point of Gasparilla
is the Parade of Pirates, which is held on the last Saturday in January and
is often referred to as *the* Gasparilla Parade. On Gasparilla Day, members
of Ye Mystic Krewe of Gasparilla "invade" downtown aboard their large

"pirate ship" and celebrate their "conquest" of the city by staging what has become the third largest parade in the United States, with a local economic impact of over $20 million and an average attendance of about 300,000.

Tampa is approximately 130 miles north of Cape Coral, Florida. Being that close to my sister Sheryl, Sandie and I planned a short visit with her and her husband, Jim. As we were the guests of the Tampa Convention and visitor's Bureau for the Gasparilla event, they provided round-trip air-fare between Vernon Hills, Illinois and Tampa, Florida. So we rented a car and drove down to Cape Coral. Time spent with Sheryl was always special due to the distance involved in getting to her.

NMMA gave me a retirement party at the Union League Club in Downtown Chicago in late February of 2016. The party was well attended and I appreciated the gesture. One of my goals during my sixteen-year NMMA tenure was to pay for myself through revenues brought in and/or savings realized through my contracting prowess. I feel confident that goal was accomplished each year of my tenure and in some years most if not my entire department was paid for through these efforts.

I thought a short speech to be appropriate for the occasion:

"Thank you, everyone.

I have a lot to be grateful for as I'm truly blessed, beginning with my wonderful wife Sandie standing here. I've enjoyed two great careers, one in hotel management and the other in trade shows/meetings management. I'm not sure how much Sandie is looking forward to my retirement because as Ella Harris put it 'A retired husband is often a wife's full-time job.'

It's difficult to believe that following fifty-two years of continuous employment, I'm here this afternoon with retirement just days away. NMMA has played a huge role in my life these past sixteen years. It is a time and experience that I will hold close to me in the future.

Having served in two industries and experienced over a dozen work environments, I can honestly say that the climate here is the best I've experienced. You all know that I worked with Thom at IPC prior to NMMA. At his going-away party, I mentioned that he provided a work climate allowing others to succeed. Well, he along with the NMMA executive staff has provided that here and I consider it an honor and privilege having been a part of it.

Sandie and I are looking forward to our Tennessee relocation, future travels, and the next chapter in our lives. I'd like to take this moment to thank each of you for your dedication, commitment, and professionalism. You've made my experience here a great one. Thank you."

My retirement became official on March 1, 2016. We put our Vernon Hills townhouse up for sale as we had decided on Clarksville, Tennessee, as the destination we would relocate to. Selling your home can't help but be somewhat disruptive. Our townhouse was in relatively good shape as we made several capital improvements during our tenure there, minimizing the need for upgrades.

In early May, we took Olivia, Sandie's oldest daughter, and her family on a road trip to Disney World. Wanting an experience similar to the Disney trip with Sandie's youngest daughter Julie and her family, we rented a van for the road trip. Apart from just having fun we wanted to bond with Olivia's family and spending nine to ten days on a trip with six of us driving in the same vehicle was a good way to accomplish that objective. The Disney "Mousemobile" pulled out of Vernon Hills for its three-day Orlando trip, stopping in Louisville, Kentucky, and Macon, Georgia, before arriving in Orlando. For this outing, we thought we'd stay on Disney property to take advantage of their transportation services and to be closer to the parks. So we shared a cabin at The Cabins at Disney's Fort Wilderness Resort.

On this trip to Disney World, Sandie and I didn't have to sit through a time-share presentation. Overnighting at a Disney hotel within the park allowed us to take their free transportation to and from the various parks, which we took full advantage of. The Vazquez and Evans families enjoyed three days at Disney World and then we began the trip back. We took our time on the way back also stopping overnight in Atlanta and Bowling Green, Kentucky, before returning home. All in all, we believe the Vazquez family of Olivia, Cesar, CJ, and Emily enjoyed their Disney World adventure.

Our Illinois home sale took some work. Initially, we had to decide upon a realtor and then that company had to perform their due diligence to ready our home for sale. They took photos, created marketing materials, and made suggestions for buyer appeal. We were fortunate to realize a seller's market needing just a few months for our townhouse to sell, including the time we spent preparing it for sale. Our only issue was the initial appraisal. The appraiser used older home sales comparisons, which didn't reflect current home values, providing an underestimated value for our residence. To address this, we offered two alternatives to our prospective buyer: (1) We'd pay for another appraisal and that would be the agreed upon selling price providing it didn't exceed our originally listed price or (2) We'd split the difference between the original appraisal and our original asking selling price. The buyer opted for option two and we were in business.

While we were in the process of selling our Vernon Hills residence, our efforts to locate our retirement home in Clarksville intensified. Pending the sale of our Vernon Hills, Illinois, home we were finally in position to seriously shop for a Clarksville, Tennessee, home. We had visited the city several times, so we had a local real estate agent there we worked with. Sandie and I journeyed down to Clarksville and looked there as well as a couple of Nashville suburbs. To say that the Nashville area was a seller's market would have been an understatement. We identified several homes in the Nashville area to walk through but most sold overnight preventing our ability to even look at them. At that time in the Nashville market, you literally needed to offer 10-20% over the seller's asking price and somehow have insider information as to what homes would be coming onto the market. We did get to preview a home in the Hendersonville suburb of Nashville but it was smaller than we wanted and backed up to a freeway.

We went through several neighborhoods in Clarksville and nothing "jumped off the page" at us. However, one property did stand out. The home at 3816 Benjamin Drive in the quiet subdivision of Tylertown had the attributes we were looking for in a home. It had three bedrooms, two baths, a two-car garage, and a bonus room. Sandie and I wanted our living space to be all on one level and with the exception of an upstairs bonus room this property fit the criteria perfectly. It had a nice sized yard with four mature trees in the rear and one in the front. The home was built in 2003 and occupied by the original owners who had taken immaculate care of it. It was on the market for 35 days listed at $180,000 but was currently listed for $169,500. With the exception of some needed cosmetic changes, the home was perfect! We settled on a price of $162,900 and signed a letter of intent with first right of refusal on the property.

Our Illinois residence hadn't yet sold so committing to the Clarksville residence before it sold meant that we could be responsible for two mortgages until our Illinois home sold. That had happened to me during the latter part of my hotel career in Minneapolis, Minnesota, nearly causing me to have to claim bankruptcy. I realized a heavy loss on the Minnesota property but did manage to avoid bankruptcy. That experience made me all the more cautious from that point forward. As the days and weeks passed, I became more concerned that we could lose the 3816 Benjamin Drive home in Clarksville without a firm commitment. Sandie had been a real trooper looking at houses with me for eight years, knowing that we weren't in the position to buy. I couldn't bear disappointing her losing out on a home that we both felt was perfect for us. Perhaps another omen: the previous owners were Mr. and Mrs. Cleaver. Yes, like the Cleavers affectionally known as June and Ward on the 1950's *Leave it to Beaver* TV sitcom. Thus, before our Illinois residence was a definite sale, we committed to our future home at 3816 Benjamin Drive in Clarksville, signing all necessary documents while paying an earnest fee.

A month or so before either of our scheduled home closings, we needed to do an inspection on our soon-to-be Tennessee home. With everything going on, I made the trip down solo for the inspection while Sandie attended to our Vernon Hills interests. The Clarksville, Tennessee, home purchase gamble paid off as our Vernon Hills home sold in a timely manner. Our next challenge was the coordination of our two closings. Our Illinois home was scheduled to close on May 19, 2016 while our new Tennessee home was scheduled for closure the next day, on May 20. We spent the evening preceding our Illinois closing at a hotel in Libertyville.

To add to our level of intensity, we noticed a flat on our Hyundai Elantra shortly after pulling into the Libertyville Holiday Inn's parking lot. We were still covered through Hyundai's "Road Assistance" program, so we contacted them and they took our vehicle to the local Hyundai dealership for repair. You would think that would have ended the repair concern for our Hyundai but unfortunately that repair created another challenge. The Hyundai dealership scratched our vehicle when they ran it through their car wash after its repair. They offered to fix it if we'd leave it for the day. We couldn't do that, as we had to begin to travel to Tennessee that day to close on our home there. Knowing this, the Lake Zurich Hyundai dealership offered to pay for the repairs via a Tennessee receipt.

Having completely moved everything out of our Vernon Hills residence, both our vehicles were crammed with household items for our Tennessee trip. When I say crammed that included each vehicle's passenger's seat, the back seats, the floorboards and the trunk/tailgate. Thus, on Thursday morning, May 19, 2016, Sandie and I drove our two vehicles to our Illinois closing in Libertyville, Illinois. The individual purchasing our home, Sheryl, was a recent widow with a younger son. Both Sandie and I liked her and wanted her to buy our home. The closing went off without a hitch and we were off with all of our worldly possessions the movers didn't transport to Tennessee for the next chapter of our lives.

During my hotel career, I was moved on numerous occasions. My employer always paid for the move and in some instances even assisted on other moving expenses. Those experiences were in the distant past and gathering moving quotes for our Tennessee move placed me in sticker shock. The cost of moving our meager three-bedroom townhouse without any appliances a mere 502 miles was in excess of $5,000! We used a local United Van Lines affiliate and they did a good job. With our household goods loaded for delivery at our new yet-to-be-confirmed Tennessee residence and the successful closing of our Illinois residence, we were ready for the next chapter of our lives.

I purchased two walkie-talkies at our local Best Buy store and after testing the units we were ready to roll. The walkie-talkies were for drive down communication and for emergencies in the event Sandie and I somehow got separated from one another during the drive. The crammed two Evans' vehicle caravan pulled out for Tennessee on Thursday morning, May 19, immediately following the successful closing of our Illinois townhouse. We worked it out where the net sale proceeds would be wired to the Clarksville, Tennessee, bank working with the Title Company on our Tennessee home purchase. I led our two-vehicle pack communicating as necessary with Sandie via our new walkie-talkies.

We broke up the trip to Clarksville, staying in Mount Vernon, Illinois on the night of May 19, then left to finish our journey on Friday, May 20. Arriving into Tennessee via Interstate 24, Clarksville, Tennessee, is just a few miles across the Kentucky state line. We reached our Clarksville destination during the late afternoon. There are four major exits off of Interstate 24 into Clarksville, Tennessee. We had reservations at a Hilton Garden Inn just off of Exit 4 so that's the exit we took. Clarksville, Tennessee, is one of the fastest growing cities in the state, providing excellent amenities for its residents. The infrastructure, however, hasn't kept pace with the growth and some roads can be hazardous to navigate. The street off Exit 4 is one of the main streets (Wilma Rudolph Boulevard) in Clarksville. From this exit, you can access numerous restaurants, hotels, gas stations, retail stores, and just about any type of other business you may need. After living in the area for a while, we realized that traveling east on Interstate 24, turning left off of Exit 4 is the most difficult of all choices. There wasn't a traffic light there at that time and while turning left in addition to regular traffic you're at the mercy of oncoming traffic needing to access Interstate 24. Realizing the situation, I got on the walkie-talkie with Sandie and asked her to stay on my tail thorough the intersection when I made the turn. We made the turn without incident but at least one motorist was unhappy with Sandie's maneuver and honked his horn at her. That was Sandie's welcome to Clarksville!

The Hilton Garden Inn we were staying at was less than a half-mile from this turn. We drove to our destination pleased overall with our trip and checked into the hotel, anxious to get to our closing the following day. These were heartening times for Sandie and me. We were going into another chapter of our lives together, and after over-twenty years of marriage/knowing each other, we were purchasing our first home together. Sandie had her own condo in the Chicago area before marrying me and moving into the townhouse that I had owned. Our Clarksville, Tennessee, home in the Tylertown subdivision was one that after eight years of looking we both decided was the right home/location for us.

The closing of our 3816 Benjamin Drive home in Clarksville was purposely scheduled for the afternoon of May 20th. We did this to provide a little time cushion in the event we ran into any difficulties between our Illinois closing and traveling down to Tennessee. Beginning the drive safely down the same day of our Illinois closing and stopping in Mount Vernon, Illinois allowed us to relax for a night and gather ourselves the next morning before closing on our dream house. Fay Whitmer from Honeycutt Realtors worked with us on each of our Clarksville excursions and was our realtor of record. Franklin American Mortgage provided our mortgage and Bankers Title & Escrow handled the actual closing. The closing went off without incident as Sandie and I proudly accepted keys to our retirement residence at 3816 Benjamin Drive, which I designated as "Sandie & Stephen's Love Nest".

The rest of May and into June, we were busy settling into our new home. It had been over twenty years since my last move and I'd forgotten the myriad of details involved on the other end of a move. It took a few days for our mover to arrive with our furniture and household goods. The electricity, Internet, water, and gas utilities had all to be arranged and put in our name. We also shopped for lawn service, trash pickup, and security companies. Of course, we also had to locate new doctors, dentists, insurance providers, etc. Additionally, we planned on and purchased new furniture for the master bedroom, living room, and kitchen. We also purchased a clothes washer and dryer. While all of this was going on, we had to contact our credit card companies and other businesses to have them change our address from Vernon Hills, Illinois, to Clarksville, Tennessee. The first couple of weeks in our new home were a revolving door with movers, setups, and deliveries being made.

With over 15,000 square feet of lawn and annual hot/dry Tennessee summers, I wanted an irrigation system to assist with law maintenance. Realizing it wouldn't be an inexpensive venture, I decided to obtain three bids for the project. As the bids came in, the importance of shopping around before committing on a major expenditure became evident. The bids ran from slightly over $4,000 to $6,600! We ended up using the same company mowing our lawn for installation of the irrigation system. The owner of that company was, for all practical purposes, a one-man operation although he did have help to install the system. We were required to obtain a separate meter for our irrigation system and pay a different rate for that water. Interesting that each month we receive two water bills: one for household water and the other for irrigation.

After purchasing the needed furniture and appliances, and finishing the irrigation project, we embarked on other improvement projects. We had new counter tops installed in the kitchen, the kitchen cabinets repainted, a tile splash guard installed in the kitchen, storage space added to our attic, and a roof installed over our backyard deck.

That August, we traveled back up to Chicago to visit Olivia, Julie, and their families. I followed up on a doctor appointment with my urologist as well as seeing my Chicago dentist for a final visit. Sandie took advantage of the Chicago visit to have breakfast with an old friend of hers. We rented a car for the trip, wanting to minimize mileage on our two vehicles to max-imize their longevity.

A few months following our Clarksville, Tennessee move my daugh-ter Janette relocated there. Janette sold her place outside Seaside, Oregon, and made the move. Before finding her eventual Clarksville home, Janette lived with us in the bonus room of our home. She ended up buying a place eight minutes away from us in August of 2016. It's an absolute delight hav-ing Janette located in the same city. I'd like to think that Sandie and my Clarksville, Tennessee, pioneering efforts was an aid in Janette meeting her move challenges.

Having been in our new Clarksville home for several months, we embarked on our first travel excursion. Our trip goal was to visit my hotel mentor, Jim Reed, in San Diego and drive from there all the way back to Clarksville visiting relatives and sites along the way. Sandie and I flew from Nashville to San Diego and rented a car for our approximate 3,500-mile trip back (counting planned detours along the way) to our new home in Clarksville.

We began our road trip by driving down to La Jolla after flying into San Diego to meet Jim Reed for lunch. We met at Duke's in La Jolla and enjoyed a panoramic ocean view while catching up and discussing old times. Having known each other for fifty-one years and he being the god-father of my oldest son Shawn, we had a lot to get caught up on. Jim looked great but mentioned that he had a couple of instances where he had fallen for no apparent reason. His doctors at the time couldn't place a cause to this although months later he was diagnosed with Parkinson's.

Our first planned stop after California was the Grand Canyon in Arizona. We stayed at a charming bed and breakfast in Valle, Arizona, for two nights. Called The Dumplin Patch, this hotel was a scant thirty minutes from the Grand Canyon. In addition to the tremendous breakfast, it adver-tised a snack bar, free Wi-Fi, cable TV, and private entrances. The Wi-Fi was sketchy at best, causing me to drive twenty minutes each morning to a McDonald's to take advantage of their free Wi-Fi. The one morning we were able to take advantage of the breakfast, it was outstanding. There literally was enough food to feed twenty guests with only Sandie and myself there that particular morning.

We had been to the Grand Canyon once before on a quickie tour that was tacked onto the end of one of my Las Vegas tradeshows. The indescribable Grand Canyon is 277 miles long, up to 18 miles wide, and reaches a depth of 6,093 feet! The Colorado River, which flows through the canyon, touches seven states, but the Grand Canyon National Park is within the Arizona state borders. It's truly a world wonder and has to be seen to be appreciated.

From the Grand Canyon, we drove to Las Vegas. My Konawaena High School class of 1964 was having a reunion there at the California Hotel. Due to my previous work schedule, it was difficult for me to attend previous reunions. Our class rotated the reunion between Kona, Hawaii, and Las Vegas, Nevada. Many of our classmates had relocated to the mainland and the thinking was that Las Vegas would not only be a draw but a central meeting spot. Sandie and I joined them for a luncheon and it was great seeing everyone in attendance.

We were less than a month away from the 2016 Presidential election. Donald Trump was running as the Republican candidate against Hillary Clinton, the Democrat candidate. This would be the beginning of true bi-party polarization in America. My political leaning has always been a bit to the right preferring the overall conservative policies to the liberal ones. However, I've always prided myself in voting for whom I consider the best person to represent our county, state, nation regardless of party affiliation.

Truth be told, I, in clear conscience, couldn't vote for either Trump or Clinton and voted for Gary Johnson instead. He was the Libertarian Party nominee for the 2016 election. Johnson was the Governor of New Mexico, with a track record that included job growth, cutting taxes, and vetoing a large number of spending bills that were not in the financial interest of the state of New Mexico. Guess I was hoping for a miracle, which of course didn't happen in our strict two-party system here in the United States.

At any rate, while in Las Vegas, we decided to drop into the new Vegas Trump Hotel out of curiosity more than anything else. As fate would have it, Trump was flying into Las Vegas on that same day for a debate with Hillary Clinton. Sandie and I walked through the hotel lobby and decided to check out the hotel's gift shop. We both had a big laugh over the Trump apparel sold in the gift shop. Looking over the red MAGA "Make America Great Again" hats, we discovered they were made in China! In November, Sandie and I were both shocked when we learned that the reality TV host actually won the election by receiving seventy-seven more electoral votes than Clinton did although he lost the popular vote count by nearly 3 million voters!

After Las Vegas, we began our 1,225-mile journey to Kerrville, Texas, to visit with my cousin Mary Lou and her husband Bill. We ventured through New Mexico, stopping in Las Cruces along the way. Little did we know that we were in for a real treat! The town of Las Cruces was having their seventh annual "Zombie Walk" the evening we were there. The event is billed as *The Living Dead Take over Downtown*. Prizes are awarded for those deemed "Most Disgusting," "Most Original," and "Best Couple or Group." There are only two rules for zombies: "Zombie attire is mandatory to be included in the walk, and all participants are asked to remain in character, communicating only in a manner consistent with zombie behavior (i.e., grunts, groans, moans, and the occasional slurred call for brains). The event included undead brides, protruding intestines, lots of fake blood, and even baby zombies. To cap it all off, the event also included food booths, craft items, and a fantastic rendition of Michael Jackson's *Thriller* dance by the Las Cruces High School Dancers.

Las Cruces, New Mexico, was 535 miles from my cousin, Mary Lou, and Bill's place. You don't get a true feel for the size of Texas until you start driving through it. We'd drive hundreds of miles barely seeing any civilization. What amazed me was the number of roadways in Texas, with an eighty-mile-an-hour speed limit. We arrived safely at our destination that Sunday evening, October 23, 2016. Greeted by Bill and Mary Lou, we settled in for a lovely two-day visit with our gracious hosts. After visiting with Mary Lou and Bill and enjoying their friendship, we continued our journey with our next scheduled stop being Oklahoma City, Oklahoma.

We arrived at our Oklahoma City destination some 7 hours and 450 miles later. This stop was simply a pause and refresh event before heading out the next morning for Highland, Illinois. Sandie's sister Janice and her brother-in-law live in Highland, which is about thirty miles across the state line of Missouri in the direction, we were traveling. This leg of our journey was 530 miles and took us around eight hours. This three-day stop allowed us not only to rest up but also to visit Janice and Bruce. Our home is approximately 250 miles from Highland, which we made in four hours. None worse for the wear, we arrived back to our Clarksville home fifteen days following our departure.

Our first post-retirement trip was an overwhelming success. We drove through nine states, visited with classmates, dear friends, and relatives who we rarely see. Hotel arrangements were made in advance and we were able to follow the set agenda at each stop without difficulty. The main travel lesson I learned from the trip was to avoid one-way auto rentals in the future. We rented through Alamo and paid a significant fee for not returning the vehicle to its rental origin.

One of my first indelible hotel memories occurred at the Opryland Hotel in Nashville. In my earlier trade show management years, I was with Bank Administration Institute. One of the trade shows that I'd managed was booked into this property as its Ryman Exhibit Hall was 260,000 square feet. I was surprised to learn that the Opryland Hotel is the largest non-casino hotel in the continental U.S with 2,888 rooms and 9 acres of indoor gardens. The size of the exhibit hall along with the hotel size provided an attractive all-inclusive, under-one-roof package. Being impressed with this property, I brought my family back to experience it for themselves. Shawn and Scott had been overwhelmed with the hotel's enormity and thoroughly enjoyed the experience. They marveled at the cascading waterfalls, a dancing water light show, and nine acres of lush gardens providing an outdoor experience all enclosed in a climate-controlled environment.

Our new Clarksville home was a scant fifty-one miles from this Nashville landmark. The year 2016 marked the hotel's thirty-third annual "A Country Christmas at Opryland" and we attended. Through hotel points, I was able to secure a room for two nights and we reveled in the Christmas atmosphere. Billed as one of the most "Christmassy destinations in the country," the resort offered special attractions like a gingerbread decorating corner, and an "Ice" exhibit that uses over two million pounds of ice, hand-carved by Chinese artisans, to depict scenes from a different Christmas classic each year. The main draw for us was the more than three million holiday lights put up inside and outdoors of the property. Their Christmas lights are so extensive they have to begin their installation in July of each year! The hotel's interior decorations are spectacular, too, with 15,000 poinsettias, 15 miles of green garland and 10 miles of hand-tied red ribbon.

While there, we took in some of the other hotel activities. The hotel's Delta Atrium held water and light shows at 6 pm, 7 pm, 8 pm and 9 pm, with choreographed music, water, and projections on a giant LED light curtain suspended above the Bellagio-like fountain inside the 4.5-acre indoor garden. The shows are "Brightest Light" and "Sounds of Christmas." We also took in the outdoor Nativity display on the beautifully lit Magnolia Lawn that featured fifty-five life-size figurines. The Nativity display included a recorded version of the Christmas story broadcast. Alongside the Nativity scene, horses and carriages transported passengers along the hotel's driveway.

An added unexpected bonus was the WSM Radio Live broadcast. It broadcasts a full-time country music format at 650 kHz and is known primarily as the home of *The Grand Ole Opry*, the world's longest running radio program. The WSM-650 AM radio studio, which broadcasts live from the hotel all day every day, is located off the Magnolia lobby. The *Nashville Today* show is also broadcasted live from there.

Sandie's oldest daughter, Olivia, and her family visited us in our new Clarksville home in the first week of February in 2017. It was their first exposure to our new locale. It was a pleasure having her, Cesar, CJ, and Emily with us. We took them to Nashville while they were in town and visited the Adventure Science Center. It's an independent, not-for-profit science and technology center dedicated to delivering innovative, dynamic learning experiences. The center is perched atop a hill with spectacular views of the city featuring 44,000 square foot of space with more than 175 hands-on exhibits focused on biology, astronomy, physics, earth science, energy, weather, sound, and space and is home to state-of-the-art Sudekum Planetarium. Serving more than 300,000 people annually, it was overflowing with visitors the day we went.

Later that month, Sandie and I decided to take advantage of an attraction in Bowling Green, Kentucky, located just a little over an hour northeast of us. The Historic Rail Park and Train Museum—formerly the Louisville and Nashville Railroad Station in Bowling Green, Kentucky— is located in the historic railroad station. The building was placed on the National Register of Historic Places in December 1979. Located on a major north–south corridor between two major cities, Bowling Green has a long history tied to the evolution of transportation in Kentucky; from steamboats traveling River Barren to the railroad, and eventually the current interstate systems. The current L&N Depot was built in 1925 to replace an older station. At one time, over twenty trains per day departed the current site, providing a hub for Bowling Green's economic foundation and exposure to travelers between Louisville, KY, and Nashville, TN. Its history was fascinating and touring the actual train cars were like actually stepping back in time.

In March 2017, my older son Shawn and I met in Phoenix, Arizona, to take in some major league spring-training baseball games. I got us a couple of rooms at the Hyatt Place Hotel in Scottsdale. The first game we took in was the Arizona Diamondbacks versus the Chicago White Sox at the beautiful Camelback Ranch Stadium in Glendale, Arizona. The White Sox won the contest 4–2. The next day, we drove over to the Peoria Sports Complex in Peoria. The San Diego Padres and the Seattle Mariners share this spring training stadium. There was plenty of action in this game as the Seattle Mariners scored three runs in the bottom of the ninth inning to edge out the Chicago Cubs 11–10.

We continued our baseball extravaganza by taking in a game on the 11th of March at Salt River Fields at Talking Stick also located in Scottsdale. This facility is shared by the hometown favorites, the Arizona Diamondbacks and the Colorado Rockies. The local favorites didn't disappoint as the Diamondbacks whipped the San Francisco Giants 5–1.

On our last full day in the valley of the sun, Shawn and I took in two games. We began the day witnessing the Los Angeles Dodgers take on the Kansas City Royals at Surprise Stadium in Surprise, Arizona. The Texas Rangers and the Kansas City Royals share surprise Stadium. The Dodgers were thumped in this contest 19–7. A common occurrence in spring training games is for teams to "split" their squads, allowing them to view more prospects and to play more than one game in a day. Such was the case on this March 12, 2017 day as during the evening we ventured back to Glendale, Arizona, to see my two favorite teams, the Los Angeles Dodgers and the Chicago White Sox, engage in an evening affair. It turned out to be another lop-sided game with the White Sox prevailing 15–5.

While you naturally cheer on your favorite team during spring training games, the organization's objective is to play as many minor-league prospects as possible to determine who may contribute on the major-league level. Established veteran players make game appearances to get into playing shape for the season and you'll also see major league team managers, general managers, and owners at these games. My main acquired treasure is the time spent with Shawn and the memories created from these experiences.

On April 4, 2017, Sandie and I headed out on a two-week road trip that would take us through eight states and even venturing into Canada for a journey that would consume over 3,000 driven miles. The highlight of the trip was a stop at Niagara Falls to celebrate our fifteenth wedding anniversary. Our first stop on this trip was in Chicago, where we visited with three of our five kids. Janette was working in Chicago at the time so we stayed with her in a downtown condo rented for her by the movie company producing the project she was working on. Neither Shawn nor Scott was in Chicago at that time, but both of Sandie's daughters were established there with their families, providing visitation opportunities to both families.

On Sunday, April 9, we headed out for Toledo, Ohio, stopping in Bangor, Michigan, along the way. Sandie's dad's significant other Pat lived there and we stopped in to visit with her and take her to lunch. The following day, we traveled to Pittsburgh, Pennsylvania. After a four-hour drive, we arrived to settle into our room at a Springhill Suites hotel located just across the street from PNC Park home to the Pittsburgh Pirates. PNC Park opened during the 2001 MLB season just east of its predecessor along the Allegheny River with a beautiful view of the Downtown Pittsburgh skyline. It was most gratifying being able to walk to the game without the worry of getting in and out of a parking lot close to the stadium. The Pirates played the Cincinnati Reds in an early regular season game. We usually root for the home team while taking in games, but unfortunately the Pirates succumbed to the Reds that evening 7–1.

The next stop on our itinerary was Cooperstown, New York, home of the National Baseball Hall of Fame. This was an absolute thrill for me being an avid baseball fan. Seeking a way to celebrate and protect baseball's history, Stephen Clark, a Cooperstown philanthropist convinced National League president Ford Frick to support the establishment of a Baseball hall of Fame. Established in 1936 the inaugural Hall of Fame class included Ty Cobb, Walter Johnson, Christy Mathewson, Babe Ruth, and Honus Wagner. The Hall of Fame's collection contains more than 40,000 three-dimensional artifacts including bats, balls, gloves, and uniforms donated by individuals wanting to preserve the game's legacy. The Museum's artifacts grow by about 400 each year. The Hall of Fame is made up of the museum, where baseball memorabilia is on display, the actual Hall of Fame, where plaques of over 300 inductees are displayed, and a library.

Niagara Falls was about 250 miles from Cooperstown, New York. Following that drive, we settled into a spectacular room at the Embassy Suites on the Canadian side of the US–Canada border. The hotel was aware of our "special occasion" and placed us in a room with a dynamic view of the famous Niagara Falls. The view was enhanced by floor to ceiling glass windows and the accommodations even included a massage chair that you could relax in while enjoying the view!

Niagara Falls was formed when glaciers receded at the end of the last ice age, and water from the newly formed Great Lakes carved a path through the Niagara Escarpment en-route to the Atlantic Ocean. Niagara Falls is famed both for its beauty and as a valuable source of hydroelectric power. Niagara Falls is a group of three waterfalls at the southern end of Niagara Gorge, between the Canadian province of Ontario and the US state of New York. The largest is Horseshoe Falls (the best view from our room), also known as Canadian Falls, which straddles the international border between Canada and the United States.

The smaller American Falls and Bridal Veil Falls lie entirely within the United States. Bridal Veil Falls are separated from Horseshoe Falls by Goat Island and from American Falls by Luna Island. Located on River Niagara, which drains Lake Erie into Lake Ontario, the combined falls have the highest flow rate of any waterfall in North America, which has a vertical drop of more than 160 feet. During peak daytime tourist hours, more than six million cubic feet of water goes over the crest of the falls every minute. Horseshoe Falls is the most powerful waterfall in North America, as measured by flow rate.

What makes Niagara Falls so impressive is the amount of water flowing over it. Most of the tallest falls in the world have very little water flowing over them. It's the combination of height and volume that makes Niagara Falls so breathtaking.

- More than 6 million cubic feet of water go over the crest line of the falls every minute during peak daytime tourist hours.

- The Canadian Horseshoe Falls drops an average of 188 feet into the Lower Niagara river.

- The crest line of the Canadian Horseshoe Falls is approximately 2,200 feet wide. The plunge pool beneath the falls is 100 feet deep.

- The height of the American Falls ranges between 70–110 feet. This measurement is taken from the top of the falls to the top of the rock pile at the base. The height of the falls from the top of the falls to the river is 188 feet. The crest line of the American Falls is approximately 850 feet wide.

The rapids above the falls reach a maximum speed of twenty-five mph, with the fastest speeds occurring at the falls themselves (recorded up to sixty-eight mph.) The water through the Whirlpool Rapids below the falls reaches thirty mph.

While staying at the Embassy Suites Niagara Falls, we treated ourselves to a special anniversary dinner at the Skylon Tower revolving restaurant. Designated as the most famous Niagara Falls restaurant, The Skylon Tower provides views 775 feet above the falls! As an added feature, admission to the Ride-to-the-Top and Observation Decks attractions were included for dining patrons. The restaurant silently rotates 360 degrees every hour, giving us a constantly changing vantage point. It is estimated that more than 3,000 square miles of scenery are viewable from the dining room. It was a spectacular view of Niagara Falls but not as breathtaking as the view from our hotel room.

Of course, our Niagara Falls visit wouldn't have been complete without a behind-the-scenes tour. Our tour took us below the falls onto a landing that when we walked out onto it, we were directly behind the powerful water falls. Included with our ticket was a historical Niagara Falls movie setting the stage for what we would be witnessing!

We took a different route back to Clarksville overnighting first in Wilmington, Delaware, following a near seven-hour drive. Our Westin hotel was just a short walk to the Christina River, providing a relaxing environment prior to a delicious Thai dinner we enjoyed that evening. The next morning, we pointed toward the last designated stop before returning home, Lynchburg, Virginia.

After over-300 miles, we arrived in Appomattox County, Virginia. Our stop in this lovely area of the country was to visit the site where Robert E. Lee surrendered to Ulysses S. Grant to end the Civil War. The signing of the surrender document occurred in the parlor of the house owned by Wilmer McLean on the afternoon of April 9, 1865. On April 12, a formal ceremony of parade and the stacking of arms led by Southern Major Gen. John B. Gordon to Federal Brig. General Joshua Chamberlain of Maine marked the disbandment of the Army of Northern Virginia with the parole of its nearly 28,000 remaining officers and men, free to return home without their major weapons but enabling men to take their horses and officers to retain their side arms (swords and pistols), and effectively ending the war in Virginia. This event triggered a series of subsequent surrenders across the South, in North Carolina, Alabama, and finally Shreveport, Louisiana, for the Trans-Mississippi Theater in the West by June, signaling the end of the four-year-long Civil War.

The site itself was mesmerizing. Closing your eyes, you could almost picture General Robert E. Lee riding into the yard, dismounting from Traveler, his white horse, and quietly walking into the McLean house to surrender his command. Evidence of this magnanimous incident was a plaque located just off the gravel road that reads, "From this spot was fired the last shot from the artillery of the army of northern Virginia, on the morning of April 9th, 1865." Adding to the event's authenticity were the actual pens used to sign the surrender document along with other memorabilia from this historic event in the museum. This part of the United States is beautiful with its rolling hills, green grass, and numerous trees. It's difficult to comprehend that only 152 years earlier, over 620,000 Americans died fighting one another in this internal conflict.

May of 2017 included a sad occasion. My cousin, Mary Ann Graham (Evans) passed away. Mary Ann was born on April 7, 1948 and passed away on May 1, 2017. Her mother Helen (my aunt) and my mother were the best of friends. My brother Floyd and I spent many days with Mary Ann and her brother Johnny due to the closeness of our respective families. Her constant energetic engaging smile is how I remember her. I attended her funeral on May 8 at the Simplicity Funeral Home in Indianapolis and learned of the kindness she displayed through her church. It was a solemn occasion but one where it was evident of the love for her by everyone in attendance.

Living as close to Nashville as we do allows us to take advantage of the entertainment scene in the "Music City." One of the prime entertainment venues in Nashville is the Grand Ole Opry. We made it to this exciting venue in both May and July of 2017. A May 30 performance was headlined by Alison Krauss who's one of my favorite singers. Also performing that night were Carly Pearce, Darius Rucker, Amanda Shires, and John Prine.

Sandie and I love the entertainment format of the Grand Ole Opry. They have up to eight performances by various artists singing two to three songs each. The format provides a nice variety while allowing attendees to witness numerous performers. We went back on July 18 as a birthday gift from my daughter Janette. That evening I saw another of my favorites, Dierks Bentley! Also preforming that night were Vince Gill, Martina McBride, Tracy Lawrence, Darius Rucker, and Diamond Rio.

Late in June of 2017 we struck out on a mini southern road-trip into Alabama, Mississippi, and Arkansas. Our first stop along this route was in Montgomery, Alabama. We were pleasantly surprised with the history and attractiveness of the city. While in Montgomery, we visited the First White House of the Confederacy, the Alabama State Capitol, the Civil Rights Memorial Center, and the Dexter Avenue King Memorial Baptist Church.

The First White House of the Confederacy was designated the "Executive Residence" by the provisional federal congress on February 21, 1861. President Jefferson Davis and his family lived there until the confederate capitol moved to Richmond, Virginia, in the summer of 1861. Many personal items of President and Mrs. Davis were in the house as well as authentic furnishings of the period. It is a Confederate house museum that tells three stories:

1. What happened during the spring of 1861 when a government was formed from few resources except cotton and courage.

2. The story of Jefferson Davis, a renowned American patriot long before The War, and his family.

3. The story of the preservation of the House.

It was an engrossing experience, producing the desire to see the Richmond, Virginia White House of the Confederacy.

The Alabama State Capitol is a truly majestic structure. Architecturally, the building is Greek Revival in style with some Beaux-Arts influences. The central core of the building, as well as the east wing to the rear of the structure, is three-stories over a below-grade basement. The north and south wings are two-stories over a raised basement. Listed on the National Register of Historic Places as the First Confederate Capitol, it's the state capitol building for Alabama located on Capitol Hill, originally Goat Hill, in Montgomery, which was declared a National Historic Landmark on December 19, 1960. Alabama has had five political capitols during its history. The current capitol building temporarily served as the Confederate Capitol while Montgomery served as the first political capital of the Confederate States of America in 1861, before being moved to Richmond, Virginia. Meeting in the Senate Chamber, the Provisional Constitution of the Confederate States was drawn up by the Montgomery Convention on February 4, 1861.

The Confederacy began in the senate chamber when delegates from southern states voted to establish a new nation in February 1861. A brass star on the west portico marks the location where Jefferson Davis stood to be inaugurated as the first and only president of the Confederacy.

A little more than a century later in the spring of 1965 the Selma to Montgomery March for voting rights culminated at the capitol steps. Dr. Martin Luther King, Jr. made one of his greatest speeches to an estimated 25,000 people there. U.S. Civil Rights Trail: The Alabama State Capitol is now recognized as an official destination on the trail along with more than 100 locations across 14 states.

The Civil Rights Memorial in Montgomery is dedicated to the forty-one people who were killed in the struggle for the equal and integrated treatment of all people, regardless of race, during the 1954–1968 civil rights movement in the United States. The memorial is sponsored by the Southern Poverty Law Center. Dr. Martin Luther King Jr's paraphrase of Amos 5:24 chiseled into the black granite of the Civil Rights Memorial is a moving tribute to all who died in the civil rights struggle: "… Until justice rolls down like waters and righteousness like a mighty stream." The museum portion of the memorial outlines and documents the civil rights movement between 1954 and 1968.

The Dexter Avenue King Memorial Baptist Church in Montgomery is one of the most recognized churches in the world, known primarily for its years in the forefront of the civil rights movement led by then-pastor Martin Luther King Jr. It was designated a national historic landmark in 1974, and the city of Montgomery added the church to its list of historic sites in 1976. It was as if Sandie and I stepped back into history when we visited the Dexter Avenue King Memorial Baptist while in Montgomery. The preserved Dexter Avenue King Memorial Baptist Church appeared as it did when Dr. Martin Luther King Jr. served there as pastor, from 1954 to 1960.

We departed Montgomery for Vicksburg, Mississippi, and traveled the reverse route used by civil right activists between Selma and Montgomery, Alabama. There were markers along the way culminating at the Edmund Pettus Bridge in Selma where large life-like bronze plaques memorialize leaders of the march. Perhaps a plaque situated at the end of the march in Montgomery best describes the march: "The Selma to Montgomery march ended here on March 25, 1965, when 25,000 civil rights marchers arrived at the Alabama State Capitol to demand the right to vote for African Americans. Dr. Martin Luther King Jr. and other civil rights leaders addressed the marchers and the nation, culminating a series of demonstrations that began in Selma on March 7—"Bloody Sunday"—when around 600 peaceful protesters were savagely beaten by lawmen as they tried to cross the Edmund Pettis Bridge.

Sandie and I toured the Vicksburg National Park on the first of July. The May 18–July 4, 1863 siege of Vicksburg was the final major military action in the Vicksburg campaign of the American Civil War. The Battle of Vicksburg, Mississippi, also called the Siege of Vicksburg, was the culmination of a long land and naval campaign by Union forces to capture a key strategic position during the American Civil War. President Abraham Lincoln recognized the significance of the town situated on a 200-foot bluff above the Mississippi River. He said, "Vicksburg is the key, the war can never be brought to a close until that key is in our pocket." Capturing Vicksburg would severe the Trans-Mississippi Confederacy from that east of the Mississippi River and opened the river to Northern traffic along its entire length. To Confederate President Jefferson Davis, Vicksburg was the "nail head that holds the South's two halves together."

Vicksburg was the last major Confederate stronghold on the Mississippi River; therefore, capturing it seriously crippled the Confederacy's war effort. It cut off the Trans-Mississippi department (containing the states of Arkansas, Texas, and part of Louisiana) from the rest of the Confederate States, effectively splitting the Confederacy in two for the duration of the war. When two major assaults against the Confederate fortifications were repulsed with heavy casualties, Grant decided to besiege the city, beginning on May 25. After holding out for more than forty days, with their supplies nearly gone, the garrison surrendered on July 4. This action, combined with the surrender of Port Hudson to Major Gen. Nathaniel P. Banks on July 9, yielded command of the Mississippi River to the Union forces, who would hold it for the rest of the Civil War.

The Confederate Vicksburg surrender on July 4 is sometimes considered, when combined with Gen. Robert E. Lee's defeat at Gettysburg by Major Gen. George Meade the previous day, the turning point of the war. Vicksburg was protected by geography, with the Mississippi creating a wide, wet, swampy valley with clear edges and higher dry grounds meeting the swamp. General Grant, whose objective was to capture Vicksburg, was facing a major challenge of getting his army to the dry ground. As was the case in numerous other civil war battles, the Vicksburg campaign was costly for both sides. The Union had 4,800 casualties while the Confederacy had 3,300 casualties with nearly 30,000 soldiers captured!

For Sandie and me, Vicksburg was a memorable experience. State Monuments were strategically placed throughout the battleground signifying each state's participation in this deciding Civil War battle. These monuments ranged from plain to downright ostentatious. The most flamboyant was from the state of Illinois. It was patterned from the design of the Roman Pantheon; the base and stairway are made of granite from Stone Mountain, Georgia, and the upper section is made of marble from north Georgia. Sitting on a hill, this fabulous structure can be seen shortly after you enter the park. Forty-seven steps make up the staircase, symbolizing the forty-seven days of the Vicksburg siege. Opulent on the outside, it gets even better on the inside—it is the only monument in the park that you can go inside. Sixty bronze tablets containing the names of every Illinois soldier at Vicksburg line the inner walls. The memorial was dedicated in October of 1906. Illinois must have been doing quite well then, as this behemoth cost nearly $200,000. Most of the other memorials in the park cost less than $20,000.

On July 3, we navigated toward Little Rock, Arkansas. Our visit objective there was to see the William J. Clinton Library & Museum. While employed at IPC, I had the privilege to meet the then President Bill Clinton while working an event in Washington, DC. The Clinton Library and Museum in Little Rock was a captivating experience. Through the permanent and rotating exhibits, one could sense what life in the White House was all about. From visualizing the timeline exhibit through seeing actual table settings for state events, to experiencing the President's daily calendar one couldn't help but to be in a sense of awe. We were also reminded of Clinton's significant contribution to the nation's economy.

When he took office following the 1992 election, the United States faced rising interest rates and large government deficits. He proposed a new three-part economic system composed of balancing the federal budget for the first time in a generation, making investments in technology, and opening new markets to products from the United States. *The country saw its largest peacetime economic expansion in history and was met with record surpluses and higher income for all economic classes.* In addition to objects and archival records, the story of this economic advancement was told with a video of President Clinton outlining his plan, and a timeline of the economic growth the country experienced.

In July of 2017, Sandie's youngest daughter, Julie and her family visited us in Clarksville. Having lived in Clarksville for a little more than a year at that point, we were excited to show our new home off to family. Knowing that Julie was a country music fan, we decided to treat them to a tour of the Country Music Hall of Fame in Nashville. The Museum has an extensive, permanent objects collection. This collection includes more than eight hundred stage costumes, over six hundred instruments, and hundreds of other objects—from microphones to automobiles—documenting the history of country music. Honoring classic and current artists, the Museum exhibits everything from Hank Williams' cherished Martin guitar to Elvis Presley's custom Cadillac limousine, to outfits and instruments from the likes of Alison Krauss and Carrie Underwood, to a showcase of today's top artists. Being an avid fan, Julie was quite pleased to view a special Tim McGraw/Faith Hill exhibit.

For young Matt's entertainment, we played a lot of cards and board games. We also went to a new family entertainment facility in downtown Clarksville called the City Forum. They had a little bit of everything from bowling to miniature golf to go-carts to arcade games. We dabbled in a couple of activities but particularly enjoyed a round of miniature golf together. We thoroughly enjoyed their six-day visit.

We had a relatively busy August 2017. The first Sunday of the month we drove up to Indianapolis to attend the annual Evans Family Reunion. While the turnout was adequate, the attendance had been dropping over the years due somewhat to a lack of interest by the generation below my age group. It's a potluck affair but the reunion committee is responsible for the pavilion rental, chicken, and drinks. For fund raising, donations are requested and there's usually a fund-raising activity at the reunion. They've had bake sales, auctions, 50/50 ticket sales, and drawings. To try and raise interest and additional funding, we've donated a $100 Kroger gift card to the last couple of events we've made. I'm hoping for the interest to be rekindled so the Evans Family Reunion won't become an ancient memory.

The trip to the Evans Family Reunion included a visit up to Chicago to visit the kids and grandkids. We try to visit them once or twice a year. With Indianapolis being conveniently located south of Chicago, we stop in there to visit with family either on the way up or on the way back from the Windy City. The Indianapolis portion of this trip, which included the Evans Family Reunion, was significant as Sandie developed appendicitis. We were going to have dinner with a friend of mine that I hadn't seen in over fifty years, Steve Verhines, the Tuesday after the reunion. However, the night before, Sandie fell sick and, after medication failed to work, we visited an urgent care center that directed us to the emergency room of nearby Franciscan Hospital for analysis. The doctors there determined that Sandie had appendicitis and removed her appendix. We enjoy adventures during our travels but this was an adventure of a different type!

Cleared by her doctors for travel, on the way back from Indianapolis we drove to Sandie's sister's place in Highland, Illinois, and visited with them for a few days. It's generally a relaxing time where we enjoy each other's company and play games after dinner. They live thirty miles from St. Louis but to that point had not attended a St. Louis Cardinal's baseball game. Thus, I decided to fix that and treated us to their August 10 game. St. Louis is an avid baseball town with an established rich history for America's favorite pastime. The Cardinals played their in-state rival that night, the Kansas City Royals. The home team Cardinals were going for their sixth consecutive win. It was a tight contest but a grand slam by the Cardinal's center fielder, Dexter Fowler, pretty much sealed an 8–6 victory for the redbirds.

August 21, 2017 was a monumental day for our new city, Clarksville, Tennessee. On that particular day, the once-in-a-lifetime solar eclipse was going to be fully visible for two and half minutes directly over our fair city. Tennessee tourism officials estimated that as many as 1.4 million visitors came to the state to view the spectacle. Sandie's sister Janice and her husband Bruce traveled to our new home to take advantage of the event.

Clarksville was in the eclipse's direct path providing the best viewing opportunities. Most every one of the county's 2,700 hotel rooms was booked and some required a minimum three-night stay. Homeowners rented out houses, rooms, and parking spaces on their lawns. The local Beachaven Winery sold plots for people to come and view the eclipse while drinking their wine and enjoying local food favorites. They even created a wine called "Blackout Blackberry" to sell as a collector's item. Nearby, Old Glory Distillery made "Solar Shine" moonshine to serve at their eclipse event while featuring live music, food trucks, and craft cocktails.

Nashville is a mere 50 miles from us and was the largest city within the entire eclipse's path and benefited tremendously by an estimated $20 million pumped into the local economy. Clarksville saw an estimated 200,000 visitors for the eclipse. It was truly a sight to behold. We experienced total darkness at approximately 1:30 pm in the afternoon!

The following month, we traveled 278 miles to Cincinnati, Ohio. The purpose of the trip was to experience a ballgame at the Great American Ballpark, home of the Cincinnati Reds. I purchased advance tickets to the game scheduled between the hometown and the Pittsburg Pirates. As an added treat, I secured accommodations at the Hilton Netherland Plaza Hotel.

During my Omni Hotel career, the Netherland Plaza was one of the chain's premiere properties. A French deco hotel masterpiece, it originally opened in 1931 and was quickly established as the city's landmark hotel. The historic hotel's mezzanine and lobby feature a half-acre of rare Brazilian rosewood, extensive use of German silver, and a stylized Egyptian décor. It was a treat staying there the weekend of September 15–17.

We arrived on Friday to relax and take in the sights as our game was scheduled for the next day. To our amazed astonishment, this particular weekend played host to the Oktoberfest Zinzinnati, an annual weekend festival in the city. Based on the original German Oktoberfest, it is billed as the largest Oktoberfest celebration in the United States! First held in 1976, it attracts an estimated 500,000 visitors every year in late September. The event took up several downtown city blocks and added tremendously to our weekend enjoyment.

Before the actual game on Saturday, we explored the downtown area and experienced the revered Cincinnati chili first hand. Both the Oktoberfest celebration and the Great American Ballpark were within walking distance from our hotel. The ballpark itself was beautiful, situated along the Mississippi River. We were treated to a home town victory as the Reds defeated the Pirates in a pitcher's duel 2–1.

In late October of 2017, Sandie and I ventured all the way to Argentina. Janette was working on an MGM production entitled *Operation Finale*, starring Ben Kingsley. Whenever we can, we enjoy visiting Janette on her movie sets as she's away from home for months at a time on projects. In addition to visiting Janette who we hadn't seen for several months, the trip also provided us with the opportunity to visit an area we had never been to but had heard so much about.

Operation Finale is a historical thriller based on the story of how a group of Israeli secret agents arrested notorious Nazi SS officer Adolf Eichmann—the man who masterminded the "Final Solution"—in Argentina. The Final Solution was a Nazi plan for the genocide of Jews during World War II. The "Final Solution to the Jewish question" was the official code name for the murder of all Jews within reach, which was not restricted to the European continent. The movie was filmed in Argentina to add to its authenticity. Eichmann was hardly alone among Nazis in finding refuge in South America after the fall of the Third Reich. According to a 2012 article in the *Daily Mail*, German prosecutors who examined secret files from Brazil and Chile discovered that as many as 9,000 Nazi officers and collaborators from other countries escaped from Europe to find sanctuary in South American countries. Brazil took in between 1,500 and 2,000 Nazi war criminals, while between 500 and 1,000 settled in Chile. According to the *Daily Mail* article, "…by far the largest number—as many as 5,000—relocated to Argentina."

Janette arranged for us to sit in on a filming session that took place in an auditorium set up as a court room. The scene being filmed was that of the prosecution confronting Eichmann on his crimes. It became apparent to me that actors work hard as the same scene was rehearsed many times as we watched. During this particular session, Ben Kingsley had no lines but his mannerisms and expressions said it all.

Argentina itself was phenomenal. We stayed in downtown Buenos Aires, a city of approximately 3,000,000 residents, with Janette in a nice apartment provided to her during her Argentina commitment. The city was modern, clean, and easy to walk. Its center is the Plaza de Mayo, lined with stately nineteenth-century buildings. It's a top tourist destination and is known for its preserved eclectic European architecture and rich cultural life. The residents were very friendly, and Sandie and I visited several areas of interest while we were there. One such attraction was the La Recoleta Cemetery, a cemetery located in the Recoleta neighborhood of the city. It contains the graves of notable people, including Eva Perón, presidents of Argentina, Nobel Prize winners, the founder of the Argentine Navy, and a granddaughter of Napoleon.

We were within walking distance of another Buenos Aires landmark, The Obelisco de Buenos Aires. The Obelisco de Buenos Aires is a national historic monument and icon of Buenos Aires. Located in the Plaza de la República in the intersection of avenues Corrientes and 9 de Julio, it was erected in 1936 to commemorate the quadricentennial of the first foundation of the city and stands 235 feet in height. While in Buenos Aires, we also visited the La Boca neighborhood. This was most satisfying. La Boca is a working-class area with a cluster of attractions near the Riachuelo River. Steakhouses and street artists surround Caminito, a narrow alley flanked by brightly painted zinc shacks that evoke the district's early immigrant days. La Bombonera is the home ground of the Boca Juniors soccer team. Modern art museum Fundación Proa has temporary exhibits and views of the old docks.

Another trip highlight was a one-day journey via ferry over to Uruguay. The population of this entire country is approximately 3,500,000 making it slightly more populated than the city of Buenos Aires. Uruguay is a South American country known for its verdant interior and beach-lined coast. The capital, Montevideo, revolves around Plaza Independencia, once home to a Spanish citadel. It leads to Ciudad Vieja (Old City), with art deco buildings, colonial homes and Mercado del Puerto, an old port market with many steakhouses. La Rambla, a waterfront promenade passes fish stalls, piers and parks.

For Thanksgiving 2017, we jaunted over to Highland, Illinois and spent it with Sandie's sister Janice and her husband Bruce. This was our second Thanksgiving since relocating to Tennessee. We stayed home for Christmas that year but continued our newly established tradition of staying a couple of nights at the Opryland Hotel in Nashville to view their beautiful Christmas displays. We went to the dinner show and were treated to the Diamond Rio group for entertainment.

Moved to Tennessee May 2016.

Sandie Grand Canyon 2016.

Buenos Aires Obelisk Monument.

Chapter 10 | 2018–2019

In early January 2018, we decided to take a one-week trip down to Biloxi, Mississippi. Biloxi is a Mississippi city on the Gulf of Mexico. While it's known for its casinos, we went down primarily to visit the Jefferson Davis Presidential Library and to relax in an ocean setting in January. Biloxi is approximately 570 miles from Clarksville, Tennessee. We thought we could spread the drive down and back over a couple of days while enjoying Biloxi for a quiet three days.

We headed out on the 10th of January and overnighted in Jackson, Mississippi. The Mississippi Civil Rights Museum is located in Jackson so we decided to visit it before departing for Biloxi. The museum shares the stories of a Mississippi movement that changed the nation. It promoted a greater understanding of the Mississippi Civil Rights Movement and its impact by highlighting the strength and sacrifices of its peoples. The museum featured the freedom struggle in eight interactive galleries that showed the systematic oppression of black Mississippians and their fight for equality that transformed Mississippi and the nation. Seven of the galleries encircled a central space called "This Little Light of Mine." There, a dramatic sculpture glows brighter and the music of the Movement swells as visitors gather.

For dinner that night, we stumbled across an out-of-the-way restaurant in Jackson called "The Iron Horse Grill." We learned that the restaurant had mysteriously burned down twice and had been abandoned since 1999. Well, it's back in fine fashion, serving delicious southern-style pub fare. Live blues-style entertainment treated us on the night we were there.

As a bonus, we discovered a museum within the facility that we toured after dinner. It was called "The Mississippi Music Experience" designed to tell the story of Mississippi, the birthplace of America's music. We progressed through a timeline starting in the 1800s, running to the current music scene.

The next day, we were off to the destination of our trip, Biloxi. We stayed at the Hyatt Place Biloxi located on the main Biloxi street, Beach Boulevard. We were given a room on the top floor that provided an outstanding ocean view. While it was too cool to swim in the Gulf of Mexico, we couldn't resist walking on the pristine sandy beach. For dinner that first evening, we discovered an on-beach restaurant called Shaggy's. Described as a fun, beach, laid-back restaurant, its menu was seafood-oriented but creative and fun. It was the type of place that you just had to have an alcoholic beverage to go with your meal. With the sign "Save water, drink beer" just above us it was appropriate to enjoy a cold, draft beer!

The next day, we journeyed over to the Beau Rivage resort to take in the theatrical showing of the production Riverdance. The show consisted mainly of traditional Irish music and dance. It originated as an interval performance act during the 1994 Eurovision Song Contest and was quite entertaining.

One of our leading aspirations for this trip was to visit the Jefferson Davis home and Library at the Beauvoir estate. Located off the main drag just a couple of miles from our hotel, it did not disappoint us. The Beauvoir estate was given that name by its then current owner Sarah Dorsey. The name "Beauvoir" signifies "beautiful view" and is most appropriate for the property. Jefferson Davis came to the Mississippi Gulf Coast in 1877, looking for a place to write his memoirs. He visited his family friend, Sarah Dorsey, at Beauvoir. When Dorsey discovered that Davis was seeking a place to write, she showed him her east cottage, which consisted of one room with a pillared gallery surrounding it. She encouraged him to stay. Davis agreed to rent the (Library) cottage for $50.00 per month (room and board) and did so for two years until he purchased all of her Beauvoir property on February 19, 1879.

In his dozen years at Beauvoir, Davis wrote his monumental two-volume memoir titled "The Rise and Fall of the Confederate Government," and he archived greatness as the symbol of the South. The pages of history reveal no other instance in which a vanquished people so idolized the leader of a cause that failed. Because of his presence, together with that of his wife (Varina) and daughter (Winnie), Beauvoir became the Mount Vernon of the Confederacy.

The night before we left, we spotted a hole-in-the-wall local barbecue joint call "Slap Ya Momma's." They proudly serve authentic dry-rubbed barbecue publicized to be so good it'll make you, yes you guessed it, "Slap Your Momma." We weren't disappointed. The food was most satisfying. We left with full bellies and smiles on our faces. The next morning, we headed back home to Clarksville. We took a different route home so we could spend a day and night in Birmingham, Alabama.

What's the saying? Turn-about is fair play? Mentioned earlier in my story was a surprise birthday visit arranged by Sandie where Janette flew in from Portland Oregon and answered the door to Sandie's condo on one of my visits. Well, on the 26th of January 2018, Sandie and I went over to Janette's in Clarksville for dinner. Sandie's youngest daughter Julie answered the door, placing Sandie in a state of bewilderment. The surprised look on her face was priceless. Janette and I conspired to bring Julie down as a birthday surprise for Sandie.

Julie stayed with us for several days, allowing Sandie and her to enjoy some late evening mother–daughter conversations. We took Julie into Nashville during her stay to provide her with the full southern experience. While in Nashville, we toured the Country Music Hall of Fame. Julie is a huge Tim McGraw–Faith Hill fan, and the museum was featuring a special exhibit on the two well-known country artists. Janette, Julie, Sandie, and I thoroughly enjoyed the extended celebration of Sandie's birthday that year!

I spent March 10–12, 2018 in Phoenix, Arizona, with Shawn, enjoying spring-training baseball. Shawn flew in from Hawaii and I flew in from Clarksville. On the 11th, we saw the Dodgers challenge the Colorado

Rockies at the Rockies, spring training facility, Salt River Fields. Much to my pleasure, the Dodgers won easily that day 13–7, scoring all of their runs during the first four innings. The next day, we witnessed the Dodgers lose 7–6 to the Milwaukee Brewers at the Dodgers spring training facility Camelback Ranch Glendale. The highlight of the game was watching the Dodger's ace, Clayton Kershaw pitch. Shawn and I even found time to bowl a couple of games while in Phoenix.

On May 4, 2018, Sandie, Janette, and I drove to Highland Illinois to attend a wedding. The next day, Brendon and Cali Rolves were getting married and we were fortunate to be in attendance. Brendon is the son of Sandie's sister, Janice. Cali lives in Highland where she and Brendon began their relationship. It was a nice ceremony and well attended. It's heart-warming witnessing a couple's lifelong commitment to one another as they enter another chapter in their lives.

May 16–27 of 2018 produced quite a memorable trip. My daughter Janette joined Sandie and me for a family vacation excursion. The nearly two-week trip took us through five states, driving roughly 2,500 miles. We flew into and out of Boise, Idaho, renting an auto while navigating through Idaho, Wyoming, Montana, North Dakota, and South Dakota.

Realizing the trip in front of the three of us I requested a vehicle upgrade at the Boise airport. To our surprise, we were upgraded to a brand new, fully loaded Cadillac SUV! The Cadillac was a breeze to drive and provided the three of with a level of comfort that added to the enjoyment of the trip. We spent our first night at a Hyatt Place close to the Boise Airport. Janette had a friend in Boise and decided to visit with her while Sandie and I unwound having a quiet dinner.

On our full first day, we traveled from Boise, Idaho, nearly 400 miles to the Grand Teton Lodge & Spa in Victor, Idaho. This resort looked and felt like a property right out of a *World's Leading Resorts* magazine. It was off-season so we were able to enjoy our fabulous accommodations and the resort itself without crowds. We chose this particular resort as it was close to the southern entrance of Yellowstone Park that we were going to tour the next day.

Yellowstone Park was an amazing adventure. We saw a section of the sprawling 3,500-square-mile area that sits atop a volcanic hot spot. Mostly in Wyoming, the park spreads into parts of Montana and Idaho (our entrance spot) too. Yellowstone features dramatic canyons, alpine rivers, lush forests, hot springs and gushing geysers, including its most famous, Old Faithful. It's also home to hundreds of animal species, including bears, wolves, bison, elk, and antelope. During our trek, we saw buffalo and elk and of course made it to Old Faithful. The famous Geyser intermittently shot a stream of water/steam high into the air, providing anxious spectators with a sight worth waiting for. It actually goes off on such a regular schedule that the park rangers post an expected "eruption" schedule that was realized fairly close to expectations. Another of nature's wonders in the area is Thermal Blue Star Spring, one of the numerous beautiful blue pools in the Upper Geyser Basin. The spring has been known to erupt on rare occasions, but is usually calm, simmering only gently.

The next day, we departed for Hardin, Montana. We purposely added this little town to the itinerary, so Janette could reconnect with her former pastor of the church she attended while living in Seaside, Oregon. He left Seaside to become pastor at Christ Evangelical & Reformed Church in downtown Hardin. We were fortunate to meet him and his family as we went to his church that Sunday and he took us around the area playing tour guide.

Not far from Hardin the battlefield Little Bighorn, where Custer's famous last stand occurred, lies in its historical setting. On Sunday, June 25 in 1876, this infamous battle occurred at this site. The pointless massacre of 265 troops along with Custer himself resulted from Custer not following orders. Custer's orders were to wait for reinforcements before attacking the Indians, but Chief Sitting Bull had been spotted nearby, and Custer was impatient to attack. The Lakota Sioux and Northern Cheyenne Indians lost approximately fifty braves during this epic well-documented battle. Visitation of the site was somewhat eerie as grave markers for each of the fallen soldiers were in place including a marker for where Custer himself died. The grave markers were symbolic as the 2nd Calvary built a granite memorial near the top of the hill where these soldiers were reinterred.

An interesting adjunct to Custer's last stand was the tribute paid to the horses that died in this battle. The 7th cavalry horse cemetery is located on this same site. Now located in the Little Big Horn Museum in Montana is a headstone that reads: "7th Cavalry Horse Cemetery-In memory of 7th cavalry horses killed during Custer's last stand June 25, 1876 and later buried here in July 1881 under supervision of Lt. Charles F. Roe of the 2nd Cavalry." Custer instructed his men to shoot their horses and use them as protection from the onslaught. They called the dead horses "breastworks," which means "a low temporary defense." Thus, the men killed their own horses for protection—which ultimately didn't work.

We left the following morning on Monday, May 21, for our next tourist experience, Fort Abraham Lincoln. This attraction was located in Mandan, North Dakota, which was nearly 400 miles away. Built in 1872 to protect survey crews and workers for the westward advancing railroad, it was renamed Fort Abraham Lincoln just a month later. In the fall of 1873, the 7th Cavalry arrived at the post under the command of Lt. Colonel George A. Custer. Their mission was to further the advancement of the railroad. Custer's campaign against the Sioux that lead to Custer's last stand originated from Fort Abraham Lincoln.

Three rebuilt blockhouses to their original Fort McKeen specifications along with the Custer house Victorian-style home sit on the site for visitors' enjoyment. The original flagpole of Fort Abraham Lincoln stands in front of the reconstructed Custer residence. Also on the site is a recreated section of the "Slant Indian Village." This village was occupied by the Mandan Indians. There are five or six earth lodges constructed on the site allowing visitors to experience the living conditions of the Mandan Indians. These earth lodges were circular with a hole in middle portion of their roof. As their namesake implies, they were built somewhat underground making them dark and very cool inside.

The next day, we traveled to Keystone, South Dakota (the closest town to Mount Rushmore), an approximate-315-mile journey for the "feature presentation of our trip." Keystone, South Dakota, was founded by those who imagined achieving their own American dreams through hard work and determination. After the discovery of gold within the mineral-rich region of the Black Hills, Keystone became a busy mining hub. With the advent of the railroad, it wasn't long before Keystone blossomed becoming the largest community in Pennington County. The railroad also allowed the easy transport of people and goods, which eventually allowed for the carving and creation of Mount Rushmore National Memorial.

The carving of Mount Rushmore commenced in 1927 and was completed in 1941. While Mount Rushmore National Memorial created revenue and jobs for local workers, few knew the true greatness that would come from this monument. In the first year of completion, 393,000 tourists ventured to view the famous and breathtaking carving. It wasn't long before Keystone discovered that tourism was (and still is) their primary industry. Today, more than 2 million people visit Mount Rushmore National Memorial each year.

After entering the park and before you get to one of the trails taking you to the Mount Rushmore spectacle, you walk through the breathtaking "Avenue of Flags" archway. Flags are powerful symbols, which remind people of their common heritage, history, and ideals. The Avenue of Flags was initially established as part of the celebration of the United States' Bicentennial in 1976 at the request of a visitor. The fifty-six flags represent the fifty states, one district, three territories, and two commonwealths of the United States. We walked one of the trails as far as was allowed due to renovations that were occurring during our visit. Every angle during our walk on the trail provided stunning views and, of course, ample photo opportunities.

Mt. Rushmore is our old friend from elementary school, and we think we know it well. Climbed upon by Cary Grant in Alfred Hitchcock's "North by Northwest." But all that supposed familiarity somewhat disintegrates once you see light at play on Washington and Jefferson's noble noses, the volume of Teddy Roosevelt's mustache, and Lincoln's sunken cheeks. It makes a startling difference, seeing this masterpiece in person versus what you've seen in pictures—especially when that sculpture sits atop a 450-foot mountain!

No visit to Mount Rushmore would be complete without sampling the famous Thomas Jefferson vanilla ice cream. While the claim that Thomas Jefferson introduced ice cream to the United States is false, he can be credited with the first known recipe recorded by an American. Jefferson also likely helped to popularize ice cream in this country when he served it at the President's House in Washington. The Thomas Jefferson vanilla ice cream didn't disappoint. Both Sandie and I agreed that it was the best tasting vanilla ice cream we've had. This was one of only ten recipes surviving in Thomas Jefferson's hand, the famous recipe for vanilla ice cream most likely dates to his time in France.

The Crazy Horse Memorial was in close proximity to Mount Rushmore so the three of us decided to check it out. Trekking a mere seventeen miles to our next stop as we entered the Crazy Horse Monument area, we were hypnotized by its mere size. The first object to stand out was the enormity of the head of Crazy Horse. The head was eighty-seven feet tall, which is twenty-seven feet taller than the Mount Rushmore sculptures. When the entire Crazy Horse monument is completed it will be 641 feet long and 563 feet tall, making it the world's largest sculpture by far.

The monument is meant to depict Tasunke Witko—best known as Crazy Horse—famous for his role in the resounding defeat of Custer and the Seventh Cavalry at the Battle of the Little Bighorn. Crazy Horse is remembered for his courage, leadership, and his tenacity of spirit in the face of near-impossible odds. The exact details of Crazy Horse's life are shrouded in mystery, but he's still remembered as one of the most prominent Native American figures of his time.

Some interesting tidbits from visiting the Cray Horse site:

- The entire project is privately funded—no government funds have been accepted.

- Although it's open as a tourist site and does feature a completed, eighty-seven-foot-tall head of Crazy Horse, the project is far from completion.

- The Crazy Horse Memorial has been under construction since 1948 and it will be at least several more decades before it's completed.

- *Korczak Ziolkowski, the project's designer (his life's work), and wife Ruth Ziolkowski are buried in the base of the monument.*

- The Crazy Horse monument is one of the largest being carved anywhere in the world.

We left Keystone South Dakota for Casper, Wyoming, the next morning. Casper was around 400 miles away. We didn't have any sightseeing planned in that area as it was simply a planned overnight rest stop. The next day we set out for Jackson Hole, Wyoming, where some sightseeing was on the agenda. Jackson Hole was a four-and-three-fourth hour drive. The country side in this part of the United States expounds beauty beyond description. Just driving along, we had to make several stops to take photos of the magnificent settings. We even took photos from our vehicle as we commuted along. The challenging aspect of this leg of our journey was the lack of services. We saw nary a gas station or restaurant for hour upon hour. Finally, giving up on coming across a place to eat lunch, we turned to Janette for our hunger salvation. Janette had enough snacks in her purse to hold us over until we were able to properly nourish ourselves.

We made it into the quaint well-known Jackson Hole anxious to explore the town. Unfortunately, the weather was not on our side as it rained the majority of the time we were there. This didn't stop us from looking around, but it did limit us somewhat to the downtown area where the buildings were closer together and provided some intermediary weather relief. We thought we'd go horseback-riding while being in the "Wild West." They were even celebrating "Old West Days" while we were there. But much to our surprise, the company that we went to for horseback riding didn't provide that activity on Sundays! The three of us were bewildered as while it wasn't the peak tourist season, it was a weekend and the town was celebrating "Old West Days."

We ventured into shops, restaurants, and art galleries, quickly realizing that the Jackson Hole visitor demographics were very much on the upper-end. Shops and art gallery pricing were reflective of this. We were fortunate to view an authentic old west stagecoach complete with a full complement of horses and a driver in complete "of the time" attire. An experience that Janette had during a previous visit and strongly recommended that Sandie and I try was having a drink at Jackson Hole's well-known Million Dollar Cowboy Bar. The bar uses actual horse saddles as their stools. The three of us got a real kick sitting at the bar as if we were sitting on a horse. After our drink, we left the saddle stools so other customers could take advantage of this high demand area. We then left Jackson Hole, Wyoming, for Boise, Idaho, to turn in our rented vehicle and fly back to Nashville following a wonderful thirteen-day trip.

Sandie had always wanted to visit New York City. In June of 2018, that wish was realized as we flew into the city and played the classical role of out-of-town tourists. One of our first stops was to take in an afternoon live Broadway style play. The theater was located in the Lincoln Center, home to the famous Juilliard School of Music. The Juilliard School of music (originally called the Institute of Musical Art) was founded in 1905. It was established on the premise that the United States did not have a premier music school and too many students were going to Europe to study music. The school has steadily added to its curriculum and now offers drama classes among its course curriculum. The play was outstanding and a positive New York experience. While I can't remember the name of the play, I'm relatively sure that it was put on by the Drama Division of Juilliard.

No visit to New York would feel complete without a visit to America's Great Lady, the Statue of Liberty. France's gift to America in 1886 represents the Roman Goddess of Freedom. She holds a torch and tablet upon which is inscribed the date of American Declaration of Independence (July 4, 1776). As you approach this magnificent statue you can't help but have a tremendous patriotic resolve along with an enormous amount of pride to be an American. The seven spikes on the crown represent the seven oceans and the seven continents of the world, indicating the universal concept of liberty.

Our tour included Ellis Island, which is in close proximity to the statue of Liberty. It was the United States' busiest immigrant inspection station from 1892 to 1954, processing approximately twelve million immigrants to the country through the Port of New York and New Jersey. Ellis Island is a federally owned island in New York Harbor, which contains a museum and former immigration inspection station. While Ellis Island is in Upper New York Bay, most of the island is in Jersey City, New Jersey. Strolling through the museum and inspection station, it was fascinating to visualize the strength, courage, and conviction these pioneers must have displayed in their desire to become American citizens. For a small fee, Sandie was able to search their vast database of passengers and found a record of someone she believes could have been her grandfather.

Unbeknownst to most, Castle Clinton located at the southern tip of Manhattan Island, a scant 10 miles away, processed immigrants before Ellis Island. We visited Castle Clinton and learned that it was originally built between 1808 and 1811 to prevent a British invasion in 1812! Castle Clinton processed more than 8 million immigrants between 1855 and 1890.

Described as a "must see" New York experience, the new One World Trade Center was our next tourist stop. One World Trade Center (WTC) is the main building of the rebuilt World Trade Center complex in Lower Manhattan. It's the tallest building in the United States, and the seventh-tallest in the world. The Observatory above the WTC provides fifty-mile views in all directions. One World Trade Center marks the rebirth of a major financial and commercial hub, re-establishing New York City as the epicenter of high-rise skyscraper design and serving as a symbol of USA freedom and revitalization in lower Manhattan.

The WTC Sky-Pod elevators climb 102 stories in 47 seconds. This astonishing ride reveals the transformation of New York City from unsettled lands to today's mass of skyscrapers. One World Trade Center is also known as the Freedom Tower. Within the WTC complex, is the $4 billion Oculus station house, designed by the Spanish architect Santiago Calatrava. It's a site to behold providing the illusion of walking through the skeleton frame of a whale. It consists of white ribs that interlock high above the ground. The interior of the station house contains two underground floors, which house part of the Westfield World Trade Center mall.

As a monument to human dignity, courage, and sacrifice, the 9/11 Memorial & Museum honors the nearly 3,000 people killed in the terrorist attacks of September 11, 2001, and February 26, 1993, recognizes the courage of those who survived, and salutes those who risked their lives to help others. The 9/11 Memorial Museum serves as the country's principal institution for examining the attacks of September 11, 2001, and documenting their continuing impact and significance.

A visit to the 9/11 Memorial Museum at the complex allowed us to learn about the history of the 9/11 attacks and 1993 World Trade Center bombing. The museum's dynamic blend of architecture, archaeology, and history creates an unforgettable encounter with the story of the attacks, their aftermath, and the people who experienced these events. It tells the story of 9/11 through artifacts, imagery, personal stories, and interactive technology. A couple of the more heart-wrenching exhibits were the remnants of a radio and TV antenna from the North Tower and the remains of a steel beam from floors 96–99 of the North Tower. The 9/11 Memorial Museum's permanent collection is an unprecedented depository consisting of material evidence, primary testimony, and historical records of response to September 11, 2001, and the ongoing repercussions of terrorist events.

We toured the actual 9/11 Memorial, which was just outside the WTC. The Memorial setting had a calm, nature-like setting to it. It's a tribute honoring the 2,977 people killed in the terror attacks of September 11, 2001 at the World Trade Center site. A deep agonizing sorrow overtook our senses as we viewed this breathtaking tribute. The memorial's design featured twin waterfall pools surrounded by a bronze protective wall that list the names of the victims of the 9/11 attacks and the 1993 World Trade Center bombing. The names engraved on the memorial are grouped by where the victims were and who they were with, rather than alphabetically. The pools are set within a plaza where several hundred swamp white oak trees grow.

In August of 2018, Sandie and I were in Indianapolis visiting my sister Sharon and her husband Joe. Missing my bio-dad's (Paul Thayer) funeral, we talked Sharon and Joe into a trip to Marion, Indiana, where he's buried in Marion National Cemetery. Marion National Cemetery is a United States National Cemetery located in the city of Marion in Grant County, Indiana. It's located approximately eighty miles northeast of Indianapolis and encompasses forty-five acres. Being a US cemetery, it's manicured perfectly. The cemetery utilizes "Section" and "Street type" markers for grave locations. Appropriately, my bio-dad's grave is near the intersection of Indiana Avenue (his home state) and Hyde Road in Section 8. We located his grave quickly enough and read the label on his headstone: "Paul J. Thayer, SI, US Navy, World War II, October 24-1925, July 16-1993."

Next on our checklist was a scheduled trip to the New England area during mid-August. All of our post-retirement trips held a level of anticipation and excitement leading up to the actual trip. When we're able to renew old acquaintances in addition to taking in the history and sights of the area it adds an element of anticipation to the adventure. Our New England trip was one such excursion. Included in our itinerary were stops in Derry, New Hampshire, and Concord, Massachusetts, to visit with friends from my Dunfey Hotels career days.

Our first stop was a lunch date with Pat and Don DuPaul at T-Bones restaurant in Derry, New Hampshire. Don was the Director of Sales at the Dunfey San Mateo, California Hotel, in the late 1970s, where I functioned as the property's Resident Manager. A special bond develops between most departmental cohorts while working diligently to achieve hotel/company goals. That was certainly the case with Don and I as our performance results were somewhat tied to each other's success. During our San Mateo experiences, I coined the nickname "Double-D" for Don that stuck with him for several years. To this day, I still refer to him with that moniker. Sandie and I had a delightful lunch with Don and his lovely wife Pat, learning that their children were, of course, fully grown by now with families of their own along and about events occurring between our last encounter and the present.

After lunch, we had some time and asked our lunch guests for touring ideas in the area. Without hesitation, Pat recommended the Budweiser Brewery located a short drive away in Merrimack. This was a pleasant diversion as it was a nice find being completely off our radar. We made it to the Brewery early enough in the afternoon to tour the entire facility. While touring the Brewery one of the first things that caught our eye was the size of the vats used to store the beer brewed there. The vats appeared to be made of stainless steel and while sitting on poles were around thirty feet in height! Witnessing the actual brewing and bottling process was worth the trip. However, we also got to walk through their Hop Garden and visit their barn where the famous Clydesdales were stabled.

A brief history of the famous Clydesdales: Farmers living in the eighteenth century along the banks of the River Clyde in Lanarkshire, Scotland, bred the Flemish Great Horse, the forerunner of the Clydesdale. These first draft horses pulled loads of more than one ton at a walking speed five miles per hour. Soon, their reputations spread beyond the Scottish borders. The Budweiser Clydesdales were formally introduced to August A. Busch and Anheuser-Busch on April 7, 1933. Prohibition had just been repealed and to commemorate the occasion he hitched the Clydesdales to a wagon and had them carry the first case of post-Prohibition beer down Pestalozzi Street from Busch's St. Louis Brewery.

After our Budweiser factory tour, we drove to Plymouth Notch, Vermont, to tour the birthplace of our 30th President, Calvin Coolidge.

After crossing the state line, the pristine appearance of Vermont became obvious. Notwithstanding the beautiful scenery, the roads were immaculate and highway services were located out-of-view offsite of the main highway so they wouldn't distract from Vermont's natural beauty.

Calvin Coolidge, the thirtieth U.S. president, led the nation through most of the Roaring Twenties, a decade of dynamic social and cultural change, materialism, and excess. He took office following the sudden death of President Warren G. Harding, whose administration was riddled with scandal. Nicknamed "Silent Cal" for his quiet, steadfast, and frugal nature, Coolidge cleaned up the rampant corruption of the Harding administration and provided a model of stability and respectability for the American people in an era of fast-paced modernization.

One of his famous quotes rang so true to me: "Nothing in this world can take the place of persistence. Talent will not; nothing is more common than unsuccessful men with talent. Genius will not; unrewarded genius is almost a proverb." This quote reaffirms the belief that hard work coupled with persistence allows the pursuer a higher life-standard. Visiting Coolidge's birthplace via a guided tour we learned an interesting backstory to his swearing in ceremony.

Vice-President Coolidge was vacationing at his beloved Vermont home during the summer of 1923 where he was wakened by his father very early in the morning with stunning news. He heard his father coming up the stairs calling his name, noticing a trembling in his voice. The tone of his father's voice was eerily similar to past incidents when death had visited the Coolidge family. His father placed his son's hand on the official report of Harding's death while explaining that President Harding had just passed away. Coolidge and his wife dressed at once, but before leaving the room he knelt in prayer asking God to bless the American people and give him the power to serve them.

He examined the Constitution to determine the requirements for taking oath of office. Finding the required form for the Constitution, he set it up on the typewriter, and the oath was administered by his father in his capacity as a notary public. The oath was taken in the sitting room by the light of a kerosene lamp, which was the most modern form of lighting at the time in the neighborhood. Beside his father officiating at the ceremony present were his wife, Senator Porter Dale, who happened to be stopping a few miles away, his stenographer, and his chauffer.

Coolidge often retreated to his beloved Plymouth Notch home to reinvigorate himself. In the summer of 1924, he was greatly stressed by the loss of his son, Calvin Jr. On the advice of his physician he left Washington in mid-August for the refreshing mountain climate of his native Plymouth. The presidential party included his wife, his son John, his secretary, his physician, two clerks, the Secret Service detachment, and a corps of twelve newsmen. Presidential duties could not be ignored, however, and Coolidge Hall was converted into a summer White House. Telephone and telegraph lines were installed, and daily reports from Washington and New York kept the President in touch with the outside world.

Amity Shlaes, a serial revisionist, portrayed "Silent Cal" in a 2013 biography as a thoughtful, reflective, and innovative president. "He was a good economist and he promulgated far better politics than he was given credit for," Shlaes said. "He was treated as though he was someone who presided over a false, champagne-bubble economy, but in fact presided over a rock-solid economy whose achievements ought to be admired today."

Of course, there's no way we could be in Vermont and not experience the original Ben & Jerry's Ice Cream Factory. A short enjoyable drive took us there. The factory tour was enlightening but the highlight of the tour was the ice cream samples at the tour's conclusion. The birth of this iconic company is an interesting story.

Initially, Ben & Jerry thought about making bagels but decided the necessary equipment was too expensive. Instead, they settled on ice cream. They decided Burlington, Vt., was an ideal location for a scoop shop because it was a college town without an ice cream parlor. They took a $5 course on ice-cream making and in 1978 opened the first Ben & Jerry's in a converted Burlington gas station. The original scoop shop became a community favorite thanks to its rich ice cream and creative flavors. Ben and Jerry also made it a point to connect with the community, hosting a free film festival and giving away free scoops on the first anniversary of the store, a tradition that still continues to this day.

One reason for the quick popularity of Ben & Jerry's was its unique flavor combinations. All new flavors were invented by Jerry, usually without any test marketing. Some 1980s' flagship flavors include Chunky Monkey, Rainforest Crunch, and Economic Crunch, scoops of which Ben & Jerry's served up for free on Wall Street following the stock market crash of October 19, 1987. The company opened its first non-Vermont franchise in Maine and signed a deal with a Boston distribution company. By the end of 1988, with the company operating shops in eighteen states, Ben and Jerry earned the distinctive award of U.S. Small Business Persons of the Year from President Ronald Reagan.

A novel Ben & Jerry's attraction near their factory is the "Flavor Graveyard." Created in 1997 for ice cream flavors that have fallen out of favor with consumers the Flavor Graveyard is designed to look like an actual cemetery. Complete with headstones for the fallen flavors, the graveyard is accessed through an archway appropriately entitled "Flavor Graveyard." It's estimated that over 250,000 visitors pay their respects annually to these fallen flavors. Being Tennesseans for a couple of years, we were disappointed to see that one of the flavors in the graveyard was Tennessee Mud. Bet that was a wonderful flavor!

Working our way northeast from Ben & Jerry's in Vermont we set our sights on Portland, Maine. While with Dunfey Hotels in the late 1970s, my second general manager's position was at their South Portland property, the Sheraton Inn. So in addition to taking in the Maine sites and eating some Maine lobster, we planned on stopping by my old hunting ground, which has since been renovated and sold.

Driving up to Portland on Interstate 95 was an eye-opener for me. The interstate leading into Maine was now five lanes each way and the traffic was very heavy leading me to believe that tourism in the state of Maine had advanced significantly following my Dunfey Hotel days. It was August and summer visitation in Maine had always done well but the bumper-to-bumper traffic indicated an absolute tourist explosion for the state.

We thought it would be a treat to stay at the hotel I managed there nearly four decades earlier. The one-tower Sheraton was now a two-tower Doubletree Hotel. What stood out to me was the growth around the hotel. During my tenure, the area was rather sparse. Not now, from other hotels to shopping malls the area was crammed with stores and retailers of all types. It was no surprise that the hotel had gone through a major transformation. In fact, I'm sure it had seen several renovations after my departure. Our room was in the newer of the two towers and we passed by the hotel's new restaurant on the way to it. It was great to stay there and there was definitely a déjà vu feel to it.

Venturing into the city of Portland, we discovered a vibrant, pulsating city by the sea. Tourists crammed the streets sampling local seafood, ice cream, and other delights. Parking was at a premium where, if you could locate a space, it was metered with a high hourly rate. Markets, boutiques, and emporiums were bustling with activity. All of this was in stark contrast to my experience there in the late 1970s.

After locating parking, we rambled along Portland's front street. Sandie and I would slip into shops along the way that piqued our interest. Exploring the city was eclectic to say the least, containing of all things a section of the actual Berlin Wall. Being adjacent to the ocean, we decided to walk out to the end of a pier to take in the majestic view of ships going and coming into the harbor. No trip to the lobster capitol of the US would have been complete without devouring a local lobster roll. For this epicurean experience, we chose the Portland Lobster Company. This iconic brand had won the prestigious "Best Lobster Roll" and "Best Outdoor Bar/Patio" honors for four consecutive years from the Portland Phoenix magazine. We certainly were not disappointed. The "Best Lobster Roll" was scrumptious.

We hit the road for approximately 150 miles south of Portland, Maine, for our next destination. Plymouth, Massachusetts, is a coastal town due south of Boston. It is the site of the first Pilgrim settlement established in 1620. Plymouth Rock, a boulder in Pilgrim Memorial State Park, marks the place where settlers were thought to have landed on shore. The Mayflower II, a full-scale replica of the ship that carried the Pilgrims across the Atlantic, is usually anchored at the park but was not there during our off-season visit.

There were significant renovations occurring during our visit to Plymouth preventing the visitation of Plimoth Plantation, a re-creation of a 1627 Pilgrim Village and some other sites. Our main objective was accomplished, however, as we were able to see the original Plymouth Rock on the location where the Mayflower ship landed. The rock was ensconced beneath a mausoleum style granite canopy. The behavior of a small percentage of our population absolutely amazes me. The actions of this small percentage of our public create obstacles for everyone else. The actual Plymouth Rock is a perfect example of this. The rock was encased in a thick mass of unbreakable plastic. A local guide informed us that this protection was due to tourists trying to chip off pieces of the famous rock to take home as souvenirs!

Our next stop was one that I had been looking forward to since planning our New England trip. We were headed to Concord Massachusetts primarily to have lunch with a past Omni Hotels boss of mine. Laurence Jeffrey was the Managing Director at the Marquette when I first met him after being assigned the General Manager's position there. We worked together for four years, all in Minneapolis split between the Marquette and NorthStar hotels. LVJ, as his staff affectionately referred to him, had retired several years earlier and was living with his wife Beth in Concord. Laurence was from that area and has a daughter, Joanna and two grandchildren.

We met him at the Papa Razzi restaurant in Concord. Beth was originally scheduled to join us but was ill and couldn't make it. Laurence was the consummate hotelier, a perfect gentleman with a European flair. He received respect and admiration from his staff through his role model example. As busy as he was with hotel activities, he always had the time to lend a helping hand to anyone outside work. Having lunch with him and reminiscing about our hotel days together was emotional and joyful.

Spending time with both Pat and Don DuPaul and Laurence Jeffrey was the highlight of this trip for me. Don't get me wrong, I thoroughly enjoyed visiting the historical sights, which will be a fond memory for years to come but there's something very special about reconnecting with colleagues that you had previous professional and personal relationships with.

Before heading back to Boston to catch a plane back to Nashville, we made two more historic stops in Concord. The first was to the Minute Man National Park. This historical setting is where the first shots of the American Revolution occurred. On the morning of April 19, 1775, the North Bridge here became a battle ground when colonial militia faced off against their King's soldiers. The site is now a National Park and has been restored to emulate the 1775 setting. The site also includes the Wayside home. The Wayside has been home to three literary families: the Alcotts, Hawthornes, and Lothrops. It's the first literary site added to the National Park Service. The Wayside is the only National Historic Landmark to have been lived in by three literary families.

Our final New England stop was to the Louisa May Alcott's Orchard House. This classical setting is best known for being where *Louisa May Alcott* wrote *Little Women* in 1868. One of the oldest, most authentically preserved historic sites in the country, it has for over a century, provided inspirational accounts of the Alcott family's contributions to the fields of literature, education, philosophy, the arts, and social justice. The Concord School of Philosophy and a Museum Store are also on the premises. With another memorable excursion under our belts Sandie and I headed back home to Clarksville, Tennessee.

We spent a relatively quiet September apart from my sister Sheryl and her husband Jim dropping in overnight on their way home from Indianapolis for an appreciated visit. In October I made a quick trek to the West Coast. The main purpose of the trip was to visit with friend and hotel mentor Jim Reed. After months of tests for poor balance and falls that led to a couple of hospital stays, he was diagnosed with Parkinson's. While conversing with him over the phone, I felt it would be timely to visit my friend

262

of over fifty years. Arriving at his condo in San Diego, I was pleased to see that he had a caretaker there to assist him with his daily routine. He was in good spirits and, being an active individual, still made a point of getting out some each day in spite of needing a walker to get around. Time spent with him that day lifted my spirits as I was leaving the caretaker pulled me to the side and informed me of how much he had looked forward to the visit and she could see that it had a positive impact on his well-being.

Since I was in California, approximately ninety miles from Huntington Beach, I decided to visit a Konawaena High School classmate. Pat Wolf (Sugai) formerly of Kona but residing in Huntington Beach for years is a high school classmate that I've kept in touch with. As a single parent in the mid-nineties, I have a fond memory of taking Janette, Shawn, and Scott over to the Wolf's residence for dinner. Shawn and Scott were both with me over that Christmas and the three of us traveled to Los Angeles to stay with Janette and have Christmas with her. When my work travels had taken me to the West Coast, I'd arrange to meet Pat and her husband Bill in town for lunch. I am sad to state that Pat lost Bill several years ago but has resisted relocating to Portland where her son Matt resides or to San Francisco where her daughter Nicole lives.

In late October of 2018, we embarked on our last road trip of the year. Our targeted cities were Richmond, Virginia, and Savannah, Georgia. On day one, we drove a little over five hours before stopping in Johnson City, Tennessee, for the night. We had dinner at a restaurant call "Cootie Brown's". The name alone was enough enticement to try out this local spot. The restaurant was described as a funky, diner-ish spot for globally inspired American fare plus dozens of beers. We weren't disappointed with either the food or the beer!

After another over-five hour drive the following day, we arrived at the first of our two targeted destinations, Richmond, Virginia. The main attraction on our tourist visitation list was the White House of the Confederacy. The White House of the Confederacy functioned as the Executive Mansion of the Confederacy when Richmond was the capital of the Confederacy.

Built in 1818, it was the main executive residence of the sole President of the Confederate States of America, Jefferson Davis, from August 1861 until April 1865. Renovations occurred, ending in 1988 to restoring the white house to its Davis-era elegance complete with period decor and objects. Walking through the house, you'd swear you were literally in the home of Jefferson Davis as it existed in that time. The home and museum rank as the most outstanding repository of Confederate memorabilia in the United States.

Around noon that same day, we drove over to tour Richmond's Hollywood Cemetery. Hollywood Cemetery is best known as the final resting place for Presidents James Monroe and John Tyler, as well as Jefferson Davis, and many major figures from the Civil War. What most people do not know is that Hollywood Cemetery also contains some of the best examples of native trees in the Commonwealth of Virginia. Although they are located in a cemetery, these historic trees are alive and well and shade the grave sites of its many famous notables. Its name was derived from the holly trees dotting the hills of the property.

Hollywood Cemetery was designed in 1847 in a rural garden style to escape the grid-like monotony of city cemeteries. A major feature of the cemetery is its many stately trees that were left untouched by its landscape designer. Garden cemeteries were designed with the living in mind and meant to be a haven for people to escape the city and enjoy a peaceful setting. The beautiful Hollywood Cemetery's paths wind over 135 acres—through valleys, over hills, and beneath stately tulip poplars and white oaks. There are over 2,000 trees in the cemetery, many of which predate the cemetery.

We broke the 512-mile trip to Savannah into two leisurely days, stopping in Spring Lake, North Carolina. Then Sandie and I spent three nights in Savannah to allow ample sightseeing opportunities. The Savannah Rock 'n' Roll Marathon was setting up during our sightseeing endeavors. This is a rather large event. The original Rock 'n' Roll Marathon was held in San Diego. It quickly became one of the largest marathons in the United States. Its success inspired the creation of other Rock 'n' Roll races. Today, the Rock 'n' Roll Marathon Series includes marathons and half marathons in twenty-three cities across the United States as well as seven in other countries.

One of our first voyager stops was at the gorgeous Forsyth Park. The park is named after its Georgia Governor at the time of the expansion in 1851, John Forsyth. Forsyth Park is a large city park that occupies thirty acres in the historic district of the city. It commemorates the American soldiers who fought in the Spanish–American War, the Boxer Rebellion, and the Philippine–American War. Its beautiful setting is home to the Confederate Memorial, a half shell theatre, a cafe, two playgrounds, and ample room for sports and events. However, people from all over come to see its most famous asset: the Forsyth fountain.

Observed in Chippewa Square was a bronze statue of James Oglethorpe. Curious of his significance to Savannah we learned that he was a British soldier, Member of Parliament, and philanthropist, as well as the founder of the colony of Georgia. As a social reformer, he attempted to resettle Britain's worthy poor in the New World, initially focusing on those in debtors' prisons. Oglethorpe led the first group of 114 colonists landing at the site of today's Savannah on February 1, 1733. The original charter banned slavery and granted religious freedom, leading to the foundation of a Jewish community in Savannah.

Taking advantage of Savannah's Trolley Tour where we could hop on and off at our discretion, we disembarked at the historic River Street area. Restaurants, shops, and museums were at the bottom of a cobble-stoned path that led from the street to the river. It's always interesting to compare and contrast the idiosyncrasies of different city destinations. Savannah provided us with a true Southern flavor. A lovely seaside setting with bountiful dazzling foliage throughout.

While walking along the riverfront area, we came across a bronze statue that caught our eye. It was a statue of a girl waving a towel toward the sea with a dog by her side. Anxious to learn the story behind this statue we discovered the statue was placed there in honor of a girl named Florence Martus. The story goes that young Florence first saw passing ships going with cargoes to the farthest corners of the globe from the old stone pier on Cockspur Island.

The small child was fascinated by these ships and waved her handkerchief as they passed by. Sailors on the ships often waved back. A few years later, Florence went to live with her brother about five miles upriver from Fort Pulaski. From this time on, she waved at every ship that passed—a table cloth or towel by day, a lantern by night. For more than forty-four years, she never missed a ship, and each ship, as it passed, returned her salute with three blasts of the whistle. Florence Martus embodied the true spirit of Southern Hospitality. Her statue is one of the most recognized historic landmarks you can see in the riverfront park. It is also the first memorial to a Georgian woman in any city park.

A short hop from the riverfront area sat Savannah's famous Pirate's House Restaurant. As it was lunch time, we decided to experience this historic eatery. Savannah's World-Famous Pirate's House is located on one of the most historic spots in Georgia. It was first opened in 1753 as an inn for seafarers, and fast became a meeting point for pirates and sailors from the Seven Seas. Pirate's House is home to some rare early edition pages of *Treasure Island*, by Robert Louis Stevenson. The pages can be seen hanging on the walls of the captain's room and the treasure room. Sandie thoroughly enjoyed their signature dish of shrimp and grits on this day. For years, the Pirate's House has been serving up traditional southern favorites with a pirate's flare. Argghhhh!

One of the attractions we had our sights set on when knowing we would visit Savannah was the Paula Dean Restaurant. Before departing on our Richmond/Savannah expedition I booked a tour through a Savannah Trolley Company that showed her original home and featured dinner in her restaurant.

Paula Dean's rags-to-riches story is an interesting one. Born in Albany, Georgia, she was a homemaker and bank teller before entering professional cooking. She divorced her first husband in 1989 shortly after moving to a modest three-bedroom home in Mid-Town Savannah, being left with only

$200 and her two teenage sons. Paula was considered a good Southern cook, so she started a small catering company called *The Bag Lady*. She would make sandwiches and other meals and have her sons deliver them. Paula avoided going out herself because she suffered from agoraphobia, a fear of public places. She believed this fear came from an incident in which she was held at gunpoint during a bank robbery during her bank teller days. *The Bag Lady* was so successful that she outgrew her home kitchen.

Paula was then hired by a Best Western Hotel in Savannah to cook. She worked there five years before opening her landmark restaurant, The Lady and Sons, in downtown Savannah. She was able to overcome her agoraphobia with her constant contact with guests. The restaurant was a huge success and later moved into a larger building in Savannah's Historic District. Since then, it has grown into a world-renowned restaurant and full service catering venue. Her restaurant, TV cooking shows, and various TV appearances made her into a multi-millionaire.

After a rest, Sandie and I headed down to Florida to visit with my sister Sheryl Pierson and her husband Jim. My brother-in-law Jim Pierson spoke highly of an auto showroom in Punta Gorda, so we decided to trek over to Muscle Car City. It's a museum showcasing over 200 muscle cars from the '50s to the '70s, plus a gift shop and a retro diner. Jim wasn't feeling well so Sheryl joined Sandie and me for the excursion. To my surprise, it was Sheryl's first visit to Muscle Car City. The three of us enjoyed stepping back in time marveling at the expansive selection of vintage 1950s to 1970s muscle cars. Following our museum exploration we found a local restaurant and enjoyed diner in a seaside setting. Watching the sun set over the Atlantic was a perfect ending to this lovely day. On our final day of our visit with Sheryl and Jim, we had the privilege of dining on some delicious pizza, homemade by Jim, a dish he prepared with great care and pride.

Hardly a week later on November 11 we sadly learned that Jim had passed away. Sheryl and her friend Shirley were staying in a cabin in southern Georgia for a weekend getaway. Jim was supposed to accompany them but begged out at the last moment as he wasn't feeling well. Sheryl couldn't reach Jim on the phone and had a friend go over to their house to check on him only to discover that Jim was lying motionless face down on the floor. A heart attack was the suspected cause of death.

One week after returning from Florida, we flew back down to comfort Sheryl and attend Jim's funeral. It was a somber period but at the same time encouraging. Encouraging because of the obvious love and support bestowed on Sheryl from family members. Almost everyone from Sheryl and Jim's immediate family made it down to console her and attend Jim's funeral. The church was overflowing for Jim's funeral eulogy. It was heartening to witness the obvious love the congregation had for Jim and the support they provided Sheryl. Family support and Sheryl's deep faith carried her through the next few days. Sheryl and Jim were married for over forty years, where an indestructible bond developed. Sandie and I took solace in the fact that Sheryl's strong faith and support of the community would serve as a cornerstone of comfort for her.

On November 23, we ended in Indianapolis to host our annual Evans Thanksgiving/Christmas dinner. With approximately twenty-five attendees in the banquet room of the Golden Corral, everyone had a grand time. We invite individuals from both sides of my family (all of Sandie's family is in Chicago) and this year my stepmom Betty Bartlett with her husband Gene were in attendance. The gathering gives everyone the opportunity to catch up with one another on family happenings and just appreciate one another during the holiday season.

Early that December, Sandie and I stayed at the Opryland Resort in Nashville for the weekend. This was our third straight year of going there following our move from Chicago. It's become a mini family tradition for Sandie and me, where we can take in the amazing Christmas decorations consisting of three million lights, gorgeously decorated Christmas trees, and Christmas decorated themes throughout the massive hotel. We always attempt to secure a room with a balcony overlooking one of the resort's beautiful, large indoor atriums.

We also attempt to a take in a dinner show at the resort over that weekend where name entertainers perform. This year, we decided to experience the original home of the Grand Ole Opry, the Ryman Auditorium. The auditorium opened as the Union Gospel Tabernacle in 1892. Its construction was spearheaded by Thomas Ryman, a Nashville businessman, who owned several saloons and a fleet of riverboats. Ryman conceived the idea of the auditorium as a tabernacle after attending a revival led by Samuel Porter Jones where 5,000 guests were in attendance.

When fearless show promoter Lula Naff leased the building and took the reins in the 1920s, the Ryman became the anchor of Nashville's cultural offerings. The venue was known as the Carnegie of the South, hosting sought-after acts including Katherine Hepburn, Harry Houdini, Charlie Chaplin, Roy Rogers, Bob Hope, and even former President Theodore Roosevelt. When the original Grand Ole Opry put down roots here in 1943, the world would never be the same as the TV show brought the likes of Elvis Presley, Hank Williams, Johnny Cash, Marty Robbins, Patsy Cline, and Roy Acuff to the stage and into living rooms around the country.

We thoroughly enjoyed the evening's entertainment. The Ryman is more intimate than the new Grand Ole Opry that sits next to the Opryland Resort. The acoustics in this famed structure were outstanding. Chris Jansen and Sawyer Brown were among the performers that evening. Sandie and I were fortunate to be in attendance at the Grand Ole Opry when Chris Jansen was inducted into their Hall of Fame. He's a gracious, family loving, God worshiping individual and is a favorite of ours.

Our 2018 Christmas was spent in our Clarksville home of nearly three years. Sandie's sister Janice and her husband Bruce drove over from Highland, Illinois, to spend the weekend with us. Janette and her boyfriend, Joe, along with Janice and Bruce joined us for games, dinner, and of course the unwrapping of gifts.

Several months of anticipation and planning led to a sixteen-day Hawaii trip in late January 2019. This was one of our larger excursions as we were touring three islands, visiting with relatives, and meeting with friends and classmates that I hadn't seen in over forty years. We were going to the islands of Oahu, Hawaii, and Kauai. My older son Shawn resided on Oahu with his fiancé Yucco. Hawaii was the island where I lived for my senior year of high school and Janette was working a movie on the island of Kauai.

Our first stop was the island of Oahu where Honolulu sits. Shawn, through his employment, secured accommodation for us at the beautiful new Grand Islander in Waikiki owned by Hilton Hotels. Located next to the Hilton Hawaiian Village the property shared resort amenities with its sister property. Our accommodations were state-of-the-art and resembled more of an apartment versus a standard hotel room. The next four days, we spent as much time with Shawn and Yucco as Shawn's work schedule allowed. Yucco is a sweet, talented, personable individual that Sandie and I immediately took to.

The first adventure we enjoyed with Yucco and Shawn was a submarine experience. We submerged 100 feet underwater on the Atlantis Waikiki submarine where it's home to many Hawaiian fish species, coral, and turtles. The submarine was specially designed to provide large solid glass viewing windows. It was a thrill of an experience that took in the coral, reef life, a sunken ship, and other artificial reefs.

The following day while Shawn worked, Sandie and I journeyed to Haleiwa on the North Shore of Oahu. We stopped at the Dole Plantation just outside of Wahiawa which was on our way. We had visited this stop many years before with Sandie's sister Janice and her husband, Bruce, and felt it warranted a return. The history of the Dole Plantation is an interesting one. James Dole used his life savings and moved to Honolulu from Massachusetts. He purchased a sixty-four-acre homestead on Oahu and experimented with several crops, finally choosing to grow pineapple. The business grew rapidly as Dole launched ad campaigns in magazines (the first consumer ad campaign in the US), invested in modern machinery to process the crops, and obtained financial backing to purchase more land to farm. He also began to ship the pineapples great distances, thanks to the trans-Atlantic aviation industry. By 1950, a small fruit stand was erected so that everyone could savor the plantation's tasty fruit. Then, in 1989, a plantation-style home was built to serve as a living museum to James Dole's work and to welcome pineapple lovers from around the globe. Today, the Dole Plantation is one of Hawaii's top attractions that we found gratifying as much on this occasion as we did on our previous visit.

From the Dole Plantation, we continued on to the North Shore on Oahu. Hawaii visitors to Oahu gravitate to Honolulu and Waikiki. Having been a past resident on two of Hawaii's Islands I can corroborate that Honolulu is similar to most big cities. In fact, if not for the weather and palm trees, it would be a challenge to differentiate it. Traffic jams there are just as bad as any major mainland city and in most cases due to the land density of Honolulu, it's even worse. Thus, it's always a treat to get away from Waikiki and travel to a more serene spot on Oahu.

Our next stop was in Haleiwa on the North Shore. The sleepy town of Haleiwa is a throwback to the true old Hawaii pre-tourism explosion. Sure, some restaurants and shops have popped up to accommodate visitors traveling to the North Shore but Haleiwa's genuine Hawaii flavor remains true. There's one highway that takes you into and out of Haleiwa. How do you know when you've arrived? Look for a long line of visitors waiting to get into a store in an old plantation town atmosphere. The store as mentioned on an earlier visit, is Matsumoto's Grocery Store. Why the line? Matsumoto's Grocery Store is home to who is professed to serve the best shave ice within the Hawaiian Islands. They have over thirty-five flavors along with combos that due to their taste "Broke the Mouth" as the locals would say.

Haleiwa means "home of the frigate birds" in the Hawaiian language. It's also known as the "surfing capital of the world." The eight miles from Haleiwa to Sunset Beach is considered to have some of the world's best surfing beaches, including Banzai Pipeline and Waimea Bay.

Surf competitions on the North Shore of Oahu are an amazing sight to see. Locals and visitors alike gather on the beach to watch the best surfers in the world pull into twenty-foot barreling waves at the legendary Banzai Pipeline. Championship tournaments are held there annually. For 2020–21, there were three such events scheduled billed as the Vans Triple Crown of Surfing. The third and final stop for this series is the world-famous Banzai Pipeline which also doubles as the final event of the World Surf League Championship Tour. There were no competitive surfing events for us to view on this trip but we were fortunate to witness pro surfing competition during an earlier Hawaii vacation.

The next day, we were having lunch with an old Brewer Resorts colleague of mine. Marylou Foley and I worked together at Brewer Resorts while she was in advertising/public relations and I was the general manager for Punalu'u Village Restaurant in the late 1970s. It was hard to believe that forty years had passed since we worked with each other on the Big Island of Hawaii. We met at Duke's Restaurant on the beach in Waikiki. Apart from being friends, the common denominator between us was our admiration for Jim Reed whom we both reported to at Brewer Resorts. During lunch we reminisced over our common work memories. The food was thoroughly enjoyable but catching up with Marylou was definitely the highlight.

Shawn and Yucco picked us up from our hotel later for an afternoon hike. Thanks to Shawn, we made a new discovery that day. Makapuu Point is a mere half hour outside of Waikiki. The scenic Makapuu Point Lighthouse Trail offers outstanding views of the island's southeastern coastline. It's about a half hour trek from the bottom to the top of the trail and the trail is paved. Once you reach the top, you're rewarded with magnificent views of the windward coast and the historic red-roofed Makapuu Lighthouse built in 1909. The lighthouse makes a stunning picture against the deep blue sea below but the lighthouse itself is off-limits. On a clear day, you may even see Molokai and Lanai. We thoroughly enjoyed the hike and were rewarded with mesmerizing photos that we'll treasure for years to come.

The next day, we flew inter-island from Oahu to Hawaii, the Big Island. This was a trip that I'd been looking forward to for some time. I graduated from Konawaena High School on the Big Island and launched the first six years of my hospitality career there. We stayed at the acclaimed five-star Mauna Kea Beach Resort the first two nights. Mauna Kea Beach Resort (MKB) employed me from 1965 through 1970. MKB was only my second employer within the hospitality industry, but my varied departmental experiences provided me with a firm foundation in hotel principles that I affectionately refer to as "obtaining my PhD in Hotel Operations." It's difficult to put into words the feeling I have for the Mauna Kea Beach Hotel. Being there creates calm, serene, at-peace feelings with the world. My sentiments align perfectly with longtime returning generation after generation guests to the property, who describe it as "There's just something magical about the place."

My heart started beating more rapidly as Sandie and turned left off the highway passing the "Mauna Kea Beach Resort" sign onto the driveway that would lead us to the resort. We headed down the driveway lined with radiant bougainvillea, toward the gleaming ocean. We turned past the third hole of the golf course where I pointed out to Sandie that this was one of the more challenging holes of the course as you had to drive your ball across an ocean water trap to land on the green. We pulled up to the front circle of MKB under palm trees holding throngs of singing birds. Everywhere one looked was beautiful flowers and plants. MKB's landscaping consists of over 200,000 plants of more than 200 varieties!

Mauna Kea Beach Hotel was the brainchild of Laurance S. Rockefeller who decided on the site location from a helicopter as at that time there were no roads that led to that locale. Being a staunch conservationist, his conception requirements were that it must blend into the natural environment to become as invisible to the extent possible. It must be open to the elements of sun and fresh air. He wanted something of an ultra-luxury retreat with the feeling of an elegant private estate focusing on nature with the comforts of fine food and first-class amenities. Rockefeller's vision was realized as Mauna Kea Beach Resort was the first world-class hotel on the island.

The lobby featured Hawaii's very first retractable roof providing a skylight that could be closed for inclement weather. The lobby also housed a multi-story garden through which coconut palms grew. Mauna Kea Beach Resort is also home to over 1,600 Pacific and Asian art pieces and artifacts from around the world. Architecturally, the integration of East and West influences was groundbreaking. The concept of positioning the hotel also as an art gallery was one of the first of its kind. The sensitivity to the Hawaiian culture and the environment was exemplary. Mauna Kea Beach Hotel won the American Institute of Architects Honor Award in 1967. *Esquire Magazine* recognized it as "One of Three Best Hotels in the World," in 1967 and *Fortune Magazine* called it one of "Ten Best Buildings of 1966." To this day, Mauna Kea Beach Resort continues to pile recognition award upon recognition award for its beach, architecture, services, amenities, and golf course.

Our Mauna Kea Beach Hotel reservation was secured through Marriott reward points that I had accumulated during my trade show career. Thank goodness for hotel incentive points, allowing the earning and banking of points for future use. Room rates at the time for Mauna Kea Beach Hotel's regular rooms were in the $800 per night category, well outside our comfortable per- night hotel spending. The Mauna Kea Beach Hotel stay was timed to celebrate Sandie's January-24 birthday. While a few months off, I made the resort aware of our anniversary. This coupled with their knowledge of my previous association with the property motivated them to provide us with a beachfront room with a killer view. The hotel management also had a bottle of champagne, a delectable fruit offering, and a personalized note from the hotel's general manager waiting for us upon our arrival.

We arrived at the Mauna Kea Beach Hotel in the afternoon on Sandie's birthday. After settling in we toured the grounds to make ourselves familiar with the location of the resort's dining facilities and amenities. Nostalgic feelings emanated throughout my body as we made our way through the property. The resort had gone through three additional ownership changes since my 1970 departure and some major renovations revealing obvious changes. To the previous owners' credit, however, the reconstruction efforts didn't interfere at all with Rockefeller's original vision.

After the tour, our experience began with dinner in the hotel's Manta restaurant where I had made a reservation, weeks earlier. For our special occasion, the hotel provided us with a patio table that provided a magnificent view of the beautiful Hawaiian sunset. Relaxation was the norm from that moment on until we departed this renowned property. We savored an outstanding dinner followed by a hotel-provided dessert personalized in recognition of Sandie's birthday. The ensuing day began with a breakfast buffet that far and away was the best that I've ever seen during my entire hotel–trade-show career. That day was set aside as a "Cabana Day" for us as we lounged in our own cabana on the beach for the entire day without a care in the world. Sadly, after another breakfast at the best breakfast buffet I've ever experienced, it was time to check out of the magical Mauna Kea Beach Hotel. It was difficult leaving such lavish accommodations but off to Kailua, Kona, we went the next day.

We had reservations in Kona at the Courtyard King Kamehameha Hotel. The King Kamehameha Hotel (referred to as the King Kam Hotel by locals) was the first major hotel built in Kona and was originally built in 1960. The initial structure was razed and replaced with a modern version of its time in 1975. In addition to being recognized as the first major hotel on the island, it's also known for its proximity to the Ahuena Heiau.

Located on a small artificial island across from the King Kamehameha Hotel in Kailua, the Ahuena Heiau—a temple of peace and prosperity— was built by King Kamehameha I between 1812 and 1813 to honor Lono, the god of fertility. It served as the king's personal refuge and was his home for the last years of his life. It is where the chief kahuna went into a deep trance and received messages from the gods. It is believed he also died here. The temple is so revered today that no one can set foot inside or on the grounds surrounding it.

We checked into an upgraded suite generously provided by the resort that overlooked Kailua-Kona's bay. Early that evening, we met Jeff Faye at a restaurant across the street from our hotel for a drink. Jeff was the Best Man at my marriage to Eileen Morinoue (Janette's mother) in 1964. He was currently operating his own charter boat business with his son. It had been fifty-five years since we had seen each other, and I just couldn't pass up the opportunity to visit with him while in Kona. We were hopeful that he would stay for dinner but he had to leave after the one drink. Sandie and I enjoyed some local fare for our dinner and after walking through downtown Kailua on a stroll called it a night.

The next day, we headed across the island to tour one of the true world wonders, the Kilauea Volcano. Remembering the dramatic effect a volcano eruption had on me years ago, I was hoping that Sandie may be able to experience the same phenomenon. Kilauea volcano is one of the world's most active volcanoes. It is a shield-type volcano that makes up the southeastern side of the Big Island of Hawaii. The summit caldera contains a lava lake known as Halemaumau that is said to be the home of the Hawaiian volcano goddess, Pele. Kilauea has had more than sixty recorded eruptions in the current cycle, according to the U.S. Geological Survey, and has been erupting on a continuous basis since 1983.

On May 3, 2018, Kilauea erupted dramatically, several hours after a magnitude-5.0 quake struck the Big Island. The eruption spewed lava into residential subdivisions in the Puna District of the Big Island, prompting mandatory evacuations of the neighboring Leilani Estates and Lanipuna Gardens subdivisions. While at the volcano site, we were scheduled to meet an old friend of mine and his wife for lunch. The route we took had us pass by old stomping grounds of mine, Punalu'u Village Restaurant.

In the mid-1970s, I managed Punalu'u Village Restaurant along with an adjacent condominium/golf course development. A 1975 massive tsunami made a direct hit on this complex, following a 7.2 magnitude earthquake. Twenty-foot waves traveling at over 600 miles per hour smashed through the area devastating everything in its path. By chance, we exited off the highway to view that area. Much to our surprise, the framework of the gutted restaurant buildings were still in place. The huge glass plated windows along with some of the walls were gone and the area had long since been overrun with vegetation. We had to carefully navigate the terrain due to broken glass and various territorial hazards. I was able to walk Sandie through the facility outlining the experience guests enjoyed while patronizing the restaurant in better times. A combination of sorrow and pride welled up inside me as Sandie and I retraced the path the restaurant's customers would have taken. It was truly a walk down memory lane for myself remembering the beehive of activity in better times of the museum, gift shop, bar, and of course the restaurant.

After a few unseen tears later, we were on our way to meet Alonzo Baker and his wife Debra for lunch at the Volcano House. Alonzo was the trifecta to Steve Verhines and me on a hitchhiking trip the three of made from Indianapolis to Louisville during my junior year of high school. I didn't learn until shortly after reconnecting with Steve Verhines that Alonzo lived on the Big Island and had for several years. It's truly ironic how life paths cross. As an Indiana kid, Hawaii was my home for more than a decade of my life at various times during the 1960s, '70s, and '80s. Decades later, an old buddy of mine relocates to the same island I lived on when I graduated from high school and we were going to reconnect more than fifty years later!

The four of us enjoyed a nice lunch in the Volcano House restaurant, followed by a self-guided mini-tour of the volcano. Alonzo and Debra have two daughters living on the mainland in different cities. Not surprisingly, there was discussion of them potentially relocating to the mainland so they wouldn't be so far away from their daughters. As the time was slipping away from us, we left Alonzo and Debra to begin our trek back to our Kona Hotel. On the way, we stopped off at my High school alma mater, Konawaena in Kealakekua. It had been so long since I'd seen the place and I hardly recognized it.

We had a planned lunch and dinner the following day. As we had the morning free we toured the Kona grounds as I pointed out areas of past interest to Sandie. As a senior at Konawaena High School, I spent a fair amount of time along Ali'i Drive in Kona. One area of attraction that was always of interest to me was a beach off of Ali'i Drive called "White Sands Beach," renowned due to an interesting natural phenomenon occurring primarily during the winter months where the sand is completely washed out to sea leaving only exposed lava rock for the beach. That's why this beach is also called "Disappearing Sands" because it quite literally vanishes. When the wave action ceases, the regular ocean currents slowly move the sand back. But this periodic and complete flushing of the sand keeps it very white. It's on this beach that I learned to body surf while living with Pat and John Peacock, a couple that my uncle knew.

Sadness welled up inside of me as the more we drove along. The realization sat in that the quiet, peaceful, beauty filled island that I once called home was now very commercialized. There was even a hotel that sprang up next to the White Sands Beach. Perhaps I should have been a little more prepared for the eventual changes that would occur over the forty years that I had been away. Added shopping malls, gift shops, restaurants, and markets are all part of progress I suppose but difficult to digest at any rate considering the fond memories of a much slower life-style.

Our lunch appointment was with Doris and Gil Tavares at a restaurant in Holualoa-Kona. Gil was a junior at Konawaena High School during my senior year when we became friends. Doris and Gil's marriage is a true high school romance story. They were going with each other in high school and married shortly after they both graduated. Over fifty years of marriage has blessed them with a beautiful family and several grandkids. Following our lunch, they guided us to the home I lived in with my uncle just off of Kuakini Highway. With the growth in local residences and vegetation, there's no way I would have found it on my own.

That evening, we were invited to dinner at the Morinoue's residence in Holualoa-Kona. Hiroki Morinoue is a well-known Big Island artist and my brother-in-law from my first marriage. During that period, I knew him as Alvin and he was a junior at Konawaena while my first wife and his sister, Eileen, and I were seniors. The entire Morinoue clan welcomed Sandie and

I into their home for an authentic Japanese style dinner that we enjoyed on their veranda. Hiroki's wife, Setsuko and Daughter Maki outdid themselves that evening with their culinary expertise. Maki's husband Jeff, son Kenzo, and sister Miho were also dinner participants. Lively conversation in a true aloha spirit fashion filled the air for a most enjoyable evening.

Our luncheon the next day was special for two reasons. First, some of my Konawaena High School 1964 graduates invited Sandie and me to lunch. Counting Sandie and me, there were a total of twenty-one guests that showed up. Among those in attendance it was great seeing Earl Ogata, Susan Morton (Texeria), her husband Jim, Pearl Gomes, Jeanette Tomono, Milton Leslie, Ray Takeguchi, and Caroline Smith again. High school stories were the order of the day, making it a delightful get together that afternoon. Second, without any input from me the organizers of the lunch decided on having it at the Kona Inn in Kailua-Kona. The Kona Inn coincidentally was the facility where my hospitality career began as a busboy in 1964! The hotel portion of the property had long since been removed but the restaurant (after a few renovations) looked just as it did in 1964. The ambience was also similar making me feel as if I were in a time-warp.

The next day, we flew to our third Hawaiian Island on our agenda, Kauai. Kauai is nicknamed "the Garden Isle" thanks to the tropical rainforest covering much of its surface. Geologically, it's the second oldest of the main Hawaiian Islands after Ni'ihau. Its dramatic cliffs and pinnacles of its Na Pali Coast have served as a backdrop for numerous Hollywood films, while ten-mile-long Waimea Canyon and the Nounou Trails traversing the Sleeping Giant mountain ridge provide beautiful scenery. Our Kauai jaunt was to visit with my daughter Janette who was working on the *Fast and Furious Presents: Hobbs & Shaw* movie there.

We arrived to the charming Koloa Landing Resort late that afternoon and checked into Janette's room. A quick tour of the Marriott Autograph Resort revealed three swimming pools situated on twenty-five acres of plush tropical foliage along with a waterfall. The rooms were oversized and nicely furnished. The amenities included three on-site restaurants, a work-out facility, and a spa. The ocean was a scant two blocks from the resort. Our stay here was certainly going to be a memorable one.

Our first self-guided tour adventure was to Waimea Falls Canyon. Waimea is Hawaiian for "reddish water," a reference to the canyon's red soil which provides a comparable Grand Canyon feel. The canyon was formed by a deep incision of the Waimea River arising from the extreme rainfall on the island's central peak which is among the wettest spots on earth. Mark Twain stood in awe of the canyons' steep valleys and called it the "Grand Canyon of the Pacific." Sandie and I were fortunate to have visited the Grand Canyon and from some scenic lookouts the views were quite similar, notwithstanding the depth differential of the two canyons.

A real treat for us was a trip to the *Hobbs & Shaw* film set with Janette serving as our tour guide. No filming was taking place, which allowed us to walk through the set at our leisure. Major props, autos, trucks, motor-cycles, and helicopters were in place. The movie used an old abandoned sugar cane factory for the main Samoan setting of the film. The other main location shoot for the film was in England. There was a cameraman cheat sheet left behind that specified what action scenes were taking place when. All in all, an authentic interesting experience.

That evening my generous daughter Janette arranged for us to attend the luau held at the Hyatt down the road. Being a former resident of Hawaii I had been to luaus but felt it a worthwhile experience for Sandie and me. In ancient Hawaii, the luau was the most significant style of celebration. The entertainment is always worthwhile as you witness authentic tradi-tional Polynesian dance rituals performed by local residents. The crowning achievement of food preparation for the luau is the roasting of a whole pig in the imu (man-made Hawaiian underground oven) where a ceremony is performed when the final product is removed from the underground oven. Unfortunately due to weather conditions, our luau was held indoors, preventing us from witnessing this time-honored tradition. Our enjoyable evening ended with Sandie having her picture taken with a couple of the local Samoan fire dancers. Of course, I had to get in on the act and have my picture taken with a hula girl performer.

The next day I went to the fitness center for my customary morning workout. My routine consisted of thirty minutes on an elliptical trainer and ten to fifteen minutes of strength conditioning. For the past several years, I had experienced an irregular heartbeat but was assured by doctors that it wasn't anything serious. Along with the irregular heartbeat came sporadic dizzy spells. These lasted just a few seconds but as the frequency of these incidents increased, they became more concerning. I finished my workout routine and headed for the hotel lobby to begin our checkout process.

Between the fitness center and the lobby, I became so weak that I had to sit down. On a balcony over my right shoulder was a boy looking out over the beautiful ocean setting. Lifting my head up to see him caused such a severe case of light headiness that I was afraid of fainting. After a while, I got up to resume my trek to the hotel lobby and it took all of my effort to make it. By this point, I was feeling so bad that I didn't know whether I could even make it back to our hotel room. My responsiveness and senses were so slow in reacting that I asked a hotel desk clerk for information on the closest hospital emergency room. He explained that the closest emergency room was thirty to forty minutes away but that there was an urgent care facility within five to ten minutes.

The only thought on my mind at that point was to make it back to our hotel room and then to the urgent care facility as quickly as possible. Truth be told, I had never experienced symptoms like this before and didn't even know if I could even make it to the Urgent Care Center. If I wasn't going to make it, I at least wanted to be with Sandie and pushed hard to make it back to our hotel room. Making it to the hotel room, Sandie sensed that there was something terribly wrong and while explaining my condition, I lied down hopeful of whatever was ailing me would somehow vanish. Instinct pushed me to drive over to the Urgent Care Center to be examined. We were scheduled to leave this day and at that point our departure was in question. The doctor on duty gave me a thorough looking over and couldn't find anything that placed me in immediate peril. For treatment, I was placed on an IV. She then suggested that I hydrate myself and rest for a bit. While that did the trick for that incident, it embedded firmly in my conscious the importance of a procedure that would remedy future such events.

A week or so after we returned from a thoroughly relaxing and memorable Hawaii excursion (excepting the heart incident), we ventured up to Indianapolis. My half-sisters on my bio-dad's side arranged for a surprise ninetieth birthday party for my step-mom Betty Bartlett. The event was held at Brandon Ferguson's (her grandson) home in the suburb of Greenwood. Around twenty guests from that side of the family were in attendance. This was a treat for Sandie and me as it's rare that we get to visit with my sisters Sheryl Pierson and Sharon Ferguson together. Betty looked and acted more like seventy than ninety and thoroughly enjoyed the evening activities. Another somewhat rare occurrence is for Sharon and Joe's younger son Chad to be at the gatherings we've attended. He was there with his wife Candice along with one of her sons.

Early that April, we ventured up to Chicago for visitations. We drove over to the Oak Lawn suburb and visited Sandie's oldest daughter Olivia and her family. While in Chicago Sandie took time out to visit with her friend Nancy who she's known since her College of Lake County days. We then drove to the Northwest Side of Chicago and visited with Sandie's youngest daughter Julie and her family. We enjoyed the time spent with Olivia, Julie, and the grandkids.

Later that April, Sandie and I were in for a real treat. Janette's sister Keturah Lowe, Keturah's husband Jason, and their two daughters, Jasmine and Keira flew in to celebrate Janette's birthday with her. They stayed in Clarksville for a few days allowing Sandie and I to get to know them better. We ventured into Nashville as a group, played cards, and just enjoyed each other's company. Such a lovely family! Jasmine and Keira are caring, friendly young ladies with clear life goals. Jason and Keturah are a hoot to be around and have obviously served as exceptional role models and nurturers of their two engaging daughters.

Sandie and I experienced a thrilling Alaskan expedition May 15–27, 2019. Our trip itinerary included Oregon, Seattle, Vancouver, and, of course, Alaska. In addition to the Oregon sites, we planned on a rendezvous with a couple of Janette's past Oregon neighbors. Janette lived in Seaside, Oregon for several years and established numerous friendships there. As was customary for early morning Nashville departures we spent the previous night in the city for easier airport access.

To begin the trip, we flew into Seattle making that our strategic west coast hub. From there, we would rent a car for travel through Washington, Oregon, and Vancouver. We would also fly between Seattle and Anchorage. We visited Seattle back in 2012 where we took in most of the city's major attractions. For this encounter our only excursion aside from using it as our west coast hub would be to take in a Seattle Mariners baseball game. We arrived into Seattle late in the day after a flight change in Oakland. The next morning, we met our Turo car renter and picked up our auto rental for the West Coast section of our trip.

The first stop of the day was nearly three hours away as we were checking into our in Portland, Oregon hotel before heading out to Seaside, Oregon. Shortly after crossing the Washington/Oregon state line, the enormity of Oregon's forests stuck out to me. We saw evidence of logging just about everywhere we looked. Oregon is one of the world's great tree-growing areas. The state's soils and climate provide ideal conditions to grow such commercially viable species as Douglas fir and ponderosa pine. Oregon is the top producer of softwood lumber producing more than 16% of the nation's softwood. Forests cover more than 30 million of Oregon's 62 million acres—almost half of the state's landmass.

It now takes one tree every year for every man, woman, and child to meet our needs for paper, packaging, fiber compounds, lumber, and panel products. Annually, every American uses a tree 16 inches in diameter by 100 foot tall. Trees harvested in Oregon use the most careful environmental protections in the world. Strict forest laws assure trees are planted and growing to replace timber harvested.

After a short but beautiful seventy-mile scenic drive through the Oregon Mountains, we arrived at our destination. Camp 18 restaurant is a log cabin-type structure that stands out from the highway. Its architecture is authentic in materials and construction techniques. This building is Gordon Smith's dream. In the early '70s, he began with a few rusty pieces of equipment, some of which were donated, others on loan and most of them purchased; which all led to the construction of the log cabin. All of the timber used in the building came from the general area. It was hauled in, hand-peeled and draw-knifed with the help of the owner's family and friends.

Sandie and I were meeting Janette's Seaside friends Susan and Dewey Bastedo, and Patty Luttrell for an early dinner. Susan and Dewey are a delightful couple. She still bakes for a local bakery and Dewey was responsible for some of the restaurant's original construction. Sandie had become Facebook friends with Susan and this was their first person-to-person meeting. Patty was Janette's next door neighbor in Seaside and her husband Rick assisted Janette with several renovations to her home. After dinner Sandie and I went over to Patty's place for a brief visit and to meet her husband Rick. Patty and Rick's yard looked as if it could have been the centerfold for a Better Home and Garden publication. The landscaping, floral displays, and lawn were immaculate. After a brief visit we headed back for our hotel in Portland. Janette later informed us that gardening is a passion of Patty's.

The next day, we reserved a tour for the acclaimed Multnomah Falls area. The tour guide picked us up from the hotel early that afternoon. Multnomah Falls is the second highest year-round waterfall in the United States and the highest in Oregon, and is Oregon's number one natural attraction. Fed by underground streams that originate miles above on Larch Mountain, this ancient 620-foot waterfall is divided into two sections; the upper falls plummets an impressive 542 feet into a pool and again drops 69 feet to form a creek that runs into the Columbia River. The falls was a spectacular site and well moderated by our tour guide. Proving his veteran status as a guide he took individual keeper photos of Sandie and me, where the falls appear to be dropping into our mouths!

The next morning, we headed out to Seattle. Our one Seattle activity this trip was a Seattle Mariners baseball game. The Mariners were playing the Minnesota Twins for this May 18, 2019 contest. We arrived at the ballpark early in the evening to allow time to explore the stadium before the first pitch. The local team's popularity was evident as there was a line of fans several blocks long waiting to get into the park. Unfortunately for the Mariners, it was a long night as the Twins shellacked the home team by an 18–4 margin.

We overnighted in Seattle before pushing on to Vancouver, British Columbia. The whole northwestern seaboard was breathtaking. Canada also didn't disappoint by any means. The last fifty miles or so in the state of Washington and the first fifty miles or so into Canada was lovely country-like driving. Driving into Vancouver presented an interesting phenomenon. Vancouver is the first major city I've ever visited that didn't have a freeway leading into it.

The lack of freeways in the City of Vancouver is primarily due to the protests of concerned citizens as the city was being developed. During the late 1950s, proposals were made by the City to put a freeway through the heart of Chinatown. It would have completely altered the city's mountain views and cut off the waterfront. The city is surrounded by water on three sides and possesses stunning mountain views. It would have been an absolute crime to destroy that ambience. Sandie and I were able to truly enjoy these spectacular views from our higher-floor hotel room and also by just walking around this friendly city.

We took a city tour the next day to make the most of our limited time in Vancouver. Vancouver has been described as "a world-class city with an ocean attached." The first thing you notice of Vancouver is the surrounding water settings buffeted by statuesque mountain ranges. Vancouver is truly one of the great scenic cities of the world. Apart from soaking in the beauty of Vancouver itself we were treated to stops at Stanley Park and Granville Island.

The highlight of the Stanley Park at the Brockton Point location was the First Nations Totem Poles display. The nine totem poles at Brockton Point in Stanley Park are British Columbia, Canada's most visited tourist attraction. The collection started at Lumberman's Arch in the 1920s, when the Park Board bought four totems from Vancouver Island's Alert Bay. More purchased totems came from the Queen Charlotte Islands to celebrate the 1936 Golden Jubilee. In the mid-1960s, the totem poles were moved to the current attractive and accessible Brockton Point.

Our mid-day stop was at Vancouver's Granville Island. Granville Island is known primarily for its Public Market, arguably the epicenter for Vancouver's culinary enthusiasm. The goods tell their own stories: strawberries straight from Fraser Valley, Okanagan cherries, fresh Coho salmon and live Dungeness crabs. No wonder Vancouver top chefs are often spotted shopping here for high-quality and rare ingredients for their menus. Luckily, even a casual visitor can partake in the abundance with a visit to the market's food court where delis, restaurants and lunch counters feature a variety of cuisines which, of course, Sandie and I took full advantage of.

Something special seems to happen when you step onto Granville Island. Despite being home to 300 businesses, studios and facilities, the marketplace retains an old-fashioned, timeless feeling. Craftsmen and artists take up residence here, and it's clear that the tradition of apprenticeship and mastery is alive and well. You can see it in the detail of a ceramic bowl or the gentle curve of a freshly blown glass vase, the intricacy of a piece of jewelry or the flick of a painter's brush. Granville Island's architecture, much of which comprises remodeled warehouses, whisper of the island's industrial past. It was the perfect addition to our city tour agenda.

The next day, we were treated once again to the beautiful Canadian and Washington state countryside as we ventured back to Seattle. Sandie and I overnighted there and returned our car rental preceding our Alaskan flight the following morning. As Vancouver held a mysterious fascination for us, Alaska most certainly did as neither Sandie nor I had the pleasure of visiting it to that point. Our Alaskan flight was appropriately on Alaska Airlines and flew into Anchorage from Seattle.

Alaska has 34,000 miles of coastline, more than the rest of the U.S. combined. Alaska is the only state to have coastlines on three different seas: the Arctic Ocean, Pacific Ocean, and Bering Sea. Most U.S. glaciers are in Alaska. Some say a picture is worth a thousand words. What do you do when a picture won't adequately capture the sheer beauty of a place? This was certainly our opinion of this grandiose state. We were determined to familiarize ourselves with as much of this state's beauty that our limited stay there would allow. Sandie and I signed up for two tours, the "Turnagain Arm" tour and the "Alaska Railroad Anchorage to Seward" tour.

The Turnagain Arm Tour was a six-hour adventure described as "A must see destination." The tour went along the scenic Seward Parkway to the Anchorage Coastal Wildlife Refuge, Beluga Point, Bird Point and Portage Valley. The Alaska Wildlife Conservation Center was a large nature preserve where injured animals were rehabilitated. Our group traveled up into the Chugach Mountains for another great vantage point on the Turnagain Arm. At the Wildlife Sanctuary we were treated to a close viewing of bears, coyotes, and elk.

The Alaska Railroad Anchorage to Seward trip the next day was a long but extremely satisfying experience. The round-trip itself took fourteen hours but, being a once in a lifetime excursion, it was well worth it. The Coastal Classic Train traveled along the Turnagain Arm from Anchorage to Seward. We viewed the Chugach Mountains, river canyons, glaciers, waterfalls, and the impressive backcountry of Alaska. In Seward, we had the option to either explore the town or take a wildlife and glacier day cruise to the Kenai Fjords. We opted for the glacier day cruise and were delighted that we did.

On the glacier boat ride, there were numerous glaciers on either side of us once we were well into the cruise. The glaciers are deceptive in size. They can be a mile wide rising 250 feet above the water line. Pictures simply cannot do them justice. Mountain peaks rose straight from the ice filled water until they seem to touch the sky. Adjacent to them are equally majestic peaks as far as the eye can see. We spotted whales, eagles and an extraordinary site; several dozen sea lions were sun bathing on the shoreline around the half-way mark of our cruise. Alaska is simply indescribably beautiful.

Our northwest/Alaska trip was satisfying to us on so many levels. Time seemed to roll by as we soaked in everything Alaska had to offer us for the few days we were there. After twelve days on the road, it was time to return to our Tennessee home of three years in Clarksville. It was sad to leave but we'll always have the memories of this outstanding experience.

The following month I had a heart procedure performed, which would hopefully correct my irregular heartbeat and prevent future "light headed" episodes similar to what I'd experienced in Hawaii the past February. The procedure was a "cardiac catheterization." Cardiac catheterization is a procedure used to diagnose and treat certain cardiovascular conditions. During cardiac catheterization, a catheter is inserted in an artery or vein in your groin, neck, or arm and threaded through your blood vessels to your heart where diagnosed damage is repaired. While the procedure was a success it didn't completely resolve my heart issue. Upon further testing and evaluation, the cardiac specialists at Vanderbilt University Hospital in Nashville indicated that I could still be at risk of future incidents. They provided two options: (1) wait for the condition to worsen risking another incident before further action or (2) schedule surgery on my heart mitral valve. Terrified from the Hawaii attack, I opted for option two and due to the anticipated recovery time and our schedule decided to have the procedure in November.

That July, Sandie and I embarked on another western road trip. This adventure was south of our previous routing to take in Utah, Colorado, Nebraska, and Kansas. The itinerary had us on the road for twelve days. We flew into Salt Lake City and rented a car for our 2,500-mile journey through four states. The car we rented was a 2019 Malibu, which turned out to be a significant issue. This vehicle had no immediate pickup when you depressed the accelerator. That was a major impediment while merging onto freeways and in my opinion was a serious safety issue. Apparently, all 2019 Malibus were engineered this way.

Wanting to feel more secure and safe on our journey, we decided to switch our vehicle. We had rented from Hertz so we felt it would be an easy process to switch at one of several nearby Hertz suburban locations by our Grand Junction, Colorado hotel. That proved to be a fallacy as we called several locations only to learn that they were out of vehicles. Frustrated, we called the main Hertz customer service number to learn the closest switch option was the Denver, Colorado airport. The last thing we wanted to do was to interrupt our trip and drive though Denver to the airport but out of a concern for safety we had no choice. After a lengthy process at the Denver airport we were switched to a brand new Subaru Forrester SUV. This vehicle was comfortable and very responsive, providing what we believed to be a safety net for the rest of our journey. Unfortunately, there would be much more to the Subaru drama but more on that after we make it into Kansas.

In relative proximity to our Golden, Colorado location was the spectacular Rim Rock Drive. We headed over the next morning to experience this wonder for ourselves. The Rim Rock Drive is described as one of the grandest scenic drives in the American West. Less than halfway through the drive it became apparent to us that this description was right on the money. The drive offered red rock canyons, crisp blue skies, and glorious views as we navigated forward. Along the way, there was access to nineteen signed viewpoints providing ample picture taking opportunities. This proved to be another one of those situations where a picture just couldn't possibly capture the natural beauty we were photographing.

We then hit the road for a four-hour drive to Westminster, Colorado. Our target just outside of Westminster was the Buffalo Bill Museum grave site and museum. The Museum is modeled after Bill Cody's house southwest of the town. The Buffalo Bill Museum's focus is on the life and times of William F. "Buffalo Bill" Cody. He was a noted guide, scout, frontiersman, showman, actor, and American icon. It took us through the history, promise, and enduring spirit of the American West. Its collection also interpreted the history of the American cowboy, dude ranching, and western conservation.

When it comes to historical characters, few embody the spirit of the American West more than Buffalo Bill. Cody left home around age eleven to become a cattle herder, and then joined the Pony Express as a rider in 1860. His resume also includes stints with the Army as a private in the 7th Kansas Calvary, and later as a scout. But his legend really began to grow as his buffalo-hunting skills became renowned, earning him the nickname Buffalo Bill. With the buzz about his exploits on the plains spreading—thanks to newspapers and dime novels, Cody parlayed his status as a national folk hero into a show-business career.

We found the fenced off Buffalo Bill's grave site to be on the same grounds as the museum. Buffalo Bill died on January 10, 1917, in Denver while visiting his sister. But because of the frozen ground, he wasn't buried until June 3, 1917, outside Golden, Colorado, with thousands of people in attendance. Though tales involving a band of body-stealing Wyomingites have been perpetuated by conspiracy theorists since the time of his funeral, Colorado's Lookout Mountain is widely regarded as the site of Cody's final resting place.

A short jaunt from Westminster, Colorado, sits the well-known Coors Brewery in Golden, Colorado. Being in such close proximity we felt it would be a shame not to visit this well-known company. Publicized as the largest single-site brewery in the world, it sits at the foot of the Rocky Mountains. The brewery boasts of a legacy of quality, innovation, and customer service. Our nominal $10 admission fee included a guided brewery tour, a historical section inclusive of old photos, retro beer cans and neon signs. Also, up to three to eight ounce beer samples along with a commemorative glass which was a no-cost extra premium!

Our next destination was North Platte, Nebraska. The one location we wanted to visit in Nebraska was the Chimney Rock National Historic site. The mundane scenery on this two-and-half hour drive made the trip non eventual to say the least. The site itself left a lot to be desired as it was simply a large vertical single free-standing rock sitting on a mountain that somewhat resembled a chimney. There was a small visitors' center accessible via the sidewalk from the parking lot. Admittedly, we were more than surprised to read warning signs after leaving our vehicle, which suggested staying on the sidewalks to avoid snakes!

Traveling between North Platte, Nebraska and Dodge City, Kansas, on July 11, 2019, was a day we'd remember for the foreseeable future. In the remote countryside of Ingalls, Kansas, Sandie had just taken over the driving chore and we pulled out onto a three way stop behind a stopped semi-truck literally in the middle of nowhere. We were stopped four to six feet behind the T&A semi-truck at this three-way stop intersection where Highways 23 and 156 intersect. The truck was stopped as was our vehicle. All of a sudden the truck's reverse lights came on and began backing up, and as the passenger I honked our horn. The truck continued to backup as I laid on the horn, continually blasting it, which he apparently couldn't hear over the roar of his diesel engine. Sandie looked into the mirror to see if there was a vehicle behind us and was reaching to put our vehicle in reverse when the truck hit us. This all occurred in a matter of seconds. The truck was driving off when another truck turning left onto 23 from Highway 156 stopped him and told him he had hit us. The semi-driver then pulled his truck off to the side of the road and we took accident photos and exchanged insurance information while I called Allstate, our insurance agency. As a precaution, I called Aidan (the semi-driver) ten minutes or so after the incident and recorded the conversation where he confirmed backing into us.

Nobody was hurt and the damage to our rental car was a slight dent on the hood and paint scraped from the hood. Our rented Subaru SUV was drivable and in fact we drove it through the rest of our trip. The incident shook up both Sandie and me as we kept picturing this 80,000-pound vehicle backing up into us. After obtaining all necessary information and settling down a bit, we drove on to Dodge City.

Damage done to our rented Subaru was in the $1,100 dollar range while there was no noticeable damage to the huge semi-truck. We were eventually cleared of any responsibility resulting from the accident, but it took nearly a year before the truck company's insurance company, Progressive, settled with Hertz and the file was actually closed. During this period, I received a couple of Hertz dunning letters threatening to revoke my Gold membership status and blackball me from renting vehicles from any of their subsidiaries. The whole incident was an ordeal that we certainly hope to avoid in the future. The main point, however, was that nobody was injured.

After resting a bit in our Dodge City hotel room, we headed over to the Boot Hill Museum & Cemetery. Boot Hill Museum is a historical museum providing an interesting interactive experience. Historical exhibits illustrated the life and times of early Dodge City and its unique characters. The Dodge City physical structures were under renovation during our visit. However, the street and museum were open allowing us to stroll down the boardwalk and peer through the windows into a time long gone by. Entering these buildings gave us a look into the past of the infamous Dodge City. We walked into and experienced an 1870s drug store, saloon, newspaper office, restaurant, and ice cream parlor of that era. Photos and wanted posters of Dodge City's most well-known citizens of that time created an "in the moment" effect.

For entertainment, we visited the original Boot Hill Cemetery located in the heart of the modern-day Dodge City. We witnessed two dramatic gunfights between the good guys and the bad guys and listened to Miss Kitty croon in the Long Branch saloon. Much to my surprise, the Can-Can girls brought me up onto the stage as they performed one of their acts. We also were treated to historical interactive displays throughout the museum that provided a unique learning experience. For instance, we learned that Wyatt Earp was born in Illinois and, before becoming the respected lawman he became known as, he was indicted in Arkansas for stealing horses!

Our final targeted landing-spot on this expedition was the Arches National Park in Moab, Utah. As this destination was eight hours from Dodge City, we broke the drive up into two days stopping halfway in Gunnison, Colorado. Arches were designated a national monument before being changed to a national park in 1971 by President Nixon. Native Americans lived in this region further back in history for thousands of years. The Arches National Park lies on top of a salt bed, which underwent extreme climate changes millions of years ago.

Arches National Park has the densest concentration of natural stone arches in the world. There are over 2,000 documented arches in the park, plus pinnacles, balanced rocks, fins, and other geologic formations. Some are more notable than others. Sandie and I were in awe, meandering through this world wonder. There were numerous pull-over spots throughout the park allowing for closer inspection of God's handiwork. Each stop seemed to offer a slightly different perspective of this beautiful creation.

We capped the day off by eating at a 1960s throwback diner called the Moab Diner. Originally named the Poor Boy Drive-Inn in the 1960s, the then popular drive-in offered 29 cent hamburgers. It was a happening place with full-service car hops and Friday and Saturday night cruisers on Main Street of Moab. To this day, locals tell nostalgic stories of high school sweethearts gathering at the local hangout enjoying the fun times and great food of the Poor Boy Drive-Inn since renamed the Moab Diner. The ambience was reminiscent of the 1960s and we thoroughly enjoyed our diner fare.

This concluded our vacation and with the accident exception it was an outstanding adventure. We completed our entire itinerary by returning the slightly damaged Subaru SUV to Hertz at the Salt Lake City Airport. After rehashing the accident with a Hertz accident investigator and filling out accident reports, Southwest Airlines flew us back to the comforts of home in Clarksville, Tennessee, via Nashville.

In September of 2019, Steve Verhines, my childhood friend of over fifty years, visited us over a long weekend. Steve and I spent the weekend reminiscing over our teenage escapades. Playing the tourist guide, we drove into Nashville to see the city. Thinking Steve would enjoy touring one of the city's museums, I purchased two yearly passes to the Musician Hall of Fame & Museum (MHOF). The MHOF honors all musicians regardless of genre or instrument. The MHOF timeline starts with the beginning of recorded music and inductees are nominated by current members of the American Federation of Musicians and by other music industry profes- sionals. One of the tour highlights was a photo and historical backdrop of the "Million Dollar Quartet" getting together on December 4, 1956 at the Sam Phillip's Studio in Memphis, Tennessee. Of course, the "Million Dollar Quartet" was comprised of Jerry Lee Lewis, Carl Perkins, Elvis Presley, and Johnny Cash!

An unexpected bonus attached to the purchase of those annual passes was an invitation to purchase tickets to the Museum's annual Induction Ceremony being held at the home of the Nashville Symphony. Sandie and I took in the October 22 performance, which featured a who's who among the music industry as performers or inductees. Special guest performers for the evening included Jason Aldean, Garth Brooks, Zac Brown, Ronnie Dunn, Vince Gill, Emmylou Harris, Paul Shaffer, and Paul Simon! The eve- ning's host was David Letterman's former music director, Paul Shaffer. A sampling of the inductees included The Safaris—Instrumental Song Award "Wipe Out," Don Everly—Iconic Riff Award "Wake up Little Susie," and Alabama—for the MHOF Lifetime Achievement Award. Not only were we treated to an evening of outstanding music performances, we also enjoyed it within the perfect acoustical setting of the Nashville Symphony hall. The highlight of the evening in my opinion was Ricky Skaggs rendition of the Everly Brother's hit song "Wake up Little Susie".

Between Steve Verhines visit and the Musicians Hall of Fame Induction ceremony, Sandie and I jaunted up to Indianapolis and then to Chicago. Sandie and I try to make it to Chicago to see the grandkids whenever we can and as Indianapolis is on the way we'll typically stop there either on the way up or on the way back to visit with my side of the family. The Indianapolis to Chicago portion of the trip was special as my sister Sheryl joined us for that leg of the journey. Sheryl was attending a wedding in southern Wisconsin and we volunteered to be her chauffeur. She flew into Indianapolis from her Cape Coral, Florida, home and was staying with her mom in Indianapolis for a visit. As always, we treasured the chance to spend time with Sheryl and the rest of our family members. Mission was accomplished for the trip. Sandie and I visited with both sides of our families and Sheryl attended the Wisconsin wedding problem-free.

Our last expedition of 2019 was in late October and originated in Newark, New Jersey. The overall purpose of the trip was to visit Franklin D. Roosevelt's Hyde Park, New York, home and Presidential Library. After settling into our accommodations we went out for one of our two dinners at the Culinary Institute of America's (CIA) primary campus located in Hyde Park, New York. The CIA also has branch campuses in St. Helena and Napa, California, San Antonio, Texas, and Singapore. If food is your passion, the Culinary Institute of America is the Gold Standard in educational pursuit. Founded in 1946 the CIA is a private, not-for-profit accredited institution recognized as the world's premier culinary college. The institution provides food-and-hospitality-focused associate, bachelor's, and master degree programs. Students rotate cooking and serving stations in one of four on-site restaurants that provide a dining experience second to none for those privileged to partake in an unforgettable gastronomical experience.

Sandie and I were among the fortunate finding our way to the CIA's scrumptious dining worldliness. Every food and beverage item consumed within the CIA's dining facilities was extraordinary. The highlight of our dining experiences was dinner in their gourmet restaurant, The Bocuse Restaurant.

We were seated within an excellent vantage point of the restaurant's open-air kitchen where we witnessed the culinary artists at work preparing feasts for their guests. Sandie had their black truffle soup under puff pastry and the market fish of the day, which was salmon served with local pole beans, caraflex cabbage, and oven-roasted tomatoes topped with pistou broth. My dinner consisted of their pate maison, and American beef wagyu served with row 7 squash, wild mushrooms, braised greens, and smoked choron. For dessert, we couldn't resist their coconut ice cream made at our table. It was one of those overall dining experiences that you never forget.

Our self-guided tour of the Franklin D. Roosevelt home and Museum was fascinating. We took our time over two separate visits to take in as much as possible. The home of Franklin D. Roosevelt National Historic Site preserves the Springwood estate in Hyde Park, New York. Springwood was FDR's birthplace, lifelong home, and burial place. During his presidency FDR made almost 200 visits to Springwood, although he eventually built Top Cottage nearby as a home of his own, separate from his mother's. The main estate functioned as a "Summer White House" where the President hosted his political associates as well as other prominent national and international figures.

Roosevelt used the estate as a retreat for himself and his political associates on the eves of three of the four elections in which he ran for president. When the incoming results indicated that he had won the election, he would go outside onto the front terrace to deliver his victory speech. The estate remained the center of Roosevelt's life in all stages of his career. Roosevelt made his last visit to Springwood in the last week of March 1945, about two weeks before his death. At his own wish, he was buried near the sundial in the Rose Garden on April 15, 1945. His wife was buried at his side after her death in 1962.

"All that is within me cries out to go back to my home on the Hudson River." For FDR, this quote captures his connection to Springwood, the estate that he loved and the place he considered home. The first US Presidential Library was started by FDR there.

A post retirement goal of ours was to visit or, in some instances, revisit all fifty states in our union. The FDR trip resulted cumulatively in our having visited forty-seven of our breathtaking fifty states. We began this crusade in May of 2016 and a mere forty-one months later embarking on as many as four annual trips accomplished this feat. By tracking trip itineraries, we realized that over these past 41 months we had driven well over 20,000 miles in our pursuit!

November of 2019 produced a memorable family event. My older son Shawn had been seeing a very sweet girl from Japan. Yucco Meroa had been living in Hawaii for a couple of years studying the English language. Extremely talented, Yucco was the lead singer of a popular group in Japan. She also produced music for her group and other groups. Shawn met her through a friend and knew almost immediately that she was the one for this forty-two-year-old bachelor.

Through conversations with Shawn and Yucco, we realized that wedding bells were in their future. Shawn had floated a few possible wedding dates, all of which were short-term in nature and difficult for Sandie and me to make the 8,600-mile round-trip. They ended up settling on November 11 to consummate their wedding vows, which presented an additional attendance challenge for Sandie and me. Heart surgery was scheduled for me later that month and I'd be prepping for the procedure. All ended well as there were but a handful of guests that witnessed this momentous occasion. My fourteen-year-old grandson Deacon served as Shawn's best man. Thus, my forty-two-year-old son Shawn Evans became the first of my three adult children to marry. Could there be grandkids from this union in our future? Stay tuned....

November 20, 2019 arrived and following an hour Uber ride from Clarksville to Nashville, we were at Vanderbilt University Medical Hospital by 6:00 am for my heart operation. I was to check in early that morning for my long anticipated mitral valve/ablation combination heart surgery. My heart surgeon Dr. Ashish Suresh Shah was the number two cardiac surgeon at John Hopkins Hospital before accepting the lead position at Vanderbilt. There was no question that I was in excellent hands. In fact, every team doctor and Vanderbilt professional on my case was exceptional before, during, and after the operation.

Admittedly, I had some pre-operation apprehension. Partly due to the procedure itself but also because the doctor couldn't inform us before he was actually well into the operation whether he could repair my mitral valve or if he'd have to replace it. Because of this a decision on the type of the new mitral valve had to made in advance. The two options were a pig's valve or a mechanical valve. The main negative point for the pig valve was that it would probably have to be replaced within ten years. The primary disadvantage of the mechanical valve was that I'd have to be on blood thinners for the rest of my life. Thus, the pig valve was chosen but by God's will it wasn't needed as my valve was repairable.

Dr. Shah informed Sandie immediately following the operation that all went well. Apparently, I was a sight to behold being on a ventilator with IVs, tubes, and wires taking over my body. I was in their ICU unit for two days before being transferred to a regular hospital room for another five days. The rigidity of hospital life following a major procedure is difficult to describe. Initially, there was a lot of pain and nausea. These were managed the best the hospital could through medication. Each day brought a little more relief but the journey was truly an ordeal. My appetite was near non-existent and wasn't helped at all by the food groups they allowed me to eat.

Bed-ridden day after day with the exception of painful bathroom excursions led to bed sores. My last tube was removed from my side four days after the operation. Mentally, this was a huge lift for me. Seeing the light at the end of the tunnel, I threw myself into the physical therapy breathing and walking exercises prescribed by the hospital staff. After seven mostly tormenting, agonizing days at Vanderbilt Hospital I was officially released to the care of a home nursing service. Elation was the feeling of the day!

When you're used to a certain level of activity, being cooped up especially in a confined situation is misery personified. The combination of practically no physical exercise combined with a very limited diet made the hospital stay tough to take. The one bright spot during my confinement was my wife Sandie. She stayed in my room by my side every day and night, providing a ray of sunshine to an otherwise discouraging daily routine. Anything I needed outside of what the hospital could provide, Sandie was there to take of it. It's impossible to describe the comfort level she provided being there. When I woke up in the morning, seeing her gave me enthusiasm to face the coming daily challenges.

The older of my two new daughters through marriage (Sandie's two girls), Olivia volunteered to help Sandie and me during the first week of my in-home recovery. We called Olivia prior to my operation to gauge her interest in flying down to help her mom and me after the procedure. It was heartwarming how Olivia immediately accepted the invitation. It was all the more significant as she had never flown on an airplane before. It's impossible to overstate the appreciation her mom and I had for the help she provided. Apart from helping around the house her presence alone was a real mental boost for both Sandie and me.

My Vanderbilt Heart team suggested continued treatment from an in-home registered nursing service. Both Sandie and I felt this would be advantageous and were led to Lifeline Home Health Care. Medicare provided for six weeks of continued treatment. Lifeline's service included twice weekly in-home registered nurse visits, physical therapy, and occupational therapy. In addition to the in-home nurse visits the company called me once a week to diagnose my current condition. Both Physical & Occupational Therapists from Lifeline made calls the first week I was home. After a few exercises and answering some questions, both determined that I wasn't in need of their services. Prior to the operation I ramped up my physical activity to be in as good of shape as possible for the procedure. This diagnosis by both of these professionals validated my pre-operation workout routines.

The operation was a total success where my heart rate was again normalized. There were however two post-op items that were concerning. The first and main concern was the weight loss I incurred as a result of the procedure. Going into the hospital, I weighed 144 pounds. Upon my release my weight was 122 pounds. I had lost 22 pounds during my hospital stay! Seven months later, I'm still hovering around 130 pounds and have accepted the fact that this will probably be my new normal going forward.

The second issue of concern was my level of sweating. The first couple weeks home from the hospital, I'd sweat so much that I'd wake up each morning feeling like I had just exited a swimming pool. My clothes were so drenched that I'd have to change them each morning simply to feel the comfort of dry clothes. The bedding didn't fare much better. Sheets and pillow cases had to be changed frequently. That for the most part after seven months dissipated. Blessed by my wife Sandie who provided invaluable support for me throughout this entire ordeal being by side every step of the way. I also appreciated the help and encouragement of Olivia, Janette, the best wishes from relatives and friends, and Barb and Elliott Watts.

My 2019 heart operation necessitated a pause to our annual Thanksgiving trips. We missed traveling to Highland, Illinois, to celebrate Thanksgiving with Sandie's sister Janice and her husband Bruce. We also had to forgo our Evans clan family Thanksgiving gathering in Indianapolis. On the brighter side, we were able to host Janette, her significant other Joe, and Sandie's sister and her husband for the Christmas holiday. We were fortunate to have Janice and Bruce visit with us for a few days. On Christmas day itself, Sandie prepared an outstanding dinner that all devoured. Conversation, games, and the opening of presents all added to the festivities of the evening. Bella, Janice, and Bruce's newly adopted dog even got into the act.

Mt Rushmore 2018 (Janette, Sandie, and Stephen).

One World Trade Center—New York.

Chapter 11 | 2020–2022

From January 27 through February 10, 2020, we ventured back to Hawaii and from there on to Napa, California. We actually had January 29 circled on our calendar for several months in hopes of attending Janette's uncle's art exhibit on Oahu. Hiroki Morinoue, my ex-brother-in-law established himself as a renowned island artist producing paintings, sculptures, and eclectic art pieces. The Napa, California, stopover on the way back home was to visit Janette who was working on the set of *13 Reasons Why* for the Netflix show's fourth and final season.

Hiroki Morinoue's Oahu exhibit turned out to be a real family affair. In addition to the entire Morinoue clan from the Big Island being in attendance relatives flew in from all over the mainland for the highly successful exhibit. As there was such a large family contingent in Hawaii for the art display a reunion was held a few days later in Holualoa-Kona on the big Island of Hawaii. This could potentially be the last gathering of this size for the Morinoue clan. Norman Sakata the family patriarch was in his nineties as was his wife Marylin. Some of the other elders were not in the best of health. The household was jammed to the rafters with family members conversing, and working their way through an amazing array of delectable Hawaiian/Asian culinary treasures. The evening was most satisfying to all in attendance. Sandie and I were honored to be invited to be a part of the festivities.

The next day, we drove over to the Kohala Coast to spend two days at the resort that launched my hotel career, Mauna Kea Beach Hotel. We were there just the year before following an absence of several decades and I just couldn't resist the magic that this prestigious resort offers. Once again, we had a stunning ocean view room. We spent most of our daylight hours relaxing on the beach. True to form our food and beverage experiences were unparalleled. The stay there was simply mythical.

Difficult as it was to leave the Big Island, we wanted to spend a couple of more days with Shawn and his new bride Yucco on Oahu. A pre-planned surprise for Sandie was a two-night stay at the renowned Royal Hawaiian Hotel on Waikiki Beach. In all my years of Hawaiian residence or hotel management tenure, I had never stayed at this historical property.

In 1927, The Royal Hawaiian opened and, ushered in a new era of luxurious resort travel to Hawaii. The six-story, 400-room structure was fashioned in a Spanish-Moorish style, popular during the period and influenced by screen star Rudolph Valentino. The first general manager of the hotel, Arthur Benaglia, presided over a staff of 300 that included lobby boys dressed in "Cathayan" costume. The Honolulu Star-Bulletin described the newly opened Royal Hawaiian as "the first resort hostelry in America."

Today, The Royal Hawaiian and its associates continue to carry on the legacy of the rich heritage and inspiring and distinctive character of the *Pink Palace of the Pacific*. Long before Waikiki was developed as a tourist destination, it was a favorite residence and recreational center for Hawaiian kings and chiefs. King Kamehameha I had his home where The Royal Hawaiian stands today, and Queen Kaahumanu's Summer Palace was previously located on what is now the resort's Coconut Grove. Built on fifteen acres of beautiful beach frontage, the luxurious hotel with its distinctive Moorish-style architecture, painted pink, was promoted world-wide as a premier visitor destination. We were given a room in the original building. While the view was good, admittedly the overall product was a letdown following our Mauna Kea Beach Hotel experience. We did take advantage of their superb beach location and rented waterfront chairs for the day. Unfortunately, the weather didn't cooperate as we had to dodge intermittent rain as the day wore on.

That evening held special meaning for us. Our only grandchild on my side of the family, Deacon, was back in Hawaii staying with his mom and we were having dinner with him. The previous year, Deacon was living on the mainland with one of his grandmothers and was unavailable to us. Shawn and Yucco picked us up from the Pink Palace and we drove over to Deacon's home in Mililani to pick him up. The five of us drove over to Mililani's California Pizza Kitchen for a most enjoyable night. Deacon is a handsome young man and is now even taller than his dad.

We invited Deacon's mom, Berna Dau, to lunch at our hotel the next day. We missed seeing her and her mother on our last trip to the islands. Berna was working in the marketing department at the Waikiki Hard Rock Café making it a short walk for her over to the Royal Hawaiian Hotel. Berna is a delightful young lady going through some challenging times. In addition to Deacon, she has two younger daughters from a previous marriage that keeps her extremely busy. It was wonderful to catch up with her and learn more of Deacon's activities.

Later in the day Shawn and Yucco took us on the Makapu'u Lighthouse Trail two-mile hike. The paved trail made for a comfortable hike. It was a mellow climb to the top of the lookout. Clear skies provided unobstructed views of the southeast part of Oahu. On a clear day you can even see the islands of Molokai, Lanai, and Maui in the distance. Sadly, this was our last day with Shawn and Yucco. However, the upside was that we were leaving the following morning for Napa, California, to visit Janette.

The trek to Napa was an interesting travel day to be sure. Our first flight left at 8:00 am from Hawaii to Los Angeles. Due to the time difference between Hawaii and California we arrived in Los Angeles late in the afternoon. Our routing then had us going from Los Angeles to Phoenix arriving early that evening. The final leg was from Phoenix to Oakland, which was the closest major airport to Napa. It was near 11:00 pm by the time we landed in Oakland after a long travel day. The routing from Los Angeles to Phoenix in lieu of Los Angeles to Oakland didn't make sense to me. One can only surmise that this particular routing benefited the airline in some fashion.

As Janette can be gone for months at a time it's always a treat to visit her on her work sites. While spending quite a bit of time in California, Napa was never on my radar. A short walk from Janette's temporary home and we were in downtown Napa for a quick tour. Napa is known for its early1900s architecture, a riverfront promenade with shops and restaurants, and its arts scene. Symbolized as the wine capitol of the United States, it had one to three wine-tasting rooms in each block. An additional town highlight was the Napa Valley Wine Train that visits area wineries via vintage Pullman cars.

Janette kindly gifted Sandie and me with two balloon rides that unfortunately, due to weather conditions, we were unable to use. There were, however, a couple of alternative activities that we pursued. Having visited the main Culinary Institute of America campus in New York State a couple of years earlier we were excited to visit the CIA's Napa campus. The Greystone campus was located twenty miles away in St. Helena, California. The campus' primary facility is a beautiful 117,000-square-foot stone building known as Greystone Cellars. The building was designed with an arched entranceway and tower, stone mullions and transoms, a low sweeping roof, well-fitted stonework, and a large and simple stone façade. It was originally built as a cooperative wine cellar and was later added to the National Register of Historic Places. It was used as a winery until its sale to the school in 1993.

Janette, Sandie, and I signed up for a guided tour of their facilities. We timed our visit perfectly as we ended up being the only individuals in our group making it a private tour. Our tour began with a brief introduction in the school's 125-seat amphitheater. The school's kitchens were comprised of all the latest industrial food service equipment and were absolutely spotless. After we pointed this out to our guide who was a student himself, he told us an interesting story. Students working the kitchen curriculum are divided into teams. Every member of each team received the same grade based upon overall team performance. A member of our tour guide's team forgot to wipe down a piece of equipment after their shift. This dropped every team member's grade one full letter causing our guide to receive a "B" for the course when he was in line for an "A." Hard lesson to learn but the message was certainly received by the entire group.

The lower level of the building was fascinating. Now appropriately called "The Barrell Room," it's used for weddings, and banquets. Huge near six-foot-tall barrels line the perimeter of the room each bearing a sign illustrating winemaking from the past. During our walk-through we noticed a private dinner setup that was obviously happening later that evening. Within the room is an amazing collection of over 1,000 corkscrews. We concluded our entertaining day there with lunch in their dining room.

One afternoon, we visited the lovely Peju winery located about half way between the Napa Culinary Institute campus and Janette's residence. Having already resided in Napa for several months Janette had toured several wineries and this was her favorite. One could see why as soon as you drove up to the building. From perfectly manicured landscaping to a cascading water fountain, you could sense that this place was special.

The Peju family purchased this 'modest' 30-acre vineyard in Rutherford, California in November of 1983. The area is regarded as the Eden of Cabernet grape growing. It was nearly 10 years after their arrival when the Peju family started construction of their masterpiece. The garage was transformed into a combination wine tasting/barrel storage facility. They installed foil-finished insulation and palm trees to divide the building into two-thirds barrel storage and one-third into their wine tasting room.

The popularity of wine and the increase in new vineyard plantings grew dramatically in the mid-90s as a result of a number of studies in the U.S. and Europe on the health benefits of wine. In 1991 their business started to take off and their popularity grew exponentially. The Peju H.B. Vineyard Cabernet scored among the top 100 Cabernets in the Wine Spectator, and Peju Province Winery won 'Top Artisan Winery' in *Wine & Spirits Magazine*. What's the saying? "When in Rome do as the Romans do." Conversely, when in Napa, California, be sure to visit a winery. Mission accomplished. After three days of area sightseeing and long overdue visiting with Janette, it was time to return home. Our return flight proved to be somewhat of a challenge.

I had purchased our airline tickets for this combo Hawaii/Napa trip nearly a year in advance of our departure date. During the months leading up to the trip American Airlines made several changes to our flight schedule. The airline would e-mail me, indicating there was a change to our itinerary. The change or changes were not detailed within the e-mail. To determine what changed, I had to log onto my American Airlines account and compare the updated ticket to the previous version. Most changes were minor where the change made the difference of a few minutes here or there. It wasn't until we were close to our trip departure that I realized one of the changes was much more dramatic than originally envisioned. For some reason, the airlines routed us from Phoenix to Miami (flying over Nashville) on our return trip, which didn't make a lot of sense to me but with fare differentials, I hadn't given it a second thought. Looking at the itinerary again, I noticed that the Miami change of planes forced us to stay overnight in Miami, which was totally unplanned for. After discussing this with the airline, they agreed to re-route us to Dallas where we would catch a direct-to-Nashville flight. While it was a long travel day, we did make it back home within the same day of departure.

Sandie is an avid *Dancing with the Stars* fan. She rarely misses the show and even then, records it on our DVR for later viewing. As a surprise birthday gift, I purchased tickets to a February 16, 2020 performance being held at the Grand Ole Opry. Entitled "Dancing with the Stars – Live Tour 2020" it was billed as an all-new production featuring fan-favorite professional dancers performing every type of dance style as seen on ABC. The advertisement also indicated that most every type of dance including show-stopping routines were choreographed just for the live show ranging from the Cha Cha, Foxtrot, Salsa, Tango—and everything in between. I'm not a *Dancing with the Stars* enthusiast but did enjoy the glitz and glitter of the routines and especially reveled in Sandie's excitement that evening.

Our sphere was turned upside down in March of 2020. We were introduced to a world-wide killer that had already caused havoc in other parts of the world. Christened with the name "Coronavirus," this pandemic was spreading like wildfire—officially labeled as "Covid-19," an acronym that stands for Coronavirus Disease 2019. After a mere few months of its existence, the coronavirus was recognized as the world's third worst ever pandemic following only the Black Death of the 1300s and the 1918 Pandemic (H1N1 virus).

The Black Death caused by Bubonic Plaque occurred in the mid-1300s. The Plague ravaged Europe, Africa, and Asia, with an estimated death toll of around 75 million people. It destroyed a higher proportion of the population than any other single known event. Thought to have originated in Asia, it most likely jumped continents via fleas living on rats that frequently lived aboard merchant ships. Major shipping ports were perfect breeding grounds for rats and fleas. In no time the bacteria spread accounting for the devastation of three continents along the way.

The 1918 Pandemic (H1N1 virus) was the most severe pandemic since the Black Death Plague. While spreading worldwide there's no consensus of its origin. It is estimated that about 500 million people or one-third of the world's population became infected with this virus. The number of deaths was estimated to be at least 50 million worldwide with about 675,000 occurring in the United States.

The coronavirus is disproportionately killing people in low-income jobs who don't have the privilege of working from home, and for the most part live in crowded buildings unlike their middle- and upper-class counterparts, preventing them from proper social distancing. While the virus originated in China the United States was hit particularly hard by failing to restrict travel from Europe, especially Italy, early enough.

One of the dozens of unexplainable moves made by the Trump Presidency was his senseless dismantling of the National Security Council (NSC) Pandemic department in 2018. The following year the world and accordingly the United States was being ravaged by this unknown coronavirus pandemic. One can only surmise that the only reason for the dismantling was because it was setup by the Obama administration. Trump, in all of his — or should I say lack of — wisdom, seemed intent on destroying anything that Obama created.

Unfortunately, the main reason the United States was and still to-date is struggling mightily against the virus is an initial lack of leadership through our federal government. President Trump, from the virus' inception, had literally said he doesn't feel it's his responsibility, but rather that it's the responsibility of each individual state. This effectively placed the handling of the pandemic on the doorstep of the governor of each state. So rather than having one central purchasing and distribution point for severely needed ventilators, masks, gowns, gloves, hospital beds, etc., states had to procure these essential items themselves.

You can well imagine the chaos this created. Rather than realizing the enormous purchasing power of one central point, in this case the federal government, individual states were bidding for these items against one-another! The net result was that supplies obtained by individual states cost significantly more than necessary, in some instances five times as much! Even more egregious was the lack of a central coronavirus policy-making command authority. This resulted in differing policies from state to state regarding stay-at-home orders, business closures, social distancing, and the wearing of masks. As if this was not confusing enough our "coward in chief," Trump, encouraged his cult followers to protest against and resist his own administration's CDC guidelines! I'd need another book to get into my distaste for this racist, sexist, sociopathic liar, narcissistic, compassionless, perjurer, dictator, and self-serving sorry excuse of a human being. But I digress.

Apart from the health consequences of the pandemic, the other major fallout was the effect it had on our economy. According to the Pew Research Center unemployment rose higher in three months of Covid-19 than it did in two years of the Great Recession from the end of 2007 to the beginning of 2010. More than 40 million people have applied for unemployment benefits during the coronavirus pandemic, and roughly 21.5

million are currently receiving them (June 2020), previously unimaginable figures that wiped out a job market that saw unemployment at historic lows as recently as February of 2020. The economic impact the virus is having on the United States is gargantuan. The economic impact discussions center on whether the United States was in a recession or a depression.

The economy was in such poor shape that in March of 2020, the government passed the Coronavirus Aid, Relief, and Economic Security Act, also known as the CARES Act. This $2 trillion U.S. stimulus package was the largest emergency relief bill in American history. The bill was designed to help individuals, families, businesses, and the economy cope with the disastrous effects of the COVID-19 pandemic. Thus, the United States was in the middle of a vexing double whammy, the pandemic playing havoc with the health of millions of Americans and the economy being dragged into a recession or depression depending on your point of view. This is where politics really reared its ugly head.

Anxious to reopen the economy, Trump acted as though the coronavirus was a thing of the past. By mid-April, most all states were several weeks into "Shelter At Home/Businesses Closed" ordered directives by each state's governor. Scientists and doctors determined that the most effective weapon against this unknown enemy was social distancing followed closely by wearing masks. By restricting business operations and residents, interacting officials hoped to get the virus under control. The states hardest hit initially were large metropolitan cities with major international airports. New York was the virus epicenter, followed by California and New Jersey. Hospitals had to place elective surgeries on hold to maximize available ICU beds for the coronavirus. Previously closed hospitals were temporarily reopened to handle the surge in coronavirus cases.

Here's where the politicizing came into play. Some states were beginning to flatten the curve when Trump made another of his asinine moves. On April 17, he made three tweets: "Liberate Minnesota," "Liberate Michigan," and "Liberate Virginia, and save your great 2nd Amendment. It is under siege." It was no accident that the governors of these three states were Democrats. What followed were rampant far right-wing protests, which white supremacists conveniently participated in. Two weeks later, during a heated protest occurring at the Michigan capitol, Trump tweeted support of the protestors, some of whom were armed.

Fox News, Trump's propaganda station, kept their millions of viewers from taking the coronavirus seriously. *Fox News* and a few other right-wing media outlets played the virus off as a hoax and preached it was a simple flu that would go away all on its own. They downright insinuated that conformance to the CDC social distancing and wearing of masks guidelines was unpatriotic. The upshot was clear: For too long, many devotees of most right-wing news decided they didn't need to stay home. Others absorbed the idea that wearing a protective mask was an act of left-leaning partisanship.

But disease shows no favoritism and leaps across the political aisle quite nimbly. It's tragic but, again, not all that surprising to see the virus was spiking in red states where governors and other public officials joined Trump and his favorite news outlets early on in downplaying the dangers. CNN senior political analyst Kirsten Powers, formerly a *Fox News* contributor, said that right-wing media's initial "refusal to accept" coronavirus as a big problem "cost a lot of lives." It's important to remember that most people are not as plugged into the news cycle as we may be and are, as a result, more susceptible to believing this spin and misinformation.

Trump's decision-making ability had been in question for some time now but this was another low. In his over-three years in office, I've learned that there's no such thing as low for him. It's obvious he doesn't have a capable staff but that's by his design. His initial inner circle members are either in jail or fired for speaking their own minds. He has only yes men and women working for him that have to be good liars to keep their positions. By September of 2019, fifty-one of the top sixty-five positions of his office had turned over. Sixteen of those had turned over twice or more!

Thus, the Trump administration went all in on pressuring states to reopen their economies in spite of the coronavirus threat. The result was that most red or Republican states did just that. By Memorial Day weekend, it was a free-for-all in most of these states with packed beaches, restaurants, and bars. By mid-June, the expected occurred. Each of these states was seeing significant spikes in the number of coronavirus cases and deaths. On June 26, the United States coronavirus cases hit 45,242 for the biggest one-day increase of the pandemic since its inception. What Trump couldn't seem to get through his head is that the economy can't fully recover until the coronavirus pandemic is under control!

It's worthwhile to note some key milestones relating to the coronavirus:

CONDENSED TIMELINE THROUGH JUNE 26, 2020

HOW THE CORONAVIRUS PANDEMIC UNFOLDED

DEC. 31, 2019
Chinese authorities treat dozens of cases of pneumonia of unknown cause

JAN. 11, 2020
China reported its first death

JAN. 20, 2020
Other countries, including the United States, confirm cases

JAN. 23, 2020
Wuhan, a city of more than 11 million, cut off by the Chinese authorities

JAN. 30, 2020
The W.H.O. (World Health Organization) declares a global
health emergency

FEB. 29, 2020
The United States reports a death

MARCH 13, 2020
United States declares a national emergency

MARCH 15, 2020

The C.D.C. recommended no gatherings of fifty or more people in the U.S.

MARCH 16, 2020

The United States advised citizens to avoid groups of more than ten. New York City's public schools with 1.1 million students announces it would close

MARCH 24, 2020

The Tokyo Olympics were delayed until 2021

MARCH 26, 2020

The United States leads the world in confirmed cases with at least 81,321 confirmed infections and more than 1,000 deaths

APRIL 2, 2020

Cases topped one million and millions lose their jobs

APRIL 17, 2020

President Trump encouraged protests against some state restrictions

APRIL 21, 2020

Officials discovered earlier known U.S. coronavirus deaths in California

APRIL 24, 2020

The president criticized over disinfectant comments

MAY 21, 2020

Reported coronavirus cases top five million worldwide

MAY 27, 2020

Coronavirus deaths in the U.S. surpasses 100,000

JUNE 24, 2020

Confirmed U.S. Cases = 2.39 Million | Confirmed U.S. Deaths = 123,000

JUNE 26, 2020

Confirmed One-Day High-U.S. Cases = 45,242

So what has this pandemic meant to the daily lives of Sandie and me? From March 2020 through March 2021, for all practical purposes, we've sheltered in place. We leave the house out of necessity only, groceries, doctor appointments, etc. When we do venture out, we go to stores during their senior hours or at times we feel the store will be less crowded. While out, we wear masks and social distance. Like a lot of other Americans, we're doing more online shopping. If buying online saves a trip to the store, we buy online.

We're playing a lot of games and catching up on some home projects. To break the monotony, we'll go on a picnic by the Cumberland River and pack a book and cards. Although our fitness center has reopened, we're avoiding it. Our fitness center has minimal staffing and we just don't have the confidence level that they're able to keep the equipment and room properly sanitized. For exercise we go on walks and I've been riding my bike in the early morning hours for a cardio workout. Sandie has both strength and cardio workout regimens that she does at home.

Zoom is used for family gatherings. We go to church and Bible Study Virtually. There was actually a silver lining to our virtual church going. With "Shelter in Place" orders being the United States standard for most of March, April, May, and June, churches were forced to have their services virtually. Wanting to surprise Sandie, I went online to see if I could track down the pastor who married us in 2002. We married at the Peace Lutheran Church in South Haven, Michigan, but knew that Pastor Robert Lindstrom had left there several years earlier. Sure enough, he was at the Trinity Lutheran Church in Grand Rapids, Michigan. We attended a virtual service of his that probably wouldn't have been possible if not for the pandemic. Finally, another way of describing most of our days: wash, rinse, repeat. The pandemic may be restricting but Sandie and I are blessed with each other, enjoy each other's company, and love our home.

January 6, 2021 produced one of the darkest days ever for American democracy. Joe Biden had defeated Donald Trump in the November 2020 Presidential election by seventy-four Electoral College votes and by over seven million popular votes. Unhappy with the results, Trump claimed the election was stolen from him, making false claims and leading up to a grand rally headed by him on January 6—held a few blocks from where Congress was scheduled to officially sanctify the election results. Trump's goal was to overturn the election.

Incited and egged on by Trump, the angry mob stormed the Capitol. The Capitol was locked down and lawmakers and staff were evacuated while rioters vandalized and occupied the building for several hours. A group of these insurrectionists looked for Vice President Mike Pence, wanting to hang him. Another group wanted to harm Nancy Pelosi. Five people died and over 140 were injured as a result of this unfortunate black stain on our democracy. Through June of 2021, over 400 arrests have been made. When all is said and done, one can only hope that appropriate justice will be served to all involved, including Trump.

February 7 of 2021 provided a monumental event. My older son Shawn and his wife Yucco became first-time parents. They welcomed Axel Boma Evans into the world, weighing 8lbs. 10 oz. Axel becomes the eighth grandchild for Sandie and me. Thinking it to be far enough into the future considering the Covid pandemic, we made arrangements for a November 2021 Hawaii trip to see our new grandchild when he would be nine months old.

We're well into 2022 as I write this, and we have broken the monotony here and there in mainly two ways. The first being overnight Nashville stays when doctor appointments necessitate visits. When we do this, we're extra careful. We clean surfaces we touch in our hotel room, wear our Covid masks, and maintain social distances. Second, during milder weather, we treat ourselves by dining out when we can do so on outside lanais. While we're nearing 500,000 Covid deaths in the United States, hope springs eternal. Joe Biden defeated Donald Trump for the presidency and assumed office on January 20, 2021. Unlike Trump, Joe Biden's presidency is addressing the pandemic. Vaccines have been purchased and distribution plans put in place. Sandie and I both should receive initial and first booster COVID vaccine injection by the end of April 2021. This will provide us with the confidence to get out more and even begin traveling again.

Our self-imposed pandemic travel restrictions caused us to miss the May 2020 high school graduations of three of our grandchildren. Olivia and Cesar's son CJ and daughter Emily graduated along with Julie and Kenny's daughter, Taylor. While we couldn't be there in person, we did acknowledge the occasion. We purchased congratulatory tributes to CJ, Emily and Taylor in the *Chicago Tribune* newspaper and setup congratulatory décor that was Facebooked to the proud graduates. Olivia and Julie transmitted CJ's and Taylors graduation ceremonies via Facebook live allowing us to attend their graduations virtually.

We took our first major trip in over a year from May 2–11, 2021. Sandie's youngest daughter, Julie had a Disney World trip planned as a graduation gift for her son Matt in early May. As both Sandie and I had our first two Pfizer Covid shots in April, I suggested meeting Julie and Matt at Disney World. It's a ten-and-half-hour drive from Clarksville to Orlando, making Atlanta an attractive stop over to break that portion of the trip up. Coincidently at this time, Janette was working a movie project in Atlanta, allowing us to both rest and visit with her.

After the visit and a peaceful night's sleep, Sandie and I were back on the road headed to Orlando. Shortly after departing Atlanta, I learned from my sister Sheryl whom we were scheduled to visit after our Orlando sojourn that she was in an accident.

Sheryl was on a well-deserved vacation in northern Atlanta with her best friend Shirley. On their way to their accommodations, they were rear-ended, causing injury to Shirley and disabling their vehicle. Knowing that we were in the general vicinity, Sheryl's daughter Denise contacted us to explain her mom's situation. Sheryl and Shirley would be without transportation following Shirley's emergency room checkup. Their location was approximately two hours north of our Atlanta location. I called Sheryl and offered to pick them up and take them home. Sheryl opted to stay to try and work things out with her insurance company. After several phone calls, Sheryl and Shirley had arrangements in place for a friend of Shirley's to pick them up and take them back to Shirley's place in Tampa. From there, a friend of Sheryl's was picking her up to take her to her Cape Coral home. We offered to skip the Cape Coral portion of our trip knowing what Sheryl currently had on her plate. However, Sheryl assured us that the accident would not be a deterrent to our visiting. In fact, she felt the family support would be comforting.

So, with concern for Sheryl on our minds, we continued our trip to Orlando and Cape Coral, as planned. We arrived to Disney's All Star Movie Resort on the afternoon of May 3. Sandie and I met Julie and Matt for dinner in the Resort's Food Court that evening. It was wonderful seeing the two of them after so long of a period due to the murderous environment created through Covid-19. After catching up over dinner, we had the next two-and-half days of Julie and Matt's company to look forward to. We used park passes for the Magic Kingdom and Hollywood Studios and Sandie joined Julie and Matt at Disney Springs later in the evenings. It was a pleasing visit and we even enjoyed some Disney activities along the way. After meeting Julie and Matt for breakfast on the morning of May 6, we began the third leg of our trip from Orlando to Cape Coral to visit with Sheryl.

Cape Coral is a leisurely three-hour drive from Orlando. We made it into Cape Coral in the early afternoon. As was the case with Julie and Matt it was great to see and visit with someone we hadn't seen in a long time frame. For what Sheryl went through and had yet to address, she looked in good spirits. She hadn't been checked out following the accident and, although Sheryl claimed to feel fine, our focus was getting her to a clinic where she could be examined. Initially, she refused to go but eventually came around to the idea. The difficulty at this point was finding a clinic that would see her and accept the forthcoming insurance from the accident's responsible party. After several attempts, she was successful in locating a clinic in Fort Myers.

We drove Sheryl to Fort Myers for her evaluation, which proved to be most fortunate. She later learned that without a timely recorded examination she could be without recourse for claims resulting from the accident. Notwithstanding the unfortunate events from the accident, we had a most enjoyable three-day visit. My sweet sister wanted to play tourist guide and show us around the area. However, considering the trauma she went through and was experiencing, Sandie and I just wanted to spend time with her enjoying her company while offering whatever support we could.

Sunday morning, May 9, we began our journey back to Clarksville. Not stopping over in Orlando as we did on the way down, we took a slightly different route back. To break up the first leg of the trip, we overnighted in Lake City, Florida. The next day, we drove nearly 300 miles to Atlanta to spend another evening with Janette. Atlanta was a good stopping off point leaving 300 miles to complete our journey. We had an engaging dinner with Janette and her boss Eric at a local indoor-outdoors Atlanta marketplace.

We began the last leg of our trip at 9 am the next morning, thinking we would be avoiding the morning commute traffic. Wrong! Not only did we not avoid it but, due to an accident, we were stuck on an area of Interstate I-75 for over an hour. Oh well, so much for our best laid plans. Overall, however, I'd have to rate this expedition a resounding success— heightened by visiting with loved ones and also gratifying to journey nearly 2,000 miles after nearly a year of self-confined imprisonment.

Sorrowful Covid-19 update as of June, 2021: The good news is that the United States is getting a handle on the pandemic with the number of cases and deaths falling tremendously under Biden's Covid plan. Regrettably, Trump's lack of leadership on one of the most important issues ever has placed the United States atop the leader board in deaths reported by country with over 600,000 confirmed deaths. The United States is followed by Brazil with over 500,000 deaths, India with nearly 400,000 deaths, and Mexico with nearly 250,000. Such an American tragedy and one that could have been better contained saving hundreds of thousands of unnecessary deaths if properly managed from the outset.

Sandie expressed an interest to visit her dad's gravesite in Michigan. Joe Spoula is buried at Fort Custer National Military Cemetery in Augusta, Michigan. The most direct route to this location from Clarksville routes us through Indianapolis, Indiana. So we journeyed roundtrip to Augusta, Michigan through Indianapolis between June 4 and 9, 2021. We were staying with my sister Sharon on our Indianapolis stopover on the way up to the Fort Custer Cemetery.

Before making our way to Sharon's apartment we had two other stops to make. My brother Floyd experienced several health issues in the past twelve to eighteen months. He was in the hospital or emergency room on several occasions from falls and heart issues. Unable to see him for over a year, I wanted to make sure to personally visit with him during this trip. Thus, we made a stop at my brother's place first on the Indianapolis agenda. We arrived in Indianapolis mid-afternoon after a mid-morning Clarksville departure. Floyd and Glenda's place was at the end of a cul-de-sac in the south Beech Grove suburb. We were amazed to see practically no parking available anywhere within the cu-de-sac due to a neighborhood garage sale.

Added to the parking density was a graduation party being held for both of Floyd and Glenda's adopted daughters, Skyla and Haley. Floyd's place was a beehive of activity as twenty or so individuals were celebrating Skyla and Haley's graduations. We were informed that Floyd was pretty much confined to bed. Sandie felt it best that I have one-on-one time with Floyd so I went straight into his bedroom for our visit. Floyd was lying down in bed eating a luncheon plate just brought into him. He looked somewhat frail. A far cry from the rock-solid athlete image I was used to seeing. I had talked with Floyd over the phone during the past months and sometimes could understand what he was saying and other times couldn't. During this personal visit, I had no difficulty in understanding him. He explained the ramifications from strokes and falls he'd experienced. He can't close one side of his mouth, which leads to unwanted drooling. One of his main issues is the undependability of his legs. He doesn't know when they will or will not support him.

Somehow or another, even his vocal cords became damaged, making his voice weaker as he converses over a period. He has a hospital-type bed at home which helps but Glenda feels that he probably needs constant nursing care. I have to admit to dual feelings here as it was awesome seeing him but disturbing to see the decline of his health.

The other stop we made was to the Daniel F. O'Reilly Funeral Home. Sandie and I have pre-planned our funerals for the burials to take place in the Young Family plot in Ladoga, Indiana. Rather than having the wake in Ladoga, Sandie felt it would work better for everyone to have that portion of the service in Indianapolis and those wanting to be present at the burial could follow the procession into Ladoga. The O'Riley Funeral home was recommended by Anthony Wireman, the Ladoga Funeral Home Director and overall coordinator of our funerals. Located on the south side of the city, we felt it would accomplish that goal and after touring it with the owner this was confirmed. Later that afternoon, we were on our way to my sister Sharon's place to meet her for dinner.

Sharon lost her husband Joe of over forty years the past year and we were anxious to see how she was coping. She decided to remain in their rented apartment in the Indianapolis suburb of Greenwood. Her youngest son Chad and wife Candice live nearby which certainly factored into her decision. Sandie and I were pleased to see Sharon doing so well. She's involved in her church and has made additional friends helping to round out her life. Our time with her was short but most enjoyable. Sandie and I enjoy Sharon's company. After an evening meal at Applebee's, we were off the next morning to the focal point of our trip, Fort Custer National Cemetery in Augusta, Michigan.

Fort Custer National Military Cemetery is approximately four hours northeast of Indianapolis. Named after General George Armstrong Custer, and originally built in 1917 as part of the military mobilization during World War I. After the war, it also served as a demobilization camp. The cemetery itself was not created until 1943. During World War II Fort

Custer was expanded to serve as a training ground and as a place to hold German prisoners of war.

Of the German POWs held during World War II, twenty-six died and were buried in the cemetery. Sixteen of them were killed when a truck carrying them from a work detail collided with a train near Blissfield, Michigan. It was not until 1981 that Fort Custer cemetery officially became Fort Custer National Cemetery, receiving a large plot of land from the Fort Custer Training Center for expansion. In 1997, another expansion was made, when sixty acres were added.

We found the cemetery outside of the small Augusta, Michigan town. It was very well laid out in a beautiful, peaceful setting. Joe Spoula, Sandie's dad's grave was easy to locate due to the section/numbering system utilized. Visiting Joe's gravesite was a sobering experience. I didn't know him long but always enjoyed being around him. His humor and quick wit were always present. I'll always be grateful that Joe was available and able to walk Sandie down the aisle at our wedding. The visit brought tears to Sandie as it had been over a decade since we were at the cemetery for his burial.

Our wedding had taken place in South Haven, Michigan. And as we were only an hour from South Haven, we planned on spending a couple of nights there during the return leg of our trip. We drove down to South Haven, and as we entered the town pleasant memories of our monumental event filled our heads. The weather was perfect that first day, allowing us to explore the touristy area of downtown South Haven. We walked the downtown area, stopping in stores of interest. We had dinner at Clementine's where we'd spent many a meal planning our wedding so many years earlier.

Built in 1896, Clementine's was originally home to the Citizens State Bank. The Ruppert family purchased it in 1989, refurbishing the interior to showcase the building's extensive brickwork, tin ceilings, and ornate woodwork. The restaurant is filled with antique relics, memorabilia from South Haven and is topped off with a Grand Golden Cupola. Best of all of course is the quality of food offered. We've always enjoyed delectable cuisine here and this meal was no exception.

We weren't as fortunate on the second day weather-wise as it rained most of the day. We traveled to Douglas, Michigan, for dinner that day to the Everyday People Café. This restaurant holds a special place in our hearts as its past chef catered our 2002 wedding. Sadly, the restaurant was closed for maintenance. Their website didn't mention this, making it a royal disappointment. We ended up settling for a restaurant within the same general vicinity. The food was okay but both Sandie and I felt it was overpriced for what we received. The next morning, we were off again to Indianapolis.

We had reservations at a south side Holiday Inn Express for the evening. There was a pre-planned sibling dinner at a Bob Evans restaurant close to our hotel. After arriving into Indianapolis and resting a bit, we took my niece Jasmine up on a visit invitation. Jasmine is Marjie's youngest daughter and is married to Tim Plahitko. They have two beautiful children, Lincoln and Parker, who we hadn't seen in over a year. We've kept up with them through Jasmine's Facebook posts. After a nice visit with Jasmine and her family, we headed out for the local Bob Evans restaurant.

My half-sisters Becky and Marjie were there along with their husbands Steve and Rod. Glenda was also in attendance but without Floyd. After visiting with Floyd, I didn't expect that he would make it although it would have been a nice surprise. We invited my sister Sharon, but she had previous commitments preventing her attendance. It was extremely gratifying to reconnect with family in person after such a long period of being unable to visit with them.

The next morning, Sandie and I had breakfast with Steve Verhines and his wife Debbie at the same Bob Evans restaurant. Steve and I reconnected with each other within the past twenty-four months after an over-fifty-year absence. He's visited us in Clarksville and I wanted to be sure to stay in touch with him. He misunderstood the location of the Bob Evans restaurant we were meeting at, making him and Debbie a half-hour late for our breakfast. They, of course, made it eventually and we enjoyed their company before heading back to Clarksville on the last leg of our trip.

Little would I realize that a month later on July 9, 2021, my brother Floyd would pass away! This was one of the hardest phone calls I've ever had to digest. The words from Kym Quick, Floyd's adopted daughter, were being received but not registering. It's taken me nearly six months before I could even add this to my bio, not wanting it to be real. Sure, Floyd was not in the best of health, evidenced by his inability to attend our recent sibling dinner. But while he wasn't the picture of health a month earlier, he did have all of his faculties. His main disability was his inability to count on his legs holding himself up while walking. To aid in this chore he had a walker.

Floyd and I were not blood-related as his dad married my mom when he was a year old and I was three. But we grew up as close as any two brothers could be to one another. He was not only my brother but my buddy, best man at my marriage to Sandie, and my best friend. Floyd was a very caring and giving individual. The times I needed him most, I could count on him being there. One particular situation comes to mind while I lived in Chicago and Floyd resided in Indianapolis. The first major conference/trade show under my supervision was scheduled for San Francisco. Being a single parent of a fifteen-year-old at the time, I arranged for a sitter while I would be out of town overseeing an event that would launch my new career out of the hotel industry.

The sitter didn't show up and couldn't be reached. At that point it was too short of a notice to obtain another sitter. At my wits end I called Floyd who agreed to drive up from Indianapolis to Chicago to pick Shawn up and keep him for the approximate week I'd be gone. Being spur of the moment, this was a sacrifice for Floyd on a few fronts not to mention his hatred for driving in Chicago traffic. Sensing my desperation, he didn't hesitate and drove up that day, allowing me to perform my occupational responsibilities with a clear head.

Toward the end of July, we embarked on another trifecta trip. We journeyed over to Highland, Illinois, to spend several nights with Sandie's sister Janice and husband Bruce. While there, we ventured to Springfield to tour the Lincoln Museum. I'm a huge fan of our sixteenth President and this

323

was our second visit to the museum. When it opened in 2005, the Abraham Lincoln Presidential Library rapidly became one of the best-attended of all the Presidential libraries and one of the most studied new museums in the world. The 200,000-square-foot complex includes an archive, library, museum, public experiences, galleries, and theater presentations that are more than 50% larger than any other presidential library. The Abraham Lincoln Presidential Museum was considered the first major Experience Museum. Designed, created, and produced by BRC Imagination Arts, the museum combines priceless historical artifacts and world class scholarship with BRC's innovative, contemporary storytelling technologies. Visitors are offered an engaging, emotional and educational experience through immersive, "You are there" exhibits.

On April 21, 1865, a train carrying the coffin of assassinated President Abraham Lincoln traveled through 180 cities and 7 states on its way back to his home state of Illinois. He was buried in Springfield on May 4. Scheduled stops for the special funeral train were published in newspapers. At each stop, Lincoln's coffin was taken off the train, place on an elaborately decorated horse-drawn hearse and led by solemn processions to a public building for viewing. Newspapers reported that people had to wait more than five hours to pass by his coffin in some cities.

While missing it during our first Lincoln Museum, we decided to visit Lincoln's tomb at Oak Ridge Cemetery in Springfield. Dedicated in 1874, Lincoln Tomb is the final resting place of Abraham Lincoln, his wife Mary, and three of their four sons, Edward, William, and Thomas. The eldest son, Robert T. Lincoln, is buried in Arlington National Cemetery. Also on the site is the public receiving vault, constructed in 1860, the scene of funeral services for Abraham Lincoln on May 4, 1865. In 1960 the Tomb was designated a National Historic Landmark and was placed on the National Register of Historic Places in 1966.

Oak Ridge Cemetery is the largest Municipal Cemetery in Illinois, with 365 acres and is the second most visited cemetery in the United States. Arlington National Cemetery holds the distinction of being the most visited US Cemetery. Oak Ridge Cemetery is a self-supporting city cemetery without sales representatives. Sales are encouraged by maintaining reasonable prices and by providing excellent care and maintenance.

After a delightful visit with Janice and Bruce we ventured to Chicago to see Olivia and Julie and their families. Living a few states away from loved ones and getting into daily routines, several months can easily pass before realizing the time spent between visits. With Sandie and I being retired, it is easier for us to travel up to Chicago to visit Olivia and Julie and their families than it is for them to venture down to Tennessee. Social media and texting helps significantly to bridge the gap between actual visits. It's always a joy to spend time with Olivia and Julie. They're loving and caring daughters and just good people.

Due to Covid and a late start by the organizers, the annual Evans family reunion was held on September 11 in 2021. Traditionally held on the first Sunday in August, this amounted to an about face for the group. Although the event was put together at the last minute, it had a decent turnout and those in attendance enjoyed themselves. Wanting to add some amusement to the celebration, I arranged for a face-painting clown to entertain the crowd. Attendees wanting their face painted started off at a snail's pace. However, my adventurous wife Sandie served as the initial subject, which started an avalanche of willing participants. Most everyone, child and adult alike, had their face painted by the end of the reunion. The face-painting clown was an enormous hit, adding to the overall success of the event.

From September 21 through September 24, Sandie and I toured Washington DC. Discounting travel time, we had a full three-and-half days to sightsee. We could have spent an additional week there and still not see all of the major sights. We did, however, make the most of the time we did have there. On the afternoon of our arrival after checking into our hotel, we taxied over to the United States Holocaust Memorial Museum. Taken from the Museum's Mission Statement: The United States Holocaust Memorial Museum is America's national institution for the documentation, study, and interpretation of Holocaust history, and serves as this country's memorial to the millions of people murdered during the Holocaust.

The Holocaust was the state-sponsored, systematic persecution and annihilation of European Jewry by Nazi Germany and its collaborators between 1933 and 1945. Jews were the primary victims—six million were murdered; Roma, people with disabilities, and Poles were also targeted for destruction or decimation for racial, ethnic, or national reasons. Millions more, including gay men, Jehovah's Witnesses, Soviet prisoners of war and political dissidents, also suffered grievous oppression and death under Nazi tyranny.

The Museum's primary mission is to advance and disseminate knowledge about this unprecedented tragedy, to preserve the memory of those who suffered, and to encourage its visitors to reflect upon the moral and spiritual questions raised by the events of the Holocaust as well as their own responsibilities as citizens of a democracy.

Touring the exhibits was a moving, unforgettable experience. One couldn't help but tear up as you viewed video, photos, and first-hand accounts of the atrocities experienced by these targeted individuals. The permanent exhibition is divided into three floors. The opening floor considered the "Nazi Assault" explores the rise of the Nazi party in Germany in 1933 through the outbreak of World War II in September 1939.

The middle floor addresses the "Final Solution," covering the period from 1940 to 1945. It examines the evolution of Nazi policy toward Jews, from ghettoization to mass murder in killing fields and gas chambers. The third and final floor displays the liberation of the Nazi camps and the Allied victory over Nazi Germany in 1945, rescue and resistance efforts, and the aftermath of the Holocaust. At the end of this floor, we sat in an exhibition theater and watched video testimonies of Holocaust survivors. It's simply beyond human comprehension that there are countless individuals who swear the Holocaust never happened.

Our first sightseeing adventure on day two was the Smithsonian National Museum of Natural History. Our first stop was into the Minerals and Gems Gallery. The highlight of the gallery was the Hope Diamond. This famous gem has more than forty-five carats and is renowned for its flawless clarity, deep blue color, and its eventful history. Numerous other rare gems were on display including a couple of stunning necklaces given by French Emperor Napoleon I to his second wife, Empress Marie Louise.

The other highlight we viewed in this museum was on the second floor entitled "Eternal Life in Ancient Egypt." We saw and learned first-hand of Egypt's handling of mummies during this early period. For more than 3,000 years, ancient Egyptians embalmed, preserved, and entombed their dead with materials they were believed to be needed for life in the next world. Offerings to the gods to help ease the deceased person's passage were often included in tombs. The exhibition included three human and sixteen animal mummies, as well as pottery vessels, jewelry, tools, and other artifacts excavated from Egyptian tombs. Modern noninvasive scanning technologies allowed scientists and visitors to explore the mummies' secrets while preserving their bodies.

The next day, we started our touring at the infamous Ford Theater where President Abraham was assassinated on April 14, 1865. Unknown to most, the Ford Theater was originally a First Baptist Church. It was purchased in 1861 by John T. Ford and was an acclaimed Civil War theater from 1861 through 1865.

Exploration of the museum revealed the timeline following Abraham Lincoln from the beginning of his presidency through his assassination. His meetings with the abolitionist Frederick Douglass were documented. We also learned first-hand of John Wilkes Booth hatred toward Lincoln and the group of individuals he recruited to overthrow the government. The museum featured artifacts related to the assassination including weapons that Booth used!

Following our Ford Theater excursion, we ventured to the Smithsonian National Museum of Air & Space. One of the world's most visited museums, the Smithsonian's Air and Space Museum has an incredible array of original artifacts from the history of flight and space exploration.

During its heyday in the late 1990s through the early 2000s, the Smithsonian's National Air and Space Museum in Washington DC was a contender for the most-visited museum in the world, besting even long-established institutions like the Louvre in Paris and the British Museum in London. In recent years, the annual tally has slipped somewhat, but it still attracts something north of five to six million visitors annually.

The museum contains the Apollo 11 Command Module *Columbia*, the *Friendship 7* capsule which was flown by John Glenn, Charles Lindbergh's *Spirit of St. Louis*, the Bell X-1, which broke the sound barrier, the model of the starship *Enterprise* used in the science fiction television show *Star Trek: The Original Series*, and the exhibit I most wanted to view, the Wright brothers' *Wright Flyer* airplane near the entrance.

Friday, September 24 was our last full touring day in DC. Wanting to make the most of our time we arranged to go on Viator's "Best of DC Tour" which lasted approximately seven hours. The itinerary was jam-packed but provided the best Washington, DC overview we could get for the time spent:

Stop 1: United States Navy Memorial and Naval Heritage Center The tour started and ended at the US Navy Memorial Plaza located just across the street from the National Archives Building

Stop 2: Grounds of the US Capitol. The US Capitol Building was closed to visitors for indoor tours. We were able to view the exterior building and grounds.

Stop 3: Dwight D. Eisenhower Memorial, a brand new memorial completed in 2020, is dedicated to the massive legacy of President Eisenhower with a large wall depicting the cliffs of Normandy behind the simple memorial designed by iconic American designer Frank Gehry.

Stop 4: The White House (also closed to visitors for inside touring). On our way there, we passed the Newseum, the Canadian Embassy, and the National Gallery of Art. We were able to see the Executive Residence of the President and his family, as well as the Eisenhower Executive Office Building.

Stop 5: Jefferson Memorial—here, we received a guided tour of the Jefferson Memorial.

Stop 6: Franklin Delano Roosevelt Memorial—we were also provided with a guided tour of FDR's Memorial, transporting us back in time to the years of 1933–1945.

Stop 7: National World War II Memorial— Symbolic of the defining event of the 20th Century, the memorial is a monument to the spirit, sacrifice, and commitment of the American people. The World War II Memorial honors the 16 million who served in the armed forces of the US, the more than 400,000 who died, and all civilians who supported the war effort. The Second World War is the only 20th Century event commemorated on the National Mall's central axis.

Stop 8: Lincoln Memorial— Stately monument honoring Abraham Lincoln, the 16th president of the United States, and "the virtues of tolerance, honesty, and constancy in the human spirit." Oh, if only our current politicians possessed these virtues!

Stop 9: Vietnam Veterans Memorial—this sight was one of Sandie's motivators for touring DC and well worth the time spent. The memorial includes the names of over 58,000 servicemen and women who gave their lives in service in the Vietnam conflict. The memorial includes the Vietnam Veterans Memorial wall, the Three Servicemen statue and the Vietnam Women's Memorial. It's the most-visited memorial on the National Mall in Washington, attracting more than 5 million people each year

Stop 10: Martin Luther King, Jr. Memorial—The Martin Luther King, Jr., Memorial was dedicated in 2011. The memorial covers four acres and includes the Stone of Hope, and a granite statue of Civil Rights Movement leader Martin Luther King Jr. carved by sculptor Lei Yixin.

Stop 11: The National Archives Museum—what a way to end the tour! We viewed the original Declaration of Independence, the Constitution, and the Bill of Rights documents! It was a busy three days in our nation's capital but one that created long-lasting memories.

In November of 2021, we embarked on our long-awaited seventeen-day Hawaii trip. We had been looking forward to the trip for several months to visit with the newest member of the family, Axel Boma Evans born on February 7, 2021, at 12:52 am. Our newest grandson weighed in at 8 pounds, 10 ounces. His mom, Yucco is tiny, and carrying Axel and delivering him had proved challenging for the new mother.

We waited until November to visit, feeling Axel would be more likely to remember us, being nine months old by then. We were not disappointed. Axel is an absolute delight. Shawn and Yucco are doing an outstanding parenting job with their bundle of joy. Yucco has Axel on a strict feeding schedule and prepares the majority of his meals from scratch!

Axel is a happy child, smiling constantly. He takes after his mother musically. Yucco is very talented as a singer and music composer. Axel enjoys listening to music and rhythmically sways to tunes of his favorite songs. He's as expected, an active child full of energy. We wish they lived closer to us so we could visit with them more frequently but understand their current need to live in Hawaii. Shawn's job is based out of there and while he could work remotely for the same company elsewhere, they also have to consider their proximity to Yucco's family in Japan.

The Hyatt Place in Waikiki was our local residence while on Oahu. My early morning routine was rewarded by discovering a Starbucks right around the corner from our hotel, which opened daily at 4 am. One observation right off the bat was the seriousness that Hawaii placed on Covid mandates as compared to our home state of Tennessee. Restaurants would not allow entrance without first proving your vaccination status along with showing your identification. On a visit to the Ala Moana (the largest open-air shopping center in the world) Sandie and I decided to refresh ourselves with an ice cream cone in their food court. After getting our cones, we went to sit down. The seating area was jam-packed so when a couple got up from their table, I rushed over to claim it only to be told by the local security guards there that there was a line we had to get into first showing our proof of vaccination and ID!

We spent a total of twelve nights on Oahu to visit with Shawn, Yucco, and Axel. We split the twelve nights up with a trip to the Big Island of Hawaii, where we enjoyed five nights at the beautiful Mauna Kea Beach Resort. We're very much at peace there as the resort provides a serenity that's truly unavailable elsewhere. So that Sandie could see more of the island, we took a couple of side excursions while there. We lunched with an old Indiana high school buddy, Alonzo Baker and wife Debra in Hilo close to their residence. On another day, we met with a group of my Hawaii high school classmates followed by a visit to Holualoa, Kona, Hawaii.

Another Hawaii observation is the cost of living there. From prior experience, we expect it to be more expensive, but when you have lunch for two on two separate locations at different spots, totaling $70 & $90, respectively, it hits you right between the eyes.

As we get older, the 4,330-mile trip between Nashville and Honolulu is becoming more and more challenging for Sandie and me. There's a four-or-five-hour time difference between the two cities, depending on whether we're on daylight savings time or not. The trip there is tiring but not as difficult as we gain time going over. The trip back is toilsome as flights leave in the evening and with the time loss, arrive the following morning. It actually takes us a few days to reacclimate ourselves into our daily routines and regain normal stamina levels. Seeing loved ones, though, makes the effort worthwhile.

For Thanksgiving 2021, we reverted to our Highland, Illinois/Indianapolis, Indiana, tradition. We stayed with Sandie's sister Janice and her husband Bruce over Thanksgiving and then ventured up to Indianapolis for an Evans family dinner the Saturday after Thanksgiving. Sandie, Janette and I treated twenty-two family members to dinner at Gray Brothers Cafeteria in Mooresville. We were most appreciative of the turnout, considering the impact Covid has had on functions.

We didn't let the dust settle much before we were back on the road again. We signed up for a Christian conference held in Williamstown, Kentucky, from December 6–9, which is four hours from us. The conference was entitled Christmas Jubilee. Apart from the speakers and program content the location was appealing as it was held at the "Ark Encounter" attraction. Visiting this site had been on my mind since its 2017 inception and this was a golden opportunity to do so. Conference registration included admission to the Ark Encounter as well as the Creation Museum.

The Ark Encounter features a full-size Noah's Ark built according to the dimensions given in the *Bible*. Spanning 510 feet long, 85 feet wide, and 51 feet high, its three floors represent a modern engineering marvel. Fun comparisons: width = 2 school buses; height = 3 giraffes stacked; length = 1.5 football fields; volume = 483 semi-trailers. Cost of the enormous project exceeded $100 million! The experience was well worth the trip.

The Creation museum was about forty minutes from the Ark Encounter in the Cincinnati suburb of Petersburg, Kentucky. Not knowing when we would make it back to the area, we wanted to see this attraction while in the vicinity. Not wanting to miss the conference closing session, we were pressed for time having to get there and back and while we got to see and experience it, we could have used more time there.

The Creation Museum is one that promotes explanation of the origin of the universe based on a literal interpretation of the Genesis creation narrative in the *Bible*. It is operated by the Christian creation apologetics organization Answers in Genesis (AiG). The 75,000-square-foot museum cost $27 million, raised through private donations, and opened on May 28, 2007. In addition to the main collection, the facility has a special effects theater, a planetarium, an *Allosaurus* skeleton and an insect collection.

Reflecting young-earth creationist beliefs, the museum depicts humans and dinosaurs coexisting, portrays the earth as approximately 6,000 years old, and disputes the theory of evolution. Scientists and educators have criticized the museum for misrepresenting science and expressed concerns that it could harm science education. Proponents of other religious beliefs about the universe's origins—including old-earth creationism, theistic evolution, and intelligent design—have said that its rejection of scientific consensus damages the credibility of Christianity and its adherents.

Tenets of young-earth creationism enjoy substantial support among the general population in the United States, however, contributing to the museum's popularity. We enjoyed the few hours we had at the facility.

Sandie and I have been attending the Legacy series at the First Baptist Church of Clarksville the first Friday of each month. The session begins with a Bible study and concludes with lunch and entertainment. Following the December 3 session, we did a self-guided tour of their parade of Christmas Trees. The church provides this exhibit annually, which includes over forty beautifully decorated trees, each telling a part of the gospel story of Jesus. The trees were dazzling and the tour was a delightful way to spend part of the afternoon.

Prior to our 3816 Benjamin Drive Christmas gathering, we navigated to the Opryland Hotel in Nashville for a couple of nights. We've tried to make this an annual tradition since retiring to Tennessee. The resort has one of our nation's best decorated facilities for the holidays. They begin decorating the resort in July and have over three-and-half million brilliant lights by the start of the holiday season. They also provide numerous adult and children Christmas-related activities that add to the festiveness.

While there, we took in a Christmas dinner-concert put on by the renowned Oak Ridge Boys. They put on a magnificent show that included some of the old hits (Elvira/Yes) as well as some original Christmas tunes. A portion of their show was quite unique. The four of them sat in rocking chairs on the stage and one by one provided background information on themselves which allowed the audience to connect closely to them. They also included Santa Claus in their performance who provided Santa hats to every child in the audience proving to be one of the biggest hits of the evening.

Not to be lost amongst all the festivities, the resort also had a parade of Christmas trees. The trees were sponsored by the Universal Music Group Nashville as a benefit for First Responders. World-renowned artists came together to showcase Christmas trees decorated by Grand Ole Opry members Alan Jackson, Carrie Underwood, Darius Rucker, Josh Turner,

Keith Urban, Reba McEntire, Eric Church, George Strait, Luke Bryan, and Mickey Guyton. Along with their trees these country music's biggest stars, each donated "Once in a Lifetime" VIP experiences (fly-away, VIP concert experiences, and other exclusive items), all to benefit First Responders Children's Foundation. Proceeds raised provided scholarships and mental health services to children who had lost a parent in the line of duty. Each tree was decorated in a particular theme and added tremendously to the overall holiday ambiance at the hotel.

We returned home on December 23 to welcome our out-of-town guests, Sandie's sister Janice and her husband Bruce. The next day, Janice and I drove to the Nashville airport to pick up another houseguest of ours, Sandie's youngest brother, Rob. Rob had lost his wife Barb recently and Sandie and I were happy that he chose to stay with us and be with family for Christmas. As usual, the Christmas dinner creation between Sandie and Janette was well received.

To add a little variety to our annual Christmas celebration, I created a Christmas Trivia game. I actually got the idea from our Bible small group Christmas party. The hosts the past couple of years played a "Family Feud" Christmas game. Our Christmas Trivia game wasn't as detailed but it was exceptionally well received and added tremendously to the evening's enjoyment.

We belong to a small Bible Study group that meets weekly. After several years with the host/hostess and several of the group's members, we've developed solid relationships with most. The group leaders are Barb and Elliott Watts and do a great job in its coordination. Other member couples include Rhonda and Ben Gupton, Shari and Mike Steele, Linda and Bryce Ellison, and Theresa and Chuck Wyatt. In 2021–2022, we meet on Tuesday evenings. The Tuesday evening before Sandie's birthday, I insisted on a birthday cake with Sandie for dessert at the study. Sandie didn't want to make a fuss over her birthday but the group got into it, enjoying the celebration.

The real gift for Sandie's sixty-seventh birthday was an occasion several months in the planning. From the October preceding her birthday through the actual celebration, I colluded with Sandie's two daughters (my new daughters) to fly them down to Tennessee from Chicago to surprise their mom. My daughter Janette was instrumental in this amazing experience. We arranged for Janette to keep Sandie busy on the afternoon of Olivia Vazquez's and Julie Douglas's arrival. We needed a three-hour window for me to travel to Nashville to pick Olivia and Julie up from the airport and get them back to Clarksville while Sandie was out with Janette.

The plan was for Janette to take Sandie to the next town over for lunch and shopping. Hopkinsville, Kentucky, was an approximate thirty-minute drive favorably adding to the desired three-hour window that Sandie would be out of the house. There wasn't any suspicion as there was a restaurant there that both of them want to try and both are accomplished shopping browsers. The Chicago to Nashville flight arrived later than expected but a text to Janette alerted her to the situation and the surprise worked to perfection.

When Janette brought Sandie back to our home, Olivia and Julie were waiting to surprise their mom in our kitchen. Julie made a funny comment while we were waiting, saying something along the lines of "my mom may need Depends due to the surprise." Sandie was blown away, with the surprise taking several minutes for the situation to settle in. Thus, a wonderful four-night stay with Olivia and Julie that extended over Sandie's birthday was launched.

The visit was all the more significant for other reasons. My two new daughters, Olivia and Julie, had only recently resumed their relationship after a hiatus of several years. An incident occurred during a family gathering that began the rift. Witnessing this feud was difficult for Sandie and me. As siblings, Olivia and Julie have only themselves. As I've mentioned in the earlier chapters, the conflict presented additional logistical challenges for us. The holidays and other family gatherings we'd have involving both families had to be arranged twice meaning we'd have two Christmas celebrations, etc.

Shortly after Olivia and Julie's reconciliation, they discussed the possibility of just the two of them taking a trip together. Thus, when I presented the idea of flying the two of them down to Tennessee, they were anxious to do so. The combination of surprising their mother and traveling together cumulated in rapid positive responses from both. Not only would all of us enjoy each other's company, the two of them would also have four days of a bonding experience. This would be the first of potentially more travels for just the two of them. Incidentally, it also was only Olivia's second airplane trip, the first occurring when she flew down to assist us following my 2019 heart surgery.

The trip also allowed the two of them relief from their daily family–work responsibilities. Both take their obligations seriously and the day-to-day demands of running a household can be exhausting. It was quite charming that the first night with us after both Sandie and I had retired for the evening, Olivia and Julie stayed up until 4 am, reminiscing. I'm an early-riser (around 4 am, a habit maintained from work) and go to bed earlier than Sandie. Olivia, Julie, and Sandie stayed up late each evening, reliving childhood memories.

As a special treat, I arranged for tickets to the Grand Ole Opry for the Saturday after their arrival. We stayed at the Hyatt Place Hotel close to the venue to fully enjoy the overall experience. This iconic venue is recognized as the number one tourist attraction in Nashville and most if not all of the south. It certainly speaks to the southern flavor of Tennessee. We were treated to an outstanding show where Kelsea Ballerina was the headline performer. Among the other acts was a newly formed group called Texas Hill. The three of them individually had been on various known TV talent shows including *The Voice* and *American Idol*. They recently joined forces and became Texas Hill. The Texas Hill trio was phenomenal previewing what will probably be an exceptional future for the group.

The four of us enjoyed each others' company, playing cards and catching up with one another. Janette hosted all of us to dinner on Sandie's actual birthday, January 24. There were birthday favors that included fun glasses making for some funny pictures. The dinner and wine were delicious. It was simply magnificent having Olivia and Julie with us for those four days. We certainly missed them after their departure to return to their families. Our home was quiet and had a sense of emptiness for a few days.

Due to the seriousness of the Covid-19 pandemic, I felt it important to provide an update as of February 3, 2022: Following several mutations to the original strain, though cases and hospitalizations are starting to decline across the United States, deaths are still rising, and community transmission is still high nationwide. The United States death total to-date exceeds 875,000. Two new CDC reports show that people who are up-to-date with their COVID-19 vaccines have the highest amount of protection against COVID. One report found that, compared to up-to-date adults, unvaccinated adults had five times the risk of infection and more than fifty times the risk of Covid-19-associated death. All this information highlights the importance of staying up to date with Covid-19 vaccinations, given how easily the variants spread.

A few interesting Covid-related United States statistics: The lowest (3.5%) and the highest (14.7%) unemployment rates in the United States since 1970 occurred 2 months apart in 2020. Retail Closings: 5,079 retail stores closed nationwide in 2021, down from a record 12,200 store closures in 2020. Worldwide, since the first coronavirus-related pneumonia outbreak in December 2019, the virus that causes the infection/disease (Covid-19) has evolved into a pandemic, and as of today, more than 100 million people globally in over 210 countries have been confirmed to have been infected and two million people have died of COVID-19! With all the scientific supporting data as well as real-life unvaccinated victim testimonies, it dumbfounds me why so many individuals still refuse the vaccines. My belief is that as long as an unacceptable percentage of the population refuses the vaccine, Covid will continue to flourish.

Thursday, January 6, 2022 marked one year since the attack on the U.S. Capitol, which disrupted a joint session of the U.S. Congress in the process of affirming the presidential election results. The government continues to investigate losses that resulted from the breach of the Capitol, including damage to the Capitol building and grounds, both inside and outside the building. According to a May 2021 estimate by the Architect of the Capitol, the attack caused approximately $1.5 million worth of damage to the U.S. Capitol building.

Under the continued leadership of the U.S. Attorney's Office for the District of Columbia and the FBI's Washington Field Office, the investigation and prosecution of those responsible for the attack continues to move forward at an unprecedented speed and scale. More than 725 defendants have been arrested in nearly all 50 states and the District of Columbia. This includes those charged in both District and Superior Court. The Department of Justice claims that they will hold accountable all those who committed crimes on January 6, 2021. I guess I'll believe it if and when Trump is held accountable as he was the main mastermind and instigator of this horrific tragedy.

Mid-February provided another welcome surprise. Janette's younger sister Sierra along with her husband Peter and daughter Eichler visited Clarksville. It was their first visit to our fair state flying all the way in from California and we enjoyed spending time with them. Janette was the consummate hostess treating them to the sights and sounds of both Clarksville and Nashville.

March 19, 2022 was a day to celebrate. Janette had officially paid off her Clarksville, Tennessee home mortgage. My thoughtful wife came up with the idea to have a "mortgage burning party" in honor of the accomplishment. The event was made even more memorable through a surprise visit by my Florida sister, Sheryl. Dinner that night was scrumptious followed by the de-facto burning of a mock mortgage by Janette to cap the evening.

To celebrate our 20th wedding anniversary Sandie and I traveled to Charleston, South Carolina for three days. Both the high and low of this trip occurred as we visited the well-known Boone Hall Plantation. The high was the fact that it was well worth the visit. As you enter the property an iconic row of ancient live oak trees welcomes you. Boone Hall is one of America's oldest living and working plantations, and one of the most famous plantations in the Southern states. The majestic Boone Hall Plantation, set on 783 acres was established in 1681, and opened to the public in 1956. It has been the filming location for dozens of movies and TV series with its historic buildings and old slave cabins still perfectly intact. We were treated to a guided tour of the elegant house, a carriage tour of the grounds and we found our own way through the slave quarters and the extensive gardens.

The low resulted from our transportation back from the plantation to our hotel which was approximately a ten-mile trip. We flew into Charleston and didn't rent a car figuring we would get around through Uber and Lyft rides. We used Lyft for the ride out to the plantation without issue and scheduled a ride back from them also. Within the plantation they have clearly marked the Uber/Lyft pickup point. To make a long story short, our ride never showed up! The same thing was happening to the woman sitting next to us in the pickup area. The three of us decided to walk two miles to the closest bus stop and get back via bus. Fortunately, after walking for twenty minutes or so in extremely hot weather a nice couple stopped and picked us up. They insisted on driving us to our desired drop off points in the city. What a blessing they were for us on that hot, humid day.

On our actual anniversary we did a city carriage ride and had dinner in one of the city's romantic restaurants. Our horse-drawn carriage tour featured a licensed guide pointing out over 350 years of Charleston's history, including antebellum mansions, churches, and gardens. He also entertained us with historical facts, lore, and humor. Wanting an unparalleled dining experience for our twentieth anniversary I selected Magnolias restaurant for its exceptional cuisine in a romantic setting. The food was outstanding and the service was exceptional topped off with a personalized anniversary chocolate treat to celebrate the occasion.

The only planned site seeing disappointment was the cancellation of our scheduled Fort Sumter tour. Heavy winds on the day of our tour forced the cancellation as the ferry couldn't navigate the choppy waters to get to the island. While able to view the fort from a distance, we wanted to witness up close where the bitter Civil War began.

This disappointment resulted in our discovering a true "diamond in the rough". The Charleston Museum founded in 1773 is commonly regarded as "America's First Museum". Inspired in part by the creation of the British Museum, the Museum was established by the Charleston Library Society. The Museum's collections now represent the most comprehensive assemblage of South Carolina materials in the nation. Its collections include natural history, historical material, culture and both documentary and photographic resources. We found the museum not only informative but highly organized. The exhibits transported you through South Carolina's history from its earliest period to our present time frame.

In May of 2022, we went on a long-anticipated expedition driving most of the Blue Ridge Parkway. The Blue Ridge Parkway is a National Parkway and All-American Road noted for its scenic beauty. The parkway, which is America's longest linear park, runs for 469 miles through 29 Virginia and North Carolina counties, linking Shenandoah National Park to Great Smoky Mountains National Park.

We began our adventure north of the Parkway's northern entrance by touring the James Monroe and Thomas Jefferson's estates. In February 1789, Monroe shared some good news with Jefferson: "It has always been my wish to acquire property near Monticello. I have lately accomplished it by the purchase acreage next to your property." The fifth president of the United States, James Monroe then had a residence next to Thomas Jefferson. Jefferson had been urging Monroe to settle near him in for several years.

Thomas Jefferson's home, called Monticello, located in Charlottesville, Virginia, is one of the most famous historic homes in the U.S. If you turn a nickel on its tail, you will see an image of Thomas Jefferson's Monticello; in many ways, the home is an American symbol. Imagine being only 25 or 26 years old, and planning to build a mansion on a plantation. That was a reality for Thomas Jefferson, a self-taught architect. We found Monticello simply enchanting. From the beautiful manicured gardens and lawns to its historical significance, Sandie and I were spellbound. After soaking in Monticello we began our Blue Ridge Parkway drive.

There are numerous outstanding sites along the route. We couldn't stop at all of them but paused at some of the most visited attractions:

Natural Bridge — The Natural Bridge of Virginia should not be missed by those traveling the Blue Ridge Parkway. Located only 15 miles from the northern section of the Parkway, it is a detour well worth the effort. It's often been listed as one of the seven Natural Wonders of the World. The spectacle is 215 feet tall, 40 feet thick, 100 feet wide and contains 450,000 cubic feet of rock weighing 72,000,000 pounds! George Washington surveyed it, and Thomas Jefferson purchased it so that it could be preserved as a national treasure.

Floyd Country Store — This old-time country store features Appalachian music and dancing every weekend, a unique selection of merchandise, and great food at its Jingle Tap Cafe counter. Since The Floyd Country Store opened for business in 1910 it has been at the heart of the Floyd Community. The store takes the responsibility of nurturing and showcasing the traditional music of the region seriously. Sandie and me enjoyed a chocolate malt at their authentic old-time soda fountain.

Mabry Mill — Ed Mabry built the mill where he and his wife Lizzy ground corn, sawed lumber, and did blacksmithing for three decades. The old mill, cultural demonstrations, and a decades-long tradition of Sunday afternoon music and dancing continue to draw visitors today. It is one of the most picturesque places on the Parkway. Mabry's original sawmill and blacksmith shop still stand as well.

Blue Ridge Music Center — The Blue Ridge Music Center is a state-of-the-art performing arts facility built to preserve and promote the historic music of Virginia and the Blue Ridge. The Blue Ridge region has produced more old-time and bluegrass musicians per capita than any other. It is the heart of many of America's living music traditions. Drawing from this rich heritage, which continues to thrive, the air at the Blue Ridge Music Center is almost always filled with music, even when there is no concert on the stage. The site features free music daily in the breezeway that we took advantage of.

Linville Falls — Its noted as the most photographed spot in the state. Trails near the Linville Falls Visitor Center led to the breathtaking three-tiered Linville Falls over the Linville Gorge via both strenuous and moderate hikes. The steep-walled Gorge is known as the "Grand Canyon of the Southern Appalachians." Linville Falls is probably the most famous waterfall in the Blue Ridge hosting over 350,000 visitors annually. The trails include four overlooks to the waterfalls, where wildflowers and foliage abound along the way.

Little Switzerland — Little Switzerland is a summer colony high in the North Carolina Mountains along the Parkway. Their town sign says "Population 46." Many buildings incorporate iconic Swiss architectural styles. Located about an hour north of Asheville, it offers a rare stop right along the Parkway for food at the Switzerland Cafe and a little shopping at the General Store or the Minerals Museum of NC.

Craggy Mountain Garden — Twisted, jagged, rocky "crags" give Craggy Gardens its name, but these high elevation summits are home to the most spectacular floral display along the 469-mile Blue Ridge Parkway corridor. For generations, visitors have headed for the Craggies in June, typically the prime time for viewing the pink and purple blooms of Catawba rhododendrons that blanket the area. Sandie and I ventured through the rocky "crags" to view the floral display but unfortunately even though we were there in June, we were a week or two too early for blooming displays. Although a treacherous rocky climb to reach a viewing summit, it was still quite the site to see.

Biltmore Estate — The luxurious family home of George and Edith Vanderbilt is a marvel of elegance and charm, as magnificent today as it was more than a century ago. Faithfully preserved and filled with original furnishings and masterpieces of art, no other residence in America offers a more authentic and inspiring view of Gilded Age life while suggesting that the Vanderbilts and their guests are still at home.

Some estate highlights: Original art by Pierre-Auguste Renoir and John Singer Sargent. Magnificent 16th century tapestries, a Library with 10,000 volumes, a Banquet Hall with a 70-foot ceiling, 65 fireplaces, an indoor pool, and a bowling alley. With thirty-five bedrooms and forty-five bathrooms, the estate was always a beehive of activity. Almost all of the priceless objects throughout the house are from George and Edith Vanderbilt's original collection!

Our Blue Ridge Parkway adventure was one of our most enjoyable trips. The scenery along the way looked as if it was painted on an artist's canvas. The drive itself was peaceful as no commercial vehicles of any type are allowed on the Parkway. This meant that we didn't see one semi-trailer along the entire Parkway! The maximum speed limit on the parkway was forty-five miles per hour adding to our travel leisure.

Needing to pick a cut-off date for this book, I'll end it here. I feel fortunate to be a healthy seventy-six-year-old as of July 2022, enjoying new adventures. My life experiences have had many ups and downs. While conversing with family and friends, we sometimes ask each other what we'd change in our past given the opportunity to go back. My straightforward answer is "Nothing." I firmly believe God has a plan for each of us. The tribulations we experience provide growth in areas of obvious need. If my life hadn't taken the turns it did, I wouldn't have the wonderful immediate and extended family that I'm blessed with.

Finally, I'll close with a sincere thank you to my family, friends, and colleagues who were and are part of my life. I'm enriched in knowing them and am truly a better person for it.

Deacon, Sandie, Me, Shawn, and Yucco 2020.

High School Classmates 2021.

Left: Grandson Axel 2022.
Right: Surprise—Olivia, Janette, Sandie, and Julie.